The South
Iron Indu
1750 - 1

Laurence Ince

Ferric Publications
147 Kineton Green Road, B92 7EG. GB.

© 1993 Ferric Publications and Author.
ISBN 0-9518165-1-9

Produced by Merton Priory Press
Page makeup by Pippin DTP Services
Printed in England by Roebuck Press
Kingston Road, Merton, SW19 1LT

Table of Contents

List of Plates iv
List of Figures v
Introduction and Acknowledgements vii
Prologue ix
Chapter One:.The Coke Iron Industry in South Wales 1750-1885. 1
Chapter Two: Blast Furnaces and Blowing Engines. 9
Chapter Three: Wrought Iron and Rolling Mills. 19
Chapter Four: The Demise of the Charcoal Iron Industry in South Wales. . . . 27
Chapter Five: The Iron Industry of Aberdare and the Cynon Valley. 33
Chapter Six: Merthyr Tydfil: The Iron Town. 47
Chapter Seven: The Homfrays of Penydarren and Tredegar. 73
Chapter Eight: The Iron Industry of the Neath Valley. 91
Chapter Nine: The Ebbw Vale Group of Ironworks. 105
Chapter Ten: The Ironworks of the Eastern Outcrop. 121
Chapter Eleven: The Ironworks of the Northern Outcrop. 129
Chapter Twelve: The Ironworks of the Southern Outcrop. 145
Chapter Thirteen: The Iron Industry of the Central Anticlinal District. . . . 151
Chapter Fourteen: The Iron Industry of West Wales. 161
Appendices 171
Bibliography 187
Index 191

List of Plates.

Plate One	A typical beam blowing engine built by the Neath Abbey Iron Company.	17
Plate Two	The remains of the furnaces at the Hirwaun Ironworks.	44
Plate Three	The Llwydcoed Ironworks photographed shortly after closure.	45
Plate Four	Crawshay Bailey, 1789-1872.	46
Plate Five	Josiah John Guest, 1785-1852. (Courtesy National Library of Wales)	69
Plate Six	Richard Crawshay, 1739-1810. (Courtesy Sir William Crawshay)	70
Plate Seven	The ruined casting houses and blowing engine house of the Ynysfach Ironworks.	71
Plate Eight	William Crawshay II, 1788-1867.	72
Plate Nine	The Penydarren Ironworks in 1813.	83
Plate Ten	Francis Homfray of Wales and Old Swinford, 1674-1737.	84
Plate Eleven	Francis Homfray of Broadwaters and Stourton Castle, 1725-1798.	84
Plate Twelve	Sir Jeremiah Homfray of Llandaff, 1759-1833.	85
Plate Thirteen	Samuel Homfray of Penydarren, 1762-1822.	86
Plate Fourteen	Watkin Homfray, 1796-1837.	87
Plate Fifteen	Samuel Homfray of Glen Usk, 1795-1882.	88
Plate Sixteen	Glen Usk, the Monmouthshire home of the Homfrays.	89
Plate Seventeen	A Homfray wedding party at Glen Usk, c1880.	90
Plate Eighteen	The remains of the Neath Abbey Furnaces which were built in 1793.	98
Plate Nineteen	Henry Habberly Price, 1794-1839.	99
Plate Twenty	Joseph Tregelles Price, 1784-1854.	100
Plate Twenty One	The works yard at the Neath Abbey Ironworks.	101
Plate Twenty Two	The remains of the double blowing engine house at the Venallt Ironworks.	102
Plate Twenty Three	The remains of a double tuyère at the Venallt Ironworks site.	103
Plate Twenty Four	The remains of an anthracite blast furnace at the Banwen Ironworks.	104
Plate Twenty Five	The massive beam of the Darby blowing engine at the Ebbw Vale Ironworks. (Courtesy Ironbridge Gorge Museum Trust)	116
Plate Twenty Six	The middle chamber of the Darby engine house. (Courtesy Ironbridge Gorge Museum Trust)	117

Plate Twenty Seven	A plate encased furnace at the Sirhowy Ironworks. (Courtesy of Welsh Industrial & Maritime Museum, Cardiff)	118
Plate Twenty Eight	A house for a beam pumping engine at the British Ironworks, Abersychan.	119
Plate Twenty Nine	The ruined Blaenavon Ironworks.	127
Plate Thirty	A cast iron tramroad bridge built in 1824 to serve the Clydach Ironworks.	143
Plate Thirty One	The Tredegar Ironworks photographed in the 1890s.	144
Plate Thirty Two	The remains of a furnace at the Llynvi Ironworks, Maesteg.	156
Plate Thirty Three	The blowing engine house of the Llynvi Ironworks, Maesteg.	157
Plate Thirty Four	John Brogden, founder of the company.	158
Plate Thirty Five	James Brogden.	159
Plate Thirty Six	The charging platform of the Ynyscedwyn Ironworks pictured in the early 1970s.	168
Plate Thirty Seven	The remains of the unfinished steel department at the Ynyscedwyn Ironworks.	169

List of Figures

Figure One	Industrial South Wales.	vi
Figure Two	The Boulton & Watt blowing engine built at Neath Abbey in 1793. (Courtesy Birmingham Central Library)	15
Figure Three	The Darby blowing engine built at the Ebbw Vale Ironworks in 1865.	16
Figure Four	A typical puddling furnace.	24
Figure Five	A typical refinery, 1870.	25
Figure Six	Trevithick's mill engine for Tredegar, 1804.	26
Figure Seven	The Glamorganshire ironworks.	31
Figure Eight	Dowlais Furnace, 1763.	68
Figure Nine	The Monmouthshire ironworks.	viii

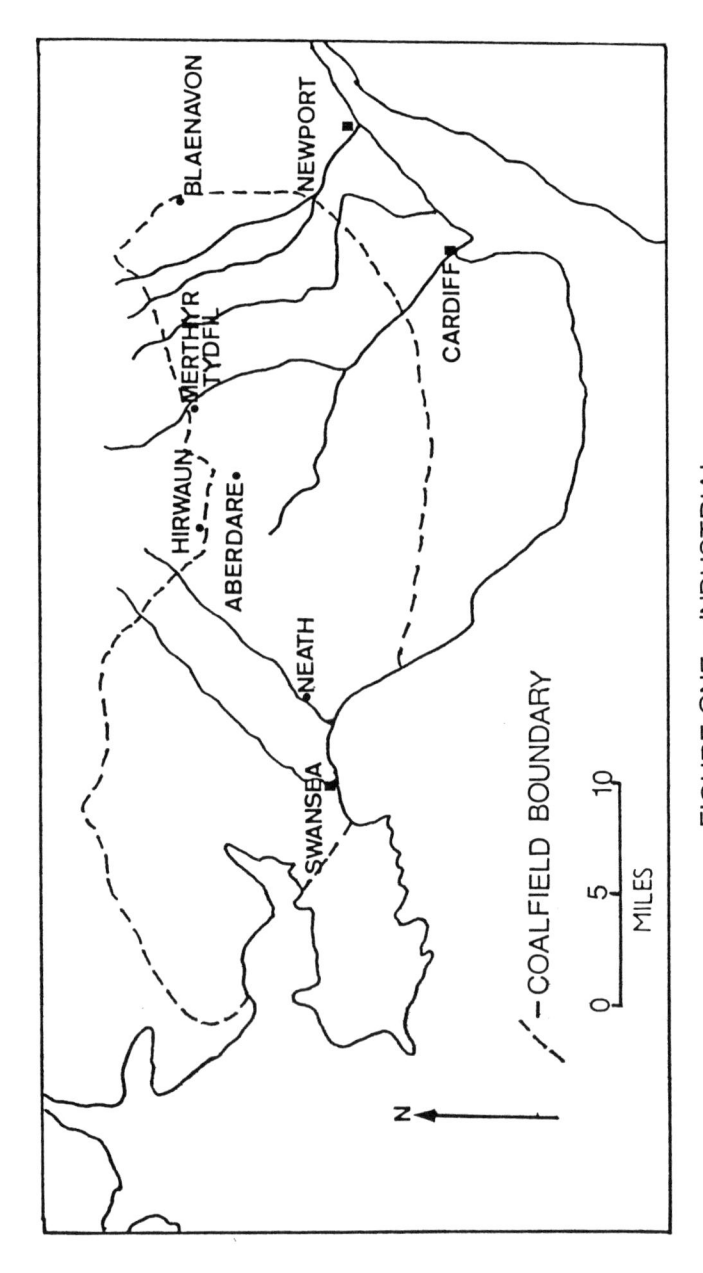

FIGURE ONE – INDUSTRIAL SOUTH WALES

Introduction and Acknowledgements.

It is now over one hundred years since the collapse of the wrought iron industry in South Wales. This industry once dominated the South Wales Coalfield changing what had been a sparsely populated area into one with a series of conurbations each relying on the fortunes of their ironworks. Often writers charting the history of this important Welsh industry have been lured into making sweeping generalisations. This is particularly true when the final years of the industry have been considered.

The early years of the coke iron industry in South Wales have received far more attention than the rest of the tale. We are often told that coke smelting, Boulton & Watt steam engines and wrought iron were the early characteristics of the industry. While examining the early history of the South Wales iron industry I became convinced of the importance of water power linked with coke smelting. It was only with later expansion did the Boulton & Watt and similar engines become an important force in the ironworks of South Wales.

By the early 1830s the main characteristics of the South Wales iron industry had come together, namely, large stone built furnaces, steam power in the form of blowing engines and rolling mill engines, the production of wrought iron and from this the manufacture of rails. These characteristics were to be found in the majority of the South Wales ironworks right up to the collapse of the wrought iron trade.

From the early 1850s onwards there is enough information available to chart the progress and demise of the industry in detail. Particularly valuable are the statistics of iron production published under the editorship of Robert Hunt. Other valuable sources of information for this period have been the weekly or bi-weekly reports on the industries of South Wales published in the Mining Journal and the Engineer.

In this volume I have concentrated on providing the reader with the story of the South Wales iron industry in technical and economic terms. I have not attempted to investigate the social changes brought about by the development of the South Wales iron industry. I have also endeavoured to give a history of each of the ironworks operating in South Wales during the period 1750-1885. For this section it would be foolish of me to believe that all my dates and figures are correct. My interest in the South Wales iron industry is still strong and I hope that local experts will get in touch with me if they can suggest corrections or additions for particular ironworks. What I sincerely hope is that this work can give interested parties a framework to pursue their own researches into the South Wales iron industry, particularly those people interested in the progress of one ironworks who wish to place its story in a wider context.

I would not have been able to complete this work without the help of librarians and archivists at various institutions around Britain. For this I would like to thank the staffs of the Gwent Record Office, the Archive Service for Glamorgan, the National Library of Wales and Birmingham Central Library. For information and help in compiling the chapter on the Homfray family I am indebted to Kenyon Homfray, John Homfray and Jeston Homfray.

I am grateful to the Welsh Industrial & Maritime Museum, Cardiff; the National Library of Wales, Aberystwyth; Cyfarthfa Castle Museum and Art Gallery, Merthyr Tydfil; Cynon Valley Library, Aberdare; Ironbridge Gorge Museum Trust and Sir William Crawshay for permission to use illustrations from their collections for this book. For permission to reproduce the Homfray portraits I must thank Kenyon Homfray, Mrs Jane S. Homfray, David Zambra, Mrs A.F. Thomas and Sir Brooke Boothby Bt.

I must also convey my heartfelt thanks to Douglas Braid of Merton Priory Press whose drive and enthusiasm have helped bring this work to publication.

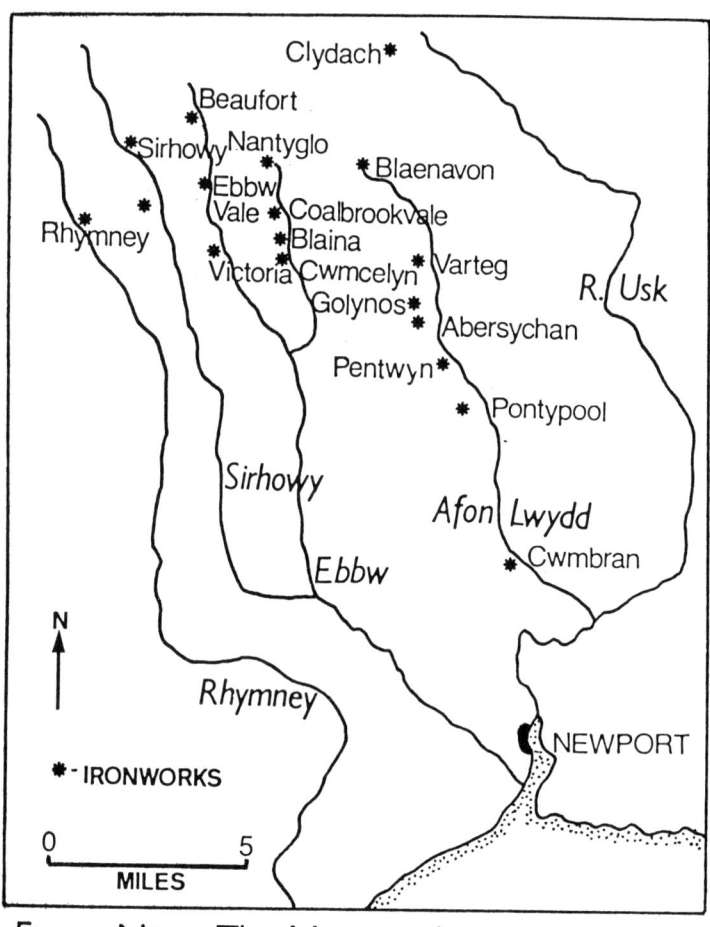

Figure Nine – The Monmouthshire Ironworks

Prologue.

The Early Charcoal Iron Industry in South Wales.

The initial development of an iron industry in South Wales can be dated to 1564 when a furnace was constructed on the River Taff at Tongwynlais. This furnace, attributed to Sir Henry Sydney, supplied iron to a forge at Rhyd-y-Gwern on the River Rhymney. Several other furnaces and forges were also founded in South Wales during the late sixteenth century. In Glamorgan the furnaces included examples at Coity, Dyffryn, Pentyrch, Blaencannaid, Cwmaman and Pontyryn.[1] Forges were also built at this time to process a proportion of the pig iron produced by the furnaces into wrought iron. The development of the iron industry in Glamorgan was largely financed by Sussex ironmasters who had been inhibited in their iron making activities in the Weald. Royal Ordinances had curtailed the ironmasters' use of Wealden timber for charcoal burning and they had searched for new iron making districts to develop. South Wales was chosen because of the abundance of timber for fuel possessed by the region, its many water power sites and the large reserves of iron ore including haematite around the lower reaches of the Taff.

Several furnaces were also built in Monmouthshire during the same period. The driving force behind this development was Richard Hanbury from Worcestershire. He built and acquired several ironworks centred on the town of Pontypool. Hanbury gained possession of a large tract of wooded land which allowed him to operate four furnaces with associated forges from 1580 onwards. Hanbury's furnaces were situated at Abercarn, Cwmffrwdoer, Monkswood and Trosnant.[2]

During the seventeenth and early eighteenth centuries several of the pioneer furnaces were forced to close. Local problems with the supply of wood and other raw materials probably contributed to this move. New furnaces were now constructed towards the north and west of the region where large reserves of timber could be utilised. In 1717 the South Wales iron industry consisted of the following furnaces and forges:

Counties	Furnaces	Forges
Breconshire	Llanelly	Clydach
-	Ynyscedwyn	Llanelly
Carmarthenshire	Kidwelly	Carmarthen
-	-	Kidwelly
-	-	Cwmbran
-	-	Llandyfan
-	-	Whitland
Glamorganshire	Caerphilly	Forest
-	Neath (Melinycwrt)	-

Counties	Furnaces	Forges
Monmouthshire	Pontypool	Machen (2)
-	Tintern	Monmouth
-	-	Pontypool
-	-	Tintern (2)
-	-	Tredegar
Pembrokeshire	-	Blackpool[3]

Most of the charcoal furnaces and forges tended to come under the ownership of a few powerful partnerships. During the eighteenth century the ironmasters faced the continual problem of finding timber to be converted into charcoal for fuel. Several other industries required charcoal for their production and also the growing of wood was rather inelastic in response to periods of great demand for iron. Land owners had soon realised the benefit of coppicing their woodlands. They cut their wood close to the ground and allowed fresh wood to grow from the old roots. However, one experienced ironmaster in the early eighteenth century recorded that wood grown in this way was cut after sixteen or seventeen years growth but it took twenty years if the wood was beech from an upland area.[4] Several experimenters had tried to use coal as a fuel but the resulting iron was of little use. The main problem was that impurities such as sulphur, which were contained in the coal, entered the iron during smelting. The answer to this problem was discovered by Abraham Darby in the early eighteenth century. He coked his coal before using it to smelt iron. The coking process drove off the bulk of the impurities and using coke Abraham Darby was able to produce a good casting iron at his Coalbrookdale Ironworks in Shropshire. It was to be this discovery that later unlocked the coalfields for development by the iron industry.

References

1. D. Morgan Rees, *The Industrial Archaeology of Wales*, Newton Abbot, 1975, pp.30-31.
2. H.R. Schubert, *History of the British Iron and Steel Industry*, 450-1775, 1957, p.177.
3. E.W. Hulme, "Statistical History of the Iron Trade", 1717-1750, *Transactions of the Newcomen Society*, Vol.9, 1928-1929, pp.21-23.
4. Gwent Record Office, Cwmbran, Misc. Ms. 448, Mr. Hanbury's Cost and Yields of Pig, Rod, Hoop and Sheet Iron, 1704.

Chapter One.

The Coke Iron Industry in South Wales 1750-1885.

One of the greatest innovations pioneered during the Industrial Revolution was the adoption of coke smelting in the iron industry. Although Darby's discovery of this method at the Coalbrookdale Ironworks is dated to 1709, it was not until the mid 1750s that the process began to spread widely through the coalfields of Britain. This was because it was not until this date that the iron manufactured with coke became acceptable at forges for conversion into wrought iron. The new iron making method rendered the coalfields to be most attractive propositions for the siting of new ironworks. South Wales with its carbon rich coal, plentiful iron ore and water power sites was in the forefront of this new investment in the British iron industry. This development started with the building of South Wales' first coke furnace at Hirwaun in 1757 and continued with the foundation of the Dowlais Ironworks in 1759, Plymouth Ironworks in 1763, Cyfarthfa Ironworks in 1765, Sirhowy Ironworks in 1778, Beaufort Ironworks in 1779, Penydarren in 1784 and several more along the northern edge of the South Wales Coalfield.

South Wales had an early advantage over other coalfields because of its carbon rich coal which kept fuel costs at a low level. The carbon content of Welsh coal exceeded 80% compared with 63% for Yorkshire, 61% for Derbyshire, 54% for Staffordshire and 34-40% for Scotland. In the early years of its history the Plymouth Furnace in Merthyr Tydfil used £0.65 of fuel per ton of iron made compared with £1.40 to £1.46 for the Horsehay Ironworks in Shropshire.[1] It is also apparent that the landlords who leased their land to the ironmasters had no idea of how valuable the minerals on their property were. In the early years of the South Wales iron industry several leases were entered into at what can only be described as a bargain price. The Cyfarthfa lease of 1765 was held for 99 years at a yearly payment of £100 and the Hirwaun lease of 1758 was held for 99 years at £23 per annum.[2] The mineral agent for the Marquess of Bute, who owned large tracts of land in the South Wales Coalfield, could recall that as late as 1823 when he took up the post that,

> your lordship had not the vestige of any mineral plans records or sections of strata; nevertheless, by perseverance I was able to give a clear view of your lordship's mineral property and was much complimented, not only by your lordship but also by your men of business and agents who had not the least conception of the great value of these minerals.[3]

However, when these long leases ran their course the landowners made sure that they would be renewed on far more favourable terms for themselves. This approach caused many serious problems to the ironmasters at a time of decline for the iron industry in South Wales.

Several common denominators can be identified when examining the make up of the partnerships that founded the South Wales iron industry. It is certainly true that all the partners had to be prosperous for not only did they have to provide money for the building and equipping of the works but they had to attract workers to what was a sparsely populated area. This necessitated the building of workers' houses and even shops. The local transport network had to be improved by promotion and investment in canals and later in railways. One important group of investors in the Welsh iron industry can be easily identified, these were the ironmasters from the English Midlands who had already witnessed the success of the coke iron industry in Shropshire. John Maybery who built the Hirwaun furnace had family links with the Powick Forge on the River Teme in Worcestershire; the Guest family who were later to control the Dowlais Ironworks came from Broseley in Shropshire and the partners of the Aberdare Ironworks included John Thompson, the Shropshire ironmaster. Another important group was made up of merchants from the cities of London and Bristol, some with little experience of the iron industry but guided by one or two experienced partners, they were willing to invest in the development of the Welsh iron industry. So we find the unlikely names of builders, grocers and teamen on early leases for some of the Welsh ironworks. A third group was made up of Quaker businessmen, a group that already had a long association with the British iron industry. The Darby family of Coalbrookdale were Quakers and many other Quakers were ironmasters. The Harfords who owned an appreciable portion of the Welsh iron industry in the late eighteenth century were Quakers and the partners that founded the Neath Abbey Iron Company were also members of the Society of Friends. An important subgroup is represented by the merchants and ironmasters who were involved in producing and selling cannon. Anthony Bacon, the founding father of the Welsh iron industry, built the Cyfarthfa furnace to supply his cannon boring mill at the same site. Such was the demand for ordnance and shot in the second half of the eighteenth century that it took the production of several other furnaces to keep the Cyfarthfa mill supplied with iron.

The Hirwaun Ironworks was built during a period of great demand for iron generated partly by the Seven Years' War. The expansion of the South Wales iron industry continued during the turbulent times of the American War of Independence and the Napoleonic Wars. A new partnership took over at Hirwaun in 1775 but the lease stipulated that they supply the lessors with 300 tons of dark grey iron yearly. This was not adhered to and the lessors complained that their forge at Brecon could use 200 tons annually "but it was impossible at present to get such a supply from the neighbouring ironworks owing to the great demand for making cannon for Government".[4] By 1800 there were at least fifteen ironworks operating in South Wales and several more planned or under construction. In 1805 South Wales produced 73,933 tons of iron which was 29.5% of the British total. Output continued to rise with cast iron and wrought iron being produced. The Merthyr ironworks had been early adopters of Cort's puddling process for making wrought iron and this was improved at Merthyr by the use of an intermediate refining stage.

The growth of the South Wales iron industry continued during the Napoleonic Wars although a temporary trade depression has been identified during 1811.[5] However, the boom in iron production came to an end with a drop in demand and prices towards the close of the Napoleonic Wars. At this time many of the smaller iron companies found themselves in financial difficulty. The proprietors of the Hirwaun Ironworks became bankrupt in 1814, the Neath Abbey Ironworks was advertised for sale in 1818 and the Cwmavon Ironworks was sold in 1820. This period of uneven demand led to the formation of a South Wales Ironmasters' Meeting which met at the King's Head Inn, Newport.[6] This body hoped to regulate prices and production of iron and to stave off the worst features of periods of recession. However, this organisation did not prove to be a success with the ever present temptation to undercut competitors difficult to shun.

Improvements to the iron trade came slowly during the early 1820s, reaching a very healthy state in 1826 when South Wales produced 223,520 tons of iron which represented 38.4% of the British make.[7] These better conditions attracted another bout of investment in the industry and during the 1820s several new works were founded including Blaina (1823), Bute (1824), Pentwyn (1825), Abersychan (1826) and Gadlys (1827). New markets for iron were developing as the material became widely used in steam engines, pipes and structural work. During the period 1825-1830 the industry also entered a trade that was to dominate the ironworks of South Wales - the supply of rails. The South Wales ironmasters were highly experienced in the production of rails and tramplates as the hilly terrain in South Wales meant that each ironworks had its network of inclines and railways to bring raw materials to the furnaces. In 1825 the Stockton and Darlington Railway, the first steam operated public railway, opened with part of its permanent way utilising cast iron rails supplied by the Neath Abbey Ironworks. In fact, the first engineer to make a survey for the line was George Overton who had at one time been a partner in the Hirwaun Ironworks. The Penydarren Ironworks also entered the rail trade at an early date for it supplied the wrought iron rails for the Liverpool and Manchester Railway. By the mid 1830s the supply of rails was dominating the order books of the South Wales works with the Dowlais Ironworks in 1836 producing 20,000 tons of rails.[8] The railway building boom saw many of the Welsh works switch production to wrought iron rails with the South Wales area becoming the largest supplier of rails for the home market during this period.

A further impetus was given to the industry in 1836 with Crane's perfection of the making of iron with anthracite coal and the hot blast. This unlocked the western valleys to development by the iron industry. The anthracite area was soon host to several ironworks such as Venallt (1839), Ystalyfera (1838) and Gwendraeth (1839). However, these ironworks were unable to enter the wrought iron rail trade and produced foundry and tinplate iron only. For several technical reasons iron production was low and the Welsh anthracite iron industry did not turn out to be a very successful branch of the trade.

The growth of the Welsh iron industry received a severe check during the period 1838-1840 with the temporary collapse of railway construction in Britain. In 1836 around 955 miles of railway had been sanctioned in Britain but 1839 only saw 54 miles approved with the Welsh iron industry producing 453,880 tons of iron.[9] Record profits were made by the Dowlais Ironworks in 1837 but this peak of £129,160 dropped to £78,066 for 1840.[10] The mid 1840s again saw a further outbreak of railway mania with South Wales iron production rising from 457,350 tons in 1843 to 706,680 tons in 1847.[11] In 1846 the South Wales works had orders for 120,000 tons of rails with the Plymouth Ironworks producing 40,000 tons alone.[12] However, the boom was to be short lived with demand falling rapidly in the late 1840s. The larger works could cushion the impact of these periods of uneven demand by stockpiling iron. At one time Robert Crawshay stockpiled 40,000 tons of puddled bars during slack times and later when prices rose he sold for £1 per ton extra, raising £40,000 alone.[13] Also at this time the large organisations had cultivated an export trade in rails. With trade depressed in the early 1840s Evans, the Dowlais representative abroad, acquired an order in 1843 for 12,000 tons of rails at £6 a ton for Poland.[14] The same works during difficult times at home won an order in about 1852 for 60,000 to 70,000 tons of rails for Russia.[15] However, the smaller works were more attuned to the domestic market and they suffered greatly in the late 1840s. The Venallt Ironworks was put up for sale in 1849, the Briton Ferry Company failed in the same year and the Garth Ironworks built in 1847 was hardly put into blast before being advertised for sale. The main product of the larger ironworks was wrought iron rails with a small amount of bar iron also being sold. The notable exceptions were the Plymouth Ironworks which produced an appreciable amount of cable iron, Gadlys which produced ductile armour plate iron and Pentyrch which was well known for its sheet iron for use in the tinplate trade. But the vast majority of Welsh iron went into the manufacture of rails, and most of these rails were exported. As early as 1857 one correspondent stated that many of the South Wales ironworks were wholly dependent on American demand.[16] The figures testify to the singleness of production at many of the works. In 1865 70% of Dowlais' production of iron went into the manufacture of rails, 90% of the Rhymney Ironworks' output was rails during the 1850s, in 1869 88% of the Aberdare Iron Company's output was rails and in the same year Blaenavon's figure was 83%.[17] It was a trade which was open to abuse for the Americans bought the worst and cheapest Welsh railway iron (this grade becoming known as American Rail).[18]

The South Wales iron industry produced about 700,000 tons in 1850 which was 31% of the British total, but at the end of the decade output had risen to 985,290 tons which however only represented 26.6% of British production.[19] This fall can be attributed to the development of other areas in Britain with large reserves of cheaper ores, the Cleveland region being in the forefront of this development. The success of the early coke iron industry in South Wales had been guaranteed because of the large supplies of cheap carbon rich coal. However, as fuel economy improved so the economic pull of coal declined. This is illustrated by the following table which shows the amount of coal needed to produce a ton of pig iron,

Date	Works	Tons of coal
1766	Plymouth	6
1817	Dowlais	5.8
1831	Rhymney	4
1839	Plymouth	2.5-3
1856	Dowlais	2.65
1857	Dowlais	2.05
1860	Abersychan	1.63
1863	Plymouth	2.25
1870	Abersychan	1.51
1881	Dowlais	1.10 [20]

South Wales' use of carbon rich coal was neutralised by the discovery by J.B. Neilson of the application of the hot blast in iron making. This invention, which was patented in 1828, produced a great improvement in fuel economy in those areas with less carbon rich coal. The use of the hot blast in South Wales with its carbon rich coals only produced moderate savings. It was now the supply of iron ore that was of paramount importance to the British iron industry. By the 1850s the richer and more easily won iron ore in South Wales was becoming exhausted. With the decline in value of their poorer carbonate ores the Welsh works increased their importation of ores from other areas of Britain and abroad. Often the importation of haematite ores from Spain could be made economically feasible by return cargoes of coal from the iron companies' pits for sale in Europe. The importation of ores to South Wales from other parts of Britain had been a feature of the industry from an early date. The Neath Abbey Ironworks was using ⅛ Lancashire ore for smelting in 1800 and in 1825 the Hills of the Plymouth Ironworks leased haematite mines in West Cumberland.[21]

The year of 1869 was a particularly bad one for the South Wales iron industry with a drop to a production figure of 800,972 tons which was 14.7% of the British make.[22] However, the early 1870s saw a world wide railway building boom, furnaces were put back into blast in South Wales and during 1871 over one million tons of iron were produced.[23] Those, however, with the ability to foresee trends could discern major changes heading for the British iron industry with the adoption of the manufacture of Bessemer steel in this country and the rise of competing industries abroad. Dowlais and Ebbw Vale were operating the Bessemer process by 1870 but at this time the method was unsuccessful when used with iron made with ore from South Wales. Even during the boom period of the early 1870s the Welsh iron companies could not keep up with Cleveland's productivity or wage scales. A fall in the price of rails took place in early 1873 and the Welsh ironmasters called for a cut in wages of 10%.[24] The ironworkers retaliated by going on strike for they realised how badly paid they were compared with the wages of the workers in the North East of England. This debilitating strike lasted from early January to mid March. Many of the South Wales works were seriously weakened by this strike and the return to work coincided with the collapse of the market for rails. The Nantyglo and Blaina Iron Company lost £50,000 to £60,000 in the year ending November 1873 and £30,000 of this was blamed on the great strike.[25] This was not an unusual occurrence as conditions progressively worsened during 1874 with the Ebbw Vale Iron Company losing no less than £160,000 on ironmaking in the year ending in March 1875.[26]

The collapse of the Welsh wrought iron trade can be dated to 1875. The year started badly with a widespread colliers' strike which lasted until May. During that year production in South Wales fell to 541,809 tons which represented only 8.5% of British output.[27] The first commercial tremor of the year occurred with the collapse of the financial empire of Richard Fothergill which closed the two Aberdare works, the Penydarren Ironworks, Treforest and Plymouth. The demand for Welsh wrought iron rails was disappearing. American consumption of rails had fallen from 1,250,000 tons in 1871 to 470,000 tons in 1876 with imports of this product falling during the same period from 515,000 tons to nothing.[28] It was now widely believed that steel was destined to take over from wrought iron for the manufacture of rails. The character of the industry was changing in many ways for in 1876 Ebbw Vale was importing large amounts of Spanish haematite from Bilbao with Welsh ore being scarcely worked at all.[29] Other changes in the industry were summed up by G.T. Clark, manager of Dowlais, in his speech given as first president of the British Iron Trade Association in 1876.[30] Clark looked back to the days of individual ownership and small partnerships when owners, mostly self made men had their attention,

> confined pretty closely to the details of their manufacture and to its sale at the nearest port. There were no labour unions then, hence no masters' union. Masters were self reliant... rough but not unpopular with the work people... and possessed that rare and great gift, the power of managing men. A sort of natural selection weeded out the weak. But the joint stock system (which had brought much capital to the industry, and in many instances worked to the advantage of us all) had changed all that. Those who supply the capital are not those who manage the trade - so the old corrective is gone.

The decline of the South Wales iron industry continued during 1876 with seventy five out of one hundred and fifteen furnaces out of blast and the closure of the Gadlys Ironworks in Aberdare announced.[31] Although output improved to 741,136 tons in 1878 the closures continued with the Nantyglo and Blaina Ironworks Company withdrawing from the iron trade.[32] In late 1878 the West of England and District Bank collapsed with the liquidation of the Blaenavon Iron and Steel Company following.[33] The collapse of this bank also forced the closure of the Pentyrch Ironworks which had borrowed heavily from this source.[34] The closures continued even though the years 1879 to 1882 saw a great improvement in the iron and steel trade. The larger works such as Tredegar, Cyfarthfa, Blaenavon and Rhymney shifted their production to steel while the smaller works who relied on the manufacture of wrought iron were forced into liquidation. In 1885 South Wales produced 792,784 tons of iron which was 10.7% of British production.[35] Except for a few specialised works the vast bulk of this iron was not going to the puddling furnace for making into wrought iron but was for conversion into steel. In the years 1872 and 1881 when production of iron in South Wales was at a similar level, the number of rolling mills fell from 142 to 103 but the number of puddling furnaces in use fell from 1241 to 589.[36] The decline in puddling continued with the Rhymney Ironworks stating in 1884 that they had abandoned puddling altogether.[37] Not only were the larger ironworks involved in steel making but smaller concerns were buying in pig iron for conversion into steel using Siemens furnaces.[38] The Welsh wrought iron industry which received its mortal blow in the mid 1870s finally limped to its death in the mid 1880s.

References.

1. C.K. Hyde, *Technological Change and the British Iron Industry 1700-1870*, Princeton, 1977, p.62 & p.157.
2. M. Atkinson & C. Baber, *The Growth and Decline of the South Wales Iron Industry 1760-1880*, Cardiff, 1987, pp.22-25.
3. J. Davies, *Cardiff and the Marquesses of Bute*, Cardiff, 1981, p.214.
4. John Lloyd, *The Early History of the Old South Wales Iron Works 1760-1840*, 1906, pp.11-18.
5. Edgar Jones, *A History of GKN, Vol.1, Innovation and Enterprise, 1759-1918*, 1987, p.37.
6. T.S. Ashton, *Iron and Steel in the Industrial Revolution*, 1963, pp.177-178. This body was instituted at Abergavenny in 1802 and was a quarterly meeting until its demise in 1824. It was revived in the 1830s.
7. *The Engineer*, February 3rd 1860, p.82.
8. A. Birch, *The Economic History of the British Iron and Steel Industry, 1784-1879*, 1967, p.168.
9. Peter Mathias, *The First Industrial Nation*, 1969, p.280.
   David Mushet, *Papers on Iron and Steel*, 1840, pp.414-415.
10. Edgar Jones, op. cit., p.60.
11. A. Birch, op. cit., p.124 & p.130.
    Harry Scrivenor, *History of the Iron Trade*, 1854, p.295.
12. A. Birch, op. cit., p.221.
13. *The Engineer*, May 16th 1879, p.359.
14&
15. A. Birch, op. cit., p.168.
16. *Mining Journal*, October 31st 1857, p.763.
17. *The Engineer*, November 3rd 1865, p.265.
    Mining Journal, October 6th 1869, p.762.
    Mining Journal, October 30th 1869, pp.821-822.
18. Duncan Burn, *The Economic History of Steel Making, 1867-1939*, Cambridge, 1961, p.58.
19. *Official Descriptive and Illustrated Catalogue of the Great Exhibition, 1851*, Vol.1, pp.150-159.
20. Edgar Jones, op. cit., pp.9-10.
    M. Atkinson & C. Baber, op. cit., p.23
    The Engineer, May 27th 1881, p.396.
21. Birmingham Reference Library (BRL), Boulton & Watt Collection (B&W), James Watt Junior's Journal of a Visit to Ironworks in South Wales, c1800.
22. Robert Hunt, *Mineral Statistics, 1869*.
23. *Mineral Statistics, 1871*.
24. *The Engineer*, January 3rd 1873, p.16.
25. *The Engineer*, November 21st 1873, p.54.
26. *The Engineer*, November 3rd 1876, p.319.
27. *Mineral Statistics, 1875*.
28. Duncan Burn. op. cit., p.28.

29. *The Engineer*, May 26th 1876, p.407.
30. Duncan Burn, op. cit., p.256.
31. *The Engineer*, August 4th 1876, p.89 & September 22nd.
32. *The Engineer*, January 4th 1878.
33. *The Engineer*, December 20th 1878, p.456.
34. Edgar L. Chappel, *Historic Melingriffith: An Account of Pentyrch Iron Works and Melingriffith Tinplate Works*, Cardiff, 1940, p.70.
35. The Journal of the Iron and Steel Institute, 1886, p.1027.
36. *Mineral Statistics, 1872 & 1881*.
37. *The Engineer*, August 22nd 1884, p. 136.
38. *Mineral Statistics, 1881*. Siemens furnaces were being operated by Wright Butler & Co. of Swansea (6); White & Challingsworth (1); E. Morewood & Co. of Llanelly, Panteg Steel Works and Engineering Co. (13); the Birchgrove Steel Company Limited, Swansea (20); the Swansea Tin Plate Co. (2) as well as the iron producers who were represented by the Landore Siemens Steel Co. (24) and the Dowlais Ironworks (6). Steel was also being manufactured in crucibles in Siemens' regenerative gas furnaces at Dowlais, Landore, Ebbw Vale and Birchgrove.

Chapter Two.

Blast Furnaces and Blowing Engines.

The use of coke as a fuel in the iron industry initiated a steady increase in the sizes of blast furnaces after 1750. Charcoal was unable to bear the weight of a large charge of iron ore and limestone but the use of coke allowed the blast furnace builders to increase the size of the structure. However, the form of the blast furnace changed very little during the eighteenth century. The furnace was usually constructed of stone blocks with a lining of fire bricks. At ground level the furnace was square but with an internal circular cross section. The widest cross section internally was called the boshes and from this point the furnace tapered upwards. There was an access arch at the front of the furnace for tapping the molten iron and slag and also an arch in the centre of one or more of the remaining walls. These arches were for openings used to blow air into the furnace and were called tuyères. Furnaces in the eighteenth century were blown through one or two tuyères, later by three. The iron ore, charcoal or coal and limestone were fed into the furnace from the top and so, often, furnaces were built into the side of a hill for ease of charging.

In the second half of the eighteenth century it is clear that larger furnaces began to be built on the South Wales Coalfield. The Cyfarthfa furnace, built in 1767, was 36ft. square externally and 50ft. high.[1] The two furnaces built at Neath Abbey in 1793 were 38ft. square externally and about 60ft. high.[2] These, however, must be viewed as examples of the largest type of furnace built at that time. In the late eighteenth century the output of blast furnaces in South Wales varied from 10 tons to 46 tons weekly.[3] With a slow but steady increase in blast furnace size the average weekly production of a South Wales furnace in 1826 varied from 35 tons to 85 tons.[4] A typical blast furnace in 1831 is represented by an example at Dowlais which was 48ft. 9in. high and 2ft. 10in. diameter across the hearth.[5] This furnace was capable of containing 8220cu.ft of material. The 1820s and 1830s saw the adoption in some areas of a cylindrical furnace made of a thin casing of masonry or bricks. This structure was known as the cupola furnace and was particularly favoured in Scotland.[6] This design seems to have little impressed the Welsh ironmasters although there was probably one example of this furnace type working in the 1820s at Morriston, Swansea. This furnace was 46ft. high and 10ft. across the boshes. The lightness of its construction was countered by the furnace being bound together by 66 wrought iron bands.[7]

Although the cupola furnace type was not widely adopted, a sort of half way design was arrived at by the Welsh iron industry from the 1830s onwards. New furnaces and rebuilds of older ones took a similar form, the base remained square being made of heavy sandstone blocks, but at approximately half its height it took on a cylindrical form of light masonry bound by wrought iron bands.

The general increase in iron production from a furnace in the nineteenth century can be gauged from the following figures for furnaces at the Cyfarthfa Ironworks. The weekly output for each furnace in the period 1810 to 1820 was 60 to 70 tons, by 1845 it was 80 tons, in 1856 it was 105 tons and in 1857 it had risen to 120 tons.[8] It was not uncommon in 1857 for furnaces on the South Wales Coalfield to be producing 200 tons each week. This increase was the result of building bigger furnaces, the adoption of hot blast and using richer ores. The early iron industry in South Wales used native Welsh ores from the coalfield which had an iron content of between 12% and 30% but its later course was dominated by the import of foreign haematite ore with an iron content of 60 + %. The general increase in furnace size continued through the 1830s and 1840s, and in the 1860s some very large furnaces of the masonry type were still being built in South Wales. The Victoria Ironworks, constructed in 1837, had furnaces 45ft. in height and 16ft. in diameter across the boshes.[9] These figures can be compared with the description made in 1867 of the Cwm Celyn furnace which was 60ft. high with a 20ft. diameter across the boshes.[10] The Aberdare Iron Company's furnaces each produced in 1863 a weekly output of between 214 tons and 349 tons of iron and in 1874 a furnace at the Ivor Ironworks, Merthyr Tydfil was built to produce 300 tons of iron weekly.[11] By this date iron cased cylindrical furnaces were coming into vogue although few were built in South Wales as the industry went into recession. Two examples of this furnace type were built at the Victoria Ironworks in 1883 and they produced 700 tons of iron weekly; another example was built at Treforest in 1880 which produced 80 tons of iron daily.[12] Several other structures would be needed also to serve the blast furnaces. Behind the furnace tops would be the area where the coal was coked in open clamps or in masonry coke ovens. Here too, would be kilns for calcining the iron ore. In front of the furnaces would be cast houses to protect the area where the iron was run out from the furnaces. These structures were basically roofs supported by columns which stopped rain and other weather interfering with the casting operations.

One area in South Wales where a different furnace practice was adopted was in the anthracite region. Here, after Crane's discovery of producing iron with anthracite coal and hot blast, smaller furnaces were built; a typical example being a furnace which was built at the Gwendraeth Ironworks, Carmarthenshire. It was 30ft. high, 12ft. in diameter across the boshes and had a 4ft. hearth. The capacity of this furnace was 1720cu.ft. of material.[13] Furnaces in the anthracite region were blown at a higher pressure than was normal on the South Wales Coalfield. The anthracite iron making district however did not prosper as output per furnace was low, even the larger ironworks such as Ystalyfera could only produce 50 to 60 tons of iron weekly from a furnace in the late 1840s.[14] This was in marked contrast to the American anthracite iron industry whose success was based upon the use of very large furnaces. Another problem facing the Welsh ironmasters was that anthracite was unsuitable for use in puddling furnaces so wrought iron could not be manufactured in the anthracite region and production revolved around foundry and other specialised irons.

To raise the temperature of the burning materials in an iron furnace to melting point a blast of air is required. In the early eighteenth century charcoal furnaces were blown by large leather bellows activated by cams from a waterwheel. The air blast was usually introduced into the furnace through a single tuyère. This system of blowing a furnace was improved in 1757 when Isaac Wilkinson took out a patent for the blowing of a furnace with cylinders operated by a waterwheel. John Smeaton later built a blowing engine which had three cylinders and pistons driven by a three throw crankshaft on a waterwheel. Often the output of these waterwheel engines was increased by having a Newcomen steam engine return water to the upstream side of the waterwheel after it had passed through. The Dowlais Ironworks had a water returning engine and the Beaufort Ironworks, built in 1780, was blown by cylinders and pistons powered by a Smeaton waterwheel. The Beaufort Ironworks later added in 1782 an atmospheric steam engine to return water.[15] During the period 1759 to 1805 the majority of Welsh ironworks built were supplied with a blast from cylinders and pistons powered by waterwheels. This design of blowing machine was favoured in the later half of the eighteenth century even though the Boulton & Watt engine was being adopted for blowing by some ironmasters.[16]

The Boulton & Watt engine was a far more efficient machine than the atmospheric steam engine for it used a separate condenser. Boulton & Watt designed the engine for the customer and manufactured some of the intricate parts but the customer, guided by Boulton & Watt, constructed his own engine. The customer was then charged a yearly sum to the value of one third of the coals saved over the cost of running a Newcomen engine. These payments in the form of a premium lapsed in 1800 when Watt's patent came to an end. Only three Welsh ironworks constructed in the period 1775 - 1805 were supplied from the outset with Boulton & Watt engines for furnace blowing. At this time a good water power site could provide enough blast for one or two furnaces. There was, however, the disadvantage of the flow of water being interrupted through drought or freezing conditions. It was only later with the expansion of the industry and the multiplication of furnaces on one site that the industry was forced to turn to steam power to provide the blast for iron making. Even with the adoption of the steam engine for blast furnace blowing, this did not mean that waterwheels became completely redundant. Several waterwheels were linked to beam blowing engines and still provided a blast. In 1798 the Cyfarthfa Ironworks had a 50in. x 9ft. beam engine for use only in the event of a scarcity of water.[17] The Llwydcoed and Plymouth Ironworks were still operating in the 1870s with waterwheels providing a portion of the blast.

A very large early beam blowing engine was built by Boulton & Watt for the Neath Abbey Iron Company in 1793. It was non-rotative and had a wooden beam. The engine had a 40in. x 8ft. steam cylinder and a 70in. blowing cylinder.[18] A further development of this Boulton & Watt design can be illustrated by the 40in. x 8ft. beam engine with an 84in. blowing cylinder supplied in 1798 to the Penydarren Ironworks, for this engine was built with an early iron beam.[19] The next development in the design of the beam blowing engine would be the addition of a flywheel. These engines blew through some form of reservoir or regulator.[20] It was thought that the use of a regulator would eliminate any pulse in the current of air. Some of the larger ironworks later did away with regulators for the long lengths of blast pipe alone could smooth out the current of air produced by the blowing engines.

The expansion of the industry saw a new maker of beam engines begin to take over the South Wales market. This was the Neath Abbey Iron Company who began to build steam engines in the early 1800s.[21] One of the most popular products built at Neath Abbey was a double acting 52½in. x 8ft. beam blowing engine. The French engineers Coste and Perdonnet in 1829 described these products in some detail.[22] The 52½in. beam blowing engine was usually supplied with a blowing cylinder of 105in. diameter although a larger cylinder of 112in. could be provided where necessary. The 105in. cylinder weighed seven tons and the engine operated at fifteen strokes per minute. These engines were suitable for blowing three furnaces and three refineries and produced 14,424cu.ft. of air per minute. In the late 1830s the Neath Abbey Ironworks began to supply slightly smaller beam blowing engines but with 122in. blowing cylinders. The typical Neath Abbey blowing engine was constructed with an upswept beam at the steam end which was connected to a large flywheel.

Another popular design for a beam blowing engine was to have the connecting rod midway between the beam support and the steam end. This method of building beam blowing engines was favoured by the Cornish foundries who supplied several cylinders and complete engines to the South Wales iron industry. Many of the furnaces in South Wales were in blast for long periods and it was important that breakdowns in the blowing engines did not curtail production. A disastrous situation could also arise if the blast air was interrupted and the contents of the furnace began to solidify. It was therefore necessary to have an over capacity in blowing engines to be able to counter any sudden breakdowns. The Tredegar Ironworks in 1869 was operating nine furnaces and had five blowing engines and in the same year the Abernant Ironworks was operating two furnaces with five blowing engines.[23] Several of the larger ironworks such as Dowlais, Blaenavon and Ebbw Vale had the resources to build their own steam engines but the complexity of casting very large cylinders was beyond their capabilities and these parts had to be bought from outside manufacturers. One of the largest beam blowing engines built in the district was the Darby engine manufactured for the Ebbw Vale Ironworks in 1865 by the Perran Foundry, Cornwall. This engine had a 72in. x 12ft. steam cylinder and a 144in. x 12ft. blowing cylinder, providing a blast at 4 psi through a receiver 40ft. long and 14ft. in diameter.[24]

The blast pressure used in South Wales was usually between 1½ to 4 psi although anthracite furnaces were blown at a higher pressure with the Ystalyfera furnaces being blown with a pressure as high as 7 psi.[25] The adoption of the hot blast in South Wales was a gradual process. No ironworks in the region could match the increase in fuel economy noted in other areas when the hot blast was introduced. The adoption of the hot blast allowed the use of raw coal at some ironworks and several ironmasters thought that this would introduce impurities into the smelting process. Many of the South Wales ironworks had switched to using hot blast by the mid 1860s although a few continued with cold blast, thinking they would not sacrifice quality for the increase in economy associated with Neilson's discovery. The use of the hot blast was made economical by using the heat from the waste gases from the blast furnaces. This development was made feasible by closing the furnace tops.

An early experimenter in closing the top of furnaces was James Palmer Budd of the Ystalyfera Ironworks. In the mid 1840s he inserted an iron cylinder into the top of the furnace and gases were drawn off from apertures below the charge level. Frederick Levick at the Cwm Celyn Ironworks was another early experimenter and by 1849 he too was using the waste gases from furnaces. He mounted an iron cylinder in the furnace throat so that it could be raised and lowered. When lowered the bottom of the cylinder closed the furnace by resting on the surface of a conical bell mounted on cross beams. Gases were extracted from ports above the charge. A final version of the closed furnace top was devised at the Ebbw Vale Ironworks where the conical bell moved up and down to allow access to the furnace (bell and hopper system). Closing the furnace tops became popular during the 1850s for the collected combustible gases could be used to heat the blast or for firing the boilers for the many steam engines present on an ironworks' site.

References.

1. D.M. Rees, *Mines, Mills and Furnaces*, 1969, p.72.
2. Laurence Ince, *The Neath Abbey Iron Company*, Eindhoven, 1984, p.91.
   Glamorgan Record Office, N.A.I., Elevations of Furnaces, 22nd April, 1829, W/4/4.
3. Harry Scrivenor, *History of the Iron Trade*, 1854, pp.95-96.
4. *The Engineer*, February 3rd 1860, p.82.
5. John Percy, *Metallurgy: Iron and Steel*, 1864, p.561.
6. Cupola was also the name given to a small vertical, coke fired furnace which was used for remelting iron.
7. Coste and Perdonnet, Sur la Fabrication de la Fonte et du Fer en Angleterre, *Annales Des Mines*, Tome V, Deuxieme Serie, 1829, pp.255-275 and 374-481.
8. A.H. John, *The Industrial Development of South Wales, 1750-1850*, Cardiff, 1950, p.154.
   The Engineer, November 13th 1868.
9. Gwent County Record Office, Ebbw Vale Collection, Sale Particulars of Victoria Ironworks, 1849, D. 454.516.
10. Gwent County Record Office, Sale Particulars of Cwm Celyn, Blaina and Coalbrookvale Ironworks, 5th June 1867, D. 1089.2.
11. John Percy, op. cit., p.556.
    Mining Journal, January 3rd 1863, p.12.
    Proceedings of the Institution of Mechanical Engineers, 1874, pp.239-241.
12. *The Engineer*, October 15th 1880, p.293.
    The Engineer, July 20th 1883, p.57.
13. Percy, op. cit., p.559
14. James Palmer Budd, On the Advantageous Use of the Gaseous Escape from the Blast Furnaces of Ystalyfera Ironworks, *Report of the Eighteenth Meeting of the British Association for the Advancement of Science*, 1848, pp.75-84.
15. *A Catalogue of the Civil and Mechanical Engineering Designs (1741-1792) of John Smeaton*, 1950, p.65.
16. Laurence Ince, Water Power and Cylinder Blowing in Early South Wales Coke Ironworks, *Historical Metallurgy*, Vol.23 No.2, 1989, pp.108-112.
17. Birmingham Reference Library (BRL), Boulton & Watt Collection (B&W), Description of Cyfarthfa Ironworks, 18th September 1798.
18. BRL, B&W, Portfolio of Drawings of Blowing Engine Supplied to R.W. Fox & Company.

19. BRL, B&W, Portfolio of Drawings of Blowing Engine Supplied to Jeremiah Homfray, Penydarren Ironworks, No. 705.
20. Later also called a receiver.
21. Laurence Ince, *The Neath Abbey Iron Company*, Eindhoven, 1984.
22. Coste and Perdonnet, op. cit., pp.255-275 & 355-481.
23. *Mining Journal*, October 6th 1869, p.762.
    Mining Journal, November 20th 1869, p.882.
24. Frederick Kohn, *Iron and Steel Manufacture*, 1869, pp.47-48.
25. Frederick Kohn, op. cit., p.44. As well as a higher pressure blast, many of the anthracite furnaces were blown through ten small tuyères. This form of furnace blowing was not adopted in the rest of the South Wales coalfield.

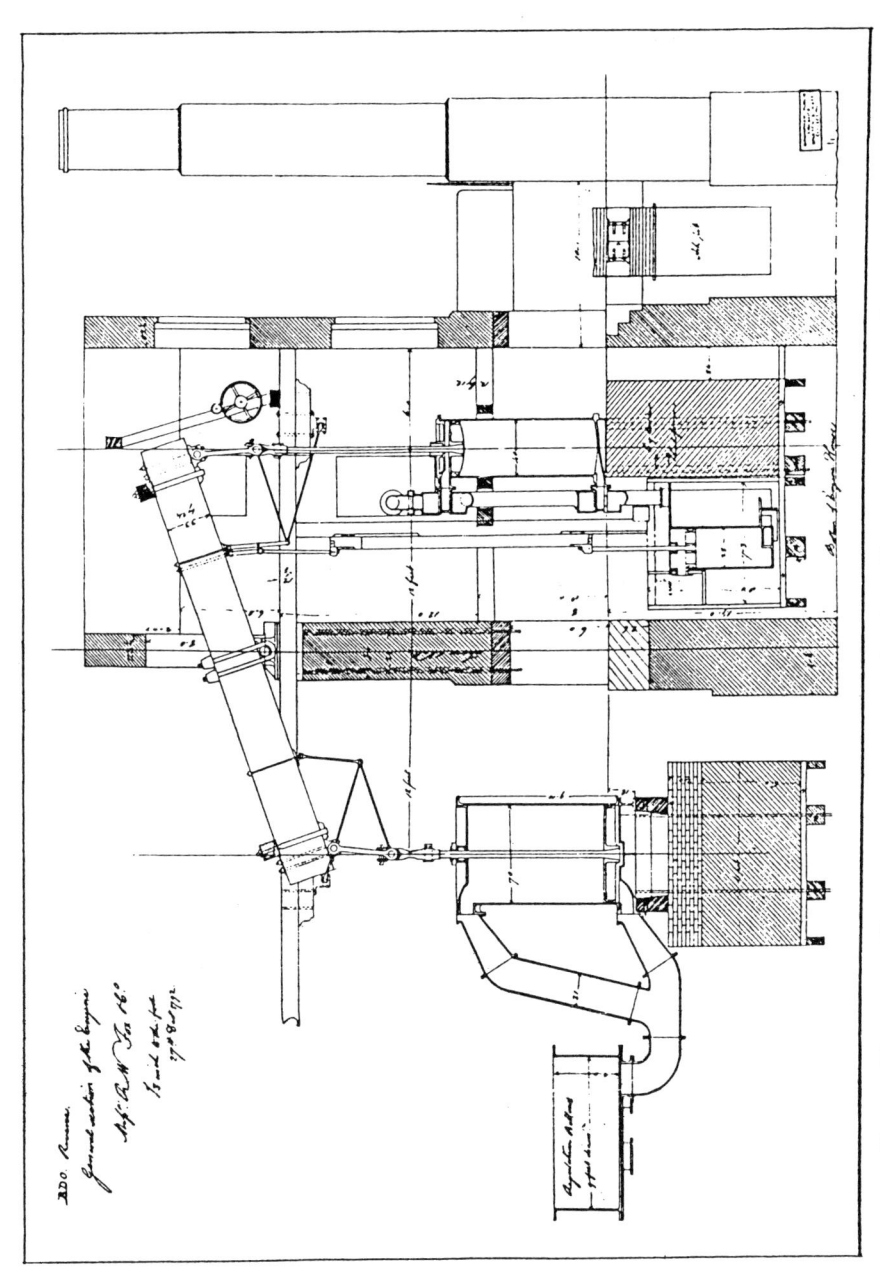

Figure Two — The Boulton & Watt Blowing Engine Built at Neath Abbey in 1793

Fig 3 — THE DARBY BLOWING ENGINE BUILT AT THE EBBW VALE IRONWORKS IN 1865

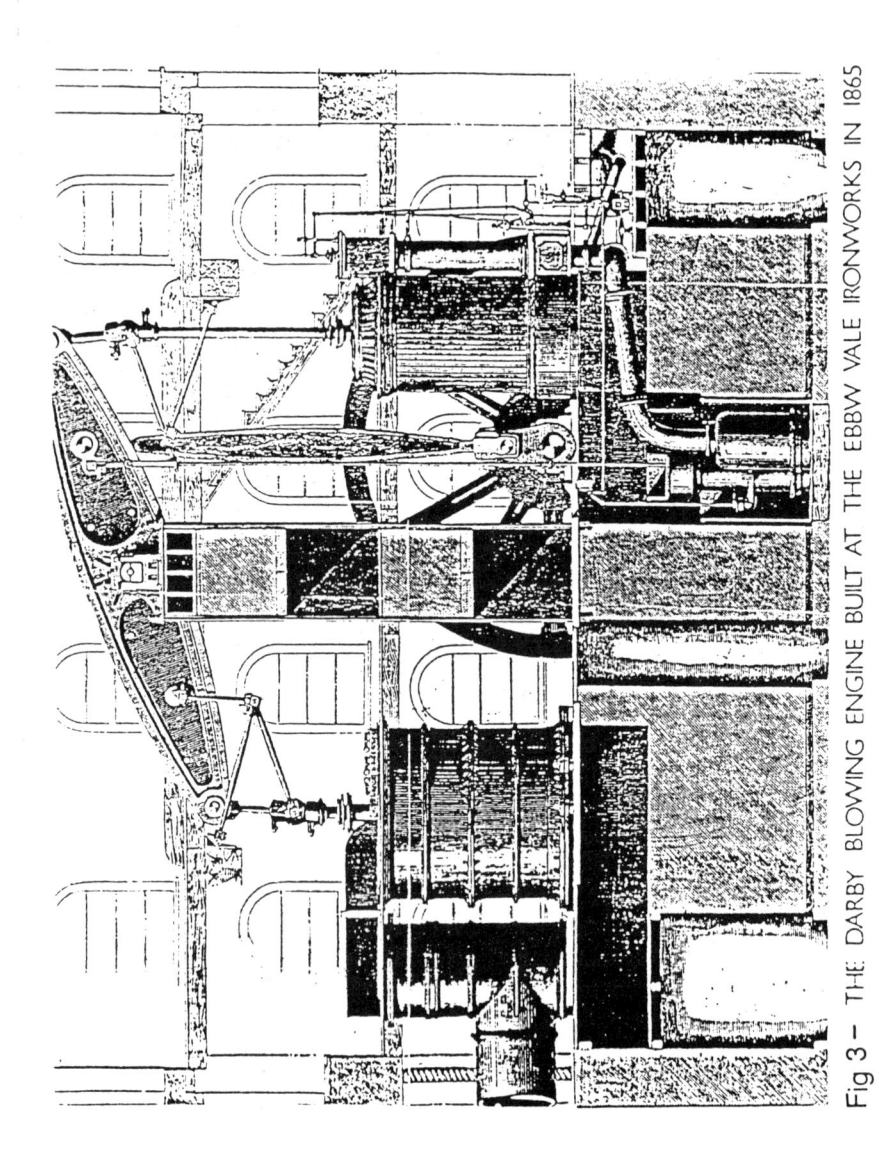

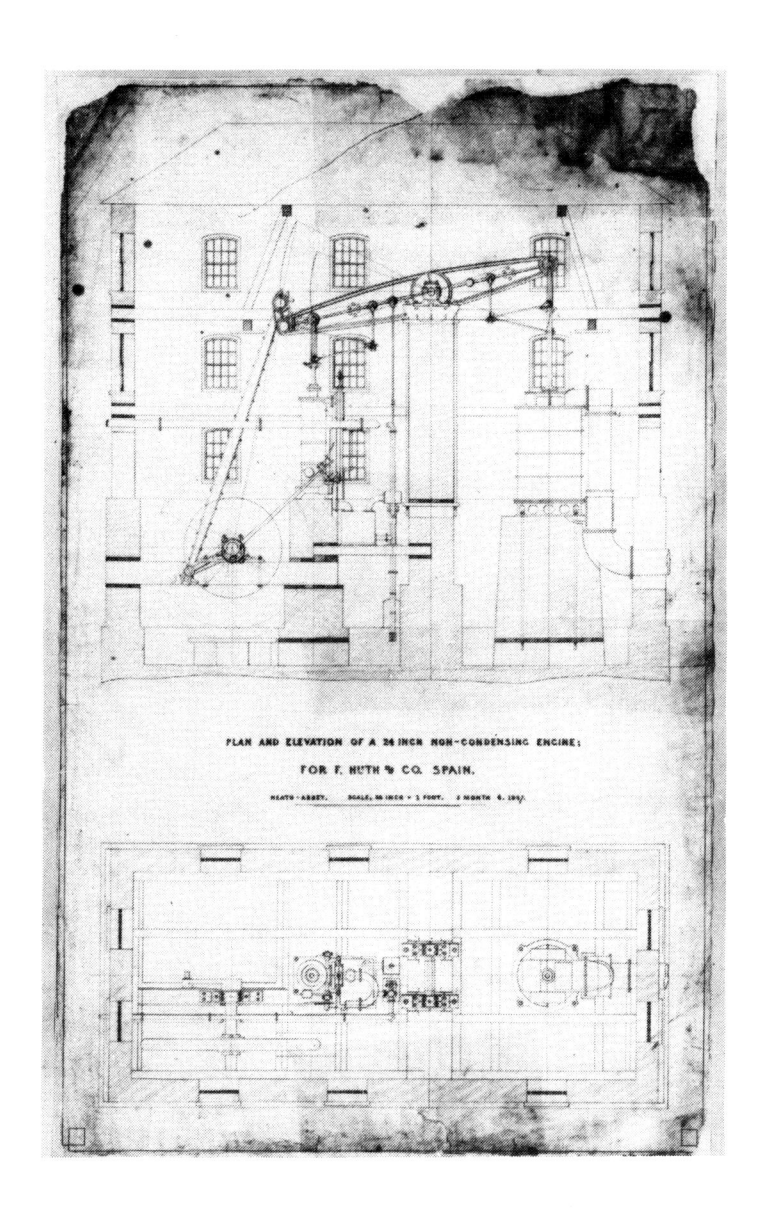

Plate One   *A typical beam blowing engine built by the Neath Abbey Iron Company. This example was a 24in. rotative non-condensing engine constructed in 1847 for Spain. (Courtesy Mr.A.W. Taylor and the Archive Service for Glamorgan)*

Chapter Three.

Wrought Iron and Rolling Mills.

One great problem still faced the expanding iron industry in the late eighteenth century when coke smelting had been established. The production of wrought iron, which was purer and more sought after than cast iron, was lagging behind the advances made in other areas of the industry. Wrought iron was an important product because it could be rolled and shaped.

In the early eighteenth century pig iron was converted into wrought iron in a forge using a charcoal fired hearth called a finery. The iron was heated and stirred while a blast of air was played on it. The oxygen in the air blast combined with the carbon in the iron and conversion took place. The iron was then heated and shaped in another hearth called a chafery. Output from the finery was low and a more efficient means of conversion had to be found if the growth of the iron industry was to be sustained.

It was soon realised that it would be necessary to expand the production of wrought iron using coal and not charcoal as the fuel. The first step forward came with the use of the stamping and potting process which allowed wrought iron to be made using coal. This helped to revolutionise the British iron industry and soon a forge at Cyfarthfa was using this method. During this process iron was heated in closed pots to stop impurities from the coal reaching the product. Several experimenters tried to discover an efficient conversion method using a reverberatory furnace in which the burning coal was separated from the melting iron.[1] One of these experimenters was Peter Onions who took out a patent for a method of making wrought iron with a reverberatory furnace while working at Merthyr Tydfil. This patent was taken out in 1783 but it was to be in the following year that Henry Cort patented his more successful method. Cort was the proprietor of the Fareham Ironworks, Hampshire and his patent not only covered the making of wrought iron but also the finishing of iron bars by the use of grooved rolls instead of by the forge hammer.

Some of the early experiments carried out with Cort's puddling process were conducted by Welsh ironmasters.[2] A trial of Cort's rolling methods was carried out in June 1784 by Francis Homfray at his rolling and slitting mill at Hyde on the River Stour. Richard Crawshay at the Cyfarthfa Ironworks also showed an early interest in Cort's process. At Cyfarthfa a forge was already working using Charles Wood's stamping and potting process but trials with Cort's methods must have taken place in 1787. During that year Crawshay came to an agreement with Cort to use his process and pay ten shillings a ton royalty. Crawshay altered his forge to make puddled wrought iron and at about the same time the Homfrays of Penydarren began to experiment with puddling. Crawshay's forge and rolling mill were designed by Henry Cort and had eight puddling furnaces capable of producing three tons of wrought iron per week. After some initial success with puddling, Crawshay's forge manager had great trouble in producing wrought iron to a constantly good standard.[3] Crawshay's iron only improved after modifications to the method were introduced at Cyfarthfa and the key to the success of puddling in South Wales proved to be the introduction of an intermediate refining stage. It is highly likely that the idea of using a refinery before puddling was the invention of Samuel Homfray of the Penydarren Ironworks.

Later, because of the activities of some of Cort's business associates his patent was seized by the Navy and the patentee died a bankrupt. Cort's family petitioned Parliament hoping for some payment for the widespread use of Cort's method by the iron industry. A Select Committee of the House of Commons met in 1812 and took evidence on the matter. However, during this enquiry the Welsh ironmasters gave evidence which would appear to have questioned the validity of the patent.[4] Certainly some of the constituent parts of Cort's process were known before the patent but it was Cort who brought them all together to radically improve the output of wrought iron in Britain. However, it is also true that the intermediate refinery stage, pioneered at Merthyr Tydfil, improved upon Cort's process by increasing production and cutting down on the time required for the operation of a charge.[5]

The refinery stage took out certain impurities from the iron manufactured by Welsh blast furnaces. A typical refinery was a shallow rectangular hearth having an area of 16 square feet and a depth of 18 inches. The back and sides were formed of hollow cast iron blocks through which water could circulate and the front consisted of a solid iron plate containing the tap hole. The rectangular space above the hearth was enclosed by two wrought iron side plates, two swing doors at the back and a single lever door in front. The complete structure was surmounted by a chimney to carry off the products of combustion. The blast of air for the refinery was supplied through six tuyères, three on each side. The tuyères were inclined downwards at an angle of between 25 to 30 degrees so as to blow into the hearth without blowing against each other. A typical refinery could handle between one and two tons of iron at a time. When the iron melted, silicon, phosphorus, sulphur and some carbon were oxidised. The molten metal was then run into a shallow iron mould under which water circulated. On cooling the 'plate metal' was then broken up and puddled.

The puddling furnace evolved into a rectangular fire-brick structure about 12ft. long, 4ft. wide and 6ft. high. The importance of the puddling furnace, which was cased in iron plates, was in its reverberatory nature which allowed burning coal and melting iron to be kept separate. The grate was at one end and was separated from the bed by a fire-bridge which stretched across the furnace. A free burning coal was used in the grate for this allowed the draught to pass through. When the making of iron with anthracite coal was pioneered in South Wales, it was soon realised that the anthracite ironworks would operate at a great disadvantage for anthracite caked on burning and was therefore unsuitable as a fuel for puddling. Puddling was a long and arduous process which entailed an operative having to mix the melting iron within the furnace and then later having to bring the molten metal together in balls. These operations were carried out by the puddler standing close to the furnace using long bars called rabbles and paddles.[6]

As early as 1818 improvements in puddling were being put forward. In that year Samuel Rogers of the Nantyglo Ironworks suggested the replacement of the solid sand bottom of the puddling furnace with a bottom composed of cast iron plates cooled from below by the circulation of air. An important step forward in the making of wrought iron by puddling was the discovery by Joseph Hall of adding iron oxide to the puddling charge in the furnace.[7] This led to the rapid oxidation of the carbon in the molten iron. In 1838 Hall with Richard Bradley and William Barrows took out a patent for calcining cinder and using it for lining or fettling the furnace bottom. This calcined product was called bull-dog. Hall's methods became known as pig boiling or wet puddling. This method cut down the time required to puddle a charge, improved the efficiency of puddling and to a large extent made the intermediate refinery stage redundant. Many ironworks adopted wet puddling but the refining of iron still took place at many of the South Wales' ironworks. Refined iron was bought by tinplate works and they themselves converted it into wrought iron using charcoal as a fuel. Charcoal iron was considered ideal for making the highest quality tinplates.

In puddling, silicon and carbon became oxidised with the carbon being released as carbon dioxide and the silicon and other elements becoming the fluid cinder. The spongy mass of refined metal drawn from the puddling furnace at the end of the process was at welding heat and wet with molten cinder. The iron had then to be shingled by hammering it to expel the slag and consolidate it into a bloom. In the early days of the Welsh iron industry shingling would be done under a tilt or helve hammer worked by waterwheels. The later course of the industry saw steam hammers in use for shingling although mechanical squeezers were preferred. In the crocodile squeezer the hot bloom of iron was forced between two heavy jaws which were made to open and close by means of a powerfully driven crank and connecting rod. The shingler was thus able to push in the ball of iron as the jaw rose so that it was gripped by the serrated under-surface of the jaw as it descended and was effectively squeezed. This was repeated until shingling was finished.

When the rough slab of iron was shingled it still was at bright red heat and was taken to a forge train (puddling rolls) where the metal was worked down to puddled bar. The bars of puddled iron were very rough looking as they contained cinder distributed through their mass in irregular patches. The bars would then be sent down to the mill to be cut into short lengths and made into piles. These piles were then raised to a welding heat in a reverberatory furnace known as a balling or reheating furnace. The piles were then worked down to the required section in a rolling mill, this product being called merchant bar. These reworkings of the wrought iron progressively improved its quality.

The wrought iron bars could then be put through a number of mill processes. The bars could be put through a primary mill called a blooming or cogging mill where the cross section would be reduced, the length increased and the structure improved by putting work into the metal. The metal could be reheated and put through a further mill to produce the final product, perhaps rails or structural ironwork. Rails would be produced by reheating piles of iron to forging temperature and passing them through a rolling mill. The rolls would have several apertures which would progressively change the iron to the rail shape as a number of passes through the mill were made. A special pair of rolls was required for each product and in 1865 the Briton Ferry Ironworks had 63 pairs of rolls in stock.[8] Most of the Welsh ironworks also had their own workshops which had roll lathes to cut and manufacture different designs of rolls.[9] Some of the Welsh ironworks had slitting mills which divided bar iron into narrow strips and in the later period guide mills were also adopted. The iron destined for a guide mill first passed through a hole in a metal block and then into the rolling mill, this process guaranteeing that the axis of the metal was in the correct position when it entered the rolls.

Many of the early rolling mills were inefficient for the metal had to be returned over the two rolls each time after a pass. This problem was solved by having a three-high mill in which a third roll was mounted above the two others. The piece of iron went between the lower and middle rolls and returned between the upper and middle; work was done in both directions and rolling time was halved.[10] In the second half of the nineteenth century the efficiency of the two-high mill was improved by being powered by a reversing engine.

Early rolling mills were powered by waterwheels, some surviving with auxiliary steam engine drive until the end of the Welsh wrought iron trade.[11] A great improvement in rolling came with the adoption of the steam engine to power the machinery. Boulton & Watt beam engines were used to power some rolling mills in South Wales, a typical example being supplied to the Dowlais Ironworks in 1808.[12] This was a 31½in. x 7ft. beam engine with an 18ft. diameter flywheel. Early Trevithick high pressure engines were also purchased by the South Wales iron industry. These were favoured for driving puddle rolls and an example of this type was the Trevithick engine supplied in 1804 to the Tredegar Ironworks.[13] This engine had a cylindrical boiler with a vertical 28in. x 6ft. steam cylinder. The typical steam engine used in South Wales for rolling iron was the beam engine and examples were manufactured by the Neath Abbey Iron Company.[14] Most of the Welsh mills were beam engine driven although examples of horizontal and vertical engines began to be installed in some ironworks from the late 1840s onwards. Certainly in the later period of the industry the twin horizontal reversing engine began to find favour among ironworks' engineers. Some very large beam engines were constructed for the iron industry and two notable examples were built at the Dowlais Ironworks in 1857.[15] These were coupled beam engines designed by Dowlais' engineers. They were 45in. x 10ft. engines working at 24 strokes per minute. The two beams were supported on eight columns, with each beam weighing 37 tons. The flywheel turned at 100r.p.m. and was 21ft. diameter with a weight of 30 tons. These engines powered the rolling mills in Dowlais' legendary Goat Mill and they provided the power to turn out weekly 1,700 tons of rails and 200 tons of bars. These high pressure beam engines were fitting examples of the many hundreds of engines of this type to be found in the South Wales iron industry in the period 1850-1885.

References.

1. R.A. Mott, *Henry Cort: The Great Finer*, 1983, pp.1-15.
2. R.A. Mott, op. cit., 51-56.
3. *The Letterbook of Richard Crawshay*, Cardiff, 1990.
4. Samuel Homfray and William Crawshay gave evidence which put Cort's patent in doubt.
5. The use of the refinery stage became known as the 'Welsh Method' and the iron produced by the refinery process was known as 'finers metal'.
6. For a description of puddling see, W.K.V. Gale, *The British Iron and Steel Industry*, Newton Abbot,1967, pp.43-47 & 62-74.
7. W.K.V. Gale, op. cit., pp.62-65.
8. C.W. Roberts, *A Legacy From Victorian Enterprise, The Briton Ferry Ironworks and Daughter Companies*, Gloucester, 1983, p.78.
9. In 1872 a medium sized ironworks such as Tredegar had five mills in use, the giant, Dowlais, operated fourteen mills.
Mineral Statistics, 1872.
10. W.K.V. Gale, op. cit., pp.81-82.
11. In 1869 Pentrebach the Plymouth Ironworks' subsidiary was still using some rolling mills powered by waterwheels. *Mining Journal*, October 2nd 1869, pp.742-743. Cyfarthfa was still operating their puddling mills with waterwheels as late as 1874.
Proceedings of the Institution of Mechanical Engineers, 1874, p.239.
12. BRL, B&W, Portfolio of Drawings for Engine No. 406, Dowlais, 1808.
13. Laurence Ince, Richard Trevithick's Patent Steam Engine, *Stationary Power*, Vol.1, 1984, p.69.
14. For a complete list of engines built at the Neath Abbey Ironworks see, Laurence Ince, *The Neath Abbey Iron Company*, Eindhoven, 1984, pp.103-111.
15. William Menelaus, Description of the Large Blowing Engine and New Rolling Mill at Dowlais Ironworks, *Proceedings of the Institution of Mechanical Engineers*, 1857, pp.112-118.

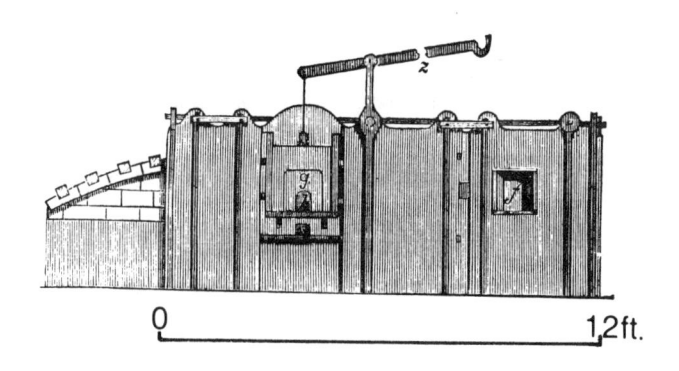

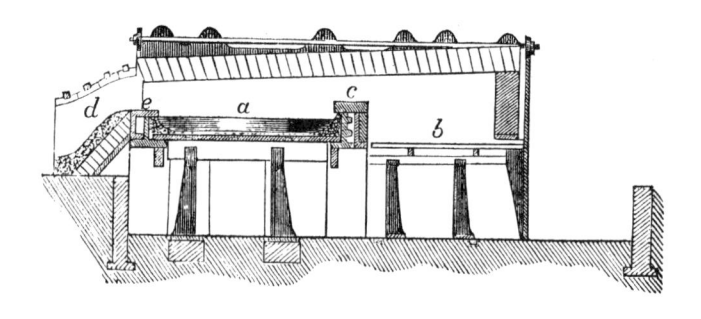

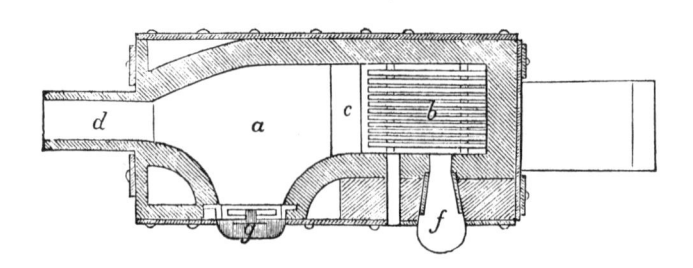

Figure Four – A Typical Puddling Furnace

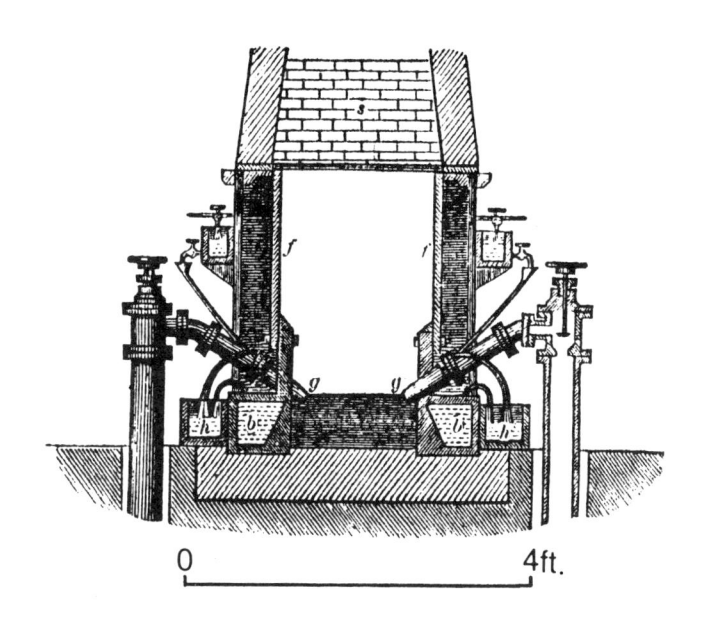

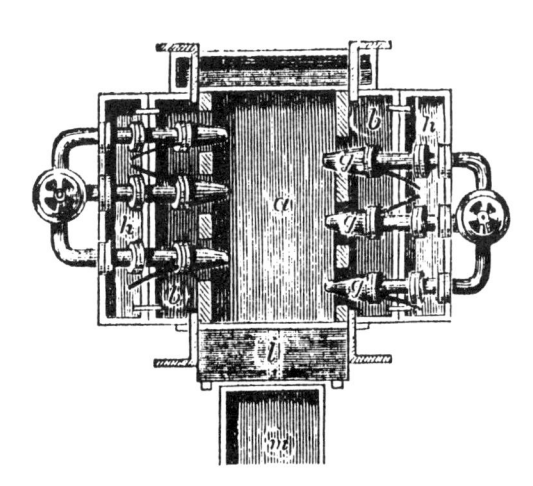

Figure Five – A Typical Refinery, 1870

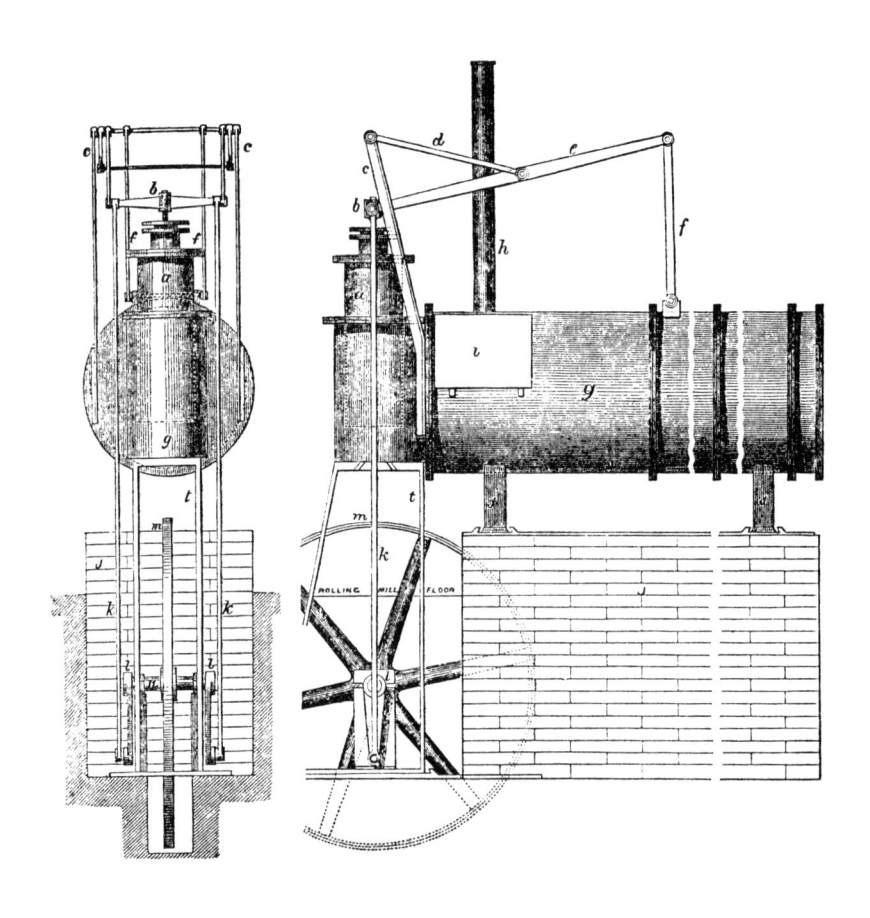

Figure Six – Trevithick's Mill Engine for Tredegar, 1804

Chapter Four.

The Demise of the Charcoal Iron Industry in South Wales.

The establishment of the coke iron industry initiated a steady decline in the production of charcoal iron in South Wales. However, this decline was to be of a prolonged nature for many of the charcoal furnaces continued in blast into the nineteenth century. The charcoal furnaces did not exist alone but were parts of extensive investment with many associated forges and mills. These ironworks were spread out to enable the ironmasters to take advantage of many differing water power sites. No doubt the charcoal iron industry managed to survive because of the large reserves of timber available in South Wales for fuel coupled with the high demand for iron during the turbulent period of war which ended in 1815. The major part of the cost of smelting iron was in acquiring charcoal for at the Llanelly Furnace in 1704 a ton of iron cost £3. 13s. 8d. to produce with £2. 9s. 10d. being expended on charcoal alone.[1] It is no wonder that the ironmasters adopted the new method of using mineral fuel which was cheaper and existed in huge quantities in combination with iron ore.

The charcoal iron industry in South Wales was characterised by groups of ironworks held by a small number of partnerships. One of the strongest was that formed in South East Wales by John Partridge of Monmouth and the Harford family of Bristol. In the late eighteenth century this Quaker partnership held furnaces at Caerphilly and at Bishopswood in the Forest of Dean with forges at Monmouth (three fineries and two chaferies), Magor (four fineries and two chaferies) and Melingriffith (three fineries, a chafery and a tin mill).[2] The principal partners of the company at that time were John Harford, James Harford, Samuel Harford and John Partridge.[3] The Harford family were later to be rare examples of charcoal ironmasters making the transition to the new flourishing coke iron industry. Wisely they did not develop their old charcoal sites but moved to invest at Ebbw Vale during this period.

The Caerphilly Furnace had a venerable history and was certainly working in the late seventeenth century. In 1717 it was producing annually two hundred tons of iron and was associated with forges at Machen and Tredegar. For a period Caerphilly was in the hands of James Pratt and in 1747 it was leased to Thomas Morgan of Ruperra, Hugh Jones and Samuel Pratt. This partnership traded as James Pratt and Company and then after the death of Samuel Pratt the partnership was known as Hugh Jones and Company. Thomas Morgan was the sole proprietor in 1754, and in 1764 the furnace was leased to John Maybery for twenty one years. Maybery was granted a further lease in 1775 and in that year a new waterwheel was built for blowing the furnace. In 1789 the ironworks was leased to James Harford, Philip Croker and

Truman Harford for twenty one years at £170 a year. The works continued under the ownership of the Harfords and John Partridge and in 1794 it consisted of a water blown charcoal furnace, a rolling mill and a slitting mill.[4] The output of iron from the furnace was 695 tons for 1796 and by this time the furnace was part of an interdependent group of works owned by Harfords and Partridge in South East Wales and the Forest of Dean.[5] The Caerphilly Furnace was probably in blast for the last time during the early years of the nineteenth century after which the site was abandoned.

Another important Quaker partnership was based in the Vale of Neath during this period. John Miers and Company operated a charcoal furnace at Melinycwrt with the iron being refined at Aberdulais (two fineries and a chafery) or at Aberavon (two fineries and a chafery). The wrought iron produced at these sites was then utilised at the partnership's tin mill at Ynysygerwyn.[6] The furnace at Melinycwrt had been built in 1708 by John Hanbury who used it to supply pig iron to his works at Pontypool.[7] In 1747 the furnace was leased to Rowland Pytt, later to Pytt and Thomas Lewis and after that the furnace was in the hands of Coles, Lewis and Company. John Miers joined the company and soon made the works his own, developing forges to convert the pig iron produced at Melinycwrt to wrought iron. The 1780s were a difficult period for John Miers and Company for Nathaniel Miers died in 1782 and John Miers died in 1787.[8] Nathaniel's son was a minor and so the concern was held by the executors of John Miers. At a later date the company's principal partners were John Nathaniel Miers and his cousin Dr. Samuel Fothergill Lettsom. The Melinycwrt Ironworks appears to have been rebuilt in 1793 for in the following year the furnace was operating with coke as a fuel. In 1796 the furnace produced 503 tons of iron and three years later the works was described as having a furnace 47ft. high and 13ft. wide, an air furnace 25ft. by 8ft. and also, a refining furnace. The blast was provided by a 38ft. diameter waterwheel and cylinders.[9] At this time the works was capable of producing 25 tons of iron per week when water was in good supply. The Melinycwrt Ironworks produced 950 tons of iron in 1805 but in around 1808 it finally closed, still held by John Miers and Company.

A similar enterprise consisting of iron furnaces, forges and tin mills was developed in West Wales by Robert Morgan (1708-1777). Morgan was the son of a coal factor from Kidwelly and before the middle of the century he had taken over an ironworks at his home town. Morgan also acquired the Priory Mills site in Carmarthen and built there a furnace and a forge. Later the Carmarthen Ironworks was enlarged by the building of a tin mill. Morgan's industrial empire grew as he developed forges at Cwmdwyfran, Cwmbran, Llandyfan, Kidwelly, Whitland and Blackpool in Pembrokeshire.[10] On Robert Morgan's death in 1777 the enterprises were run by his son John who built up a good reputation for the production of iron and tinplate. By 1794 there had been a reduction in the size of the business for Morgan was holding in that year at Carmarthen, tin mills, a furnace and a forge (two fineries and a chafery), at Kidwelly a tin mill and forge (two fineries and a chafery), at Whitland a forge (a finery and a chafery) and at Cwmdwyfran a forge (two fineries and a chafery). The output of the Carmarthen Ironworks was reported as 290 tons for 1796.[11] John Morgan transferred the running of the business to his nephew, also named John Morgan, but the enterprise began to fail and to save the situation Morgan took William and Thomas Morris as partners. The Carmarthen Furnace was blown out shortly after this event. The concern traded as John Morgan and Company and then after Morgan's death as Morris, Morgan and Company. After the expiry of the lease in 1821 the works at Carmarthen passed to Reynolds and Smith who within a few years transferred the undertaking to Aberavon. It appears that the forge at Cwmdwyfran continued in operation until at least 1836.

Another ancient charcoal furnace operated at Tintern in Monmouthshire. Certainly a furnace was operating at this site in the second half of the seventeenth century associated with a wire making works. In the eighteenth century the works was held by a succession of owners who included John Hanbury of Pontypool and David Tanner who held the lease in 1775. The Tanner family were important figures in the Welsh iron trade and at various times held interests in ironworks at Brecon, Caerleon, Blaendare and Cyfarthfa. The Tintern Furnace was operated for a period by Robert Thompson and later by William Matthews before the furnace was blown out for the last time in 1828. In the early years of the nineteenth century the furnace was producing 28 to 30 tons of charcoal forge pig iron per week, the furnace charge being composed of ⅞ Lancashire haematite and ⅛ of Forest of Dean ore. After the closure of the furnace, the forges and wireworks continued in operation until 1901. During the later period the Tintern works were being used for the production of tinplate.[12]

Although the furnace and forge at Brecon was to be a comparatively small scale venture, its later development was to have important repercussions for the course of the South Wales iron industry. The furnace was built alongside the River Honddu in the early 1720s by Benjamin Tanner, ironmonger of Brecon and Richard Wellington, gentleman of Hay. Known leases for this concern date from 1723 although the date of 1720 was cast on a lintel in the furnace. At about the same time the partners also developed a forge at Pipton near Glasbury. In 1750 the enterprise was in the hands of Benjamin Tanner's son William who assigned all interest in the works to Thomas Daniel and Richard Reynolds, merchants and dealers in iron from Bristol. Three years later Reynolds and Daniel sold their interest in the works for £400 to Thomas Maybery who conveyed the concern to his son John. The Maybery family were experienced within the iron trade for they had previously held an interest in the Powick Forge on the River Teme in Worcestershire. This business was expanded in 1757 when land was leased at Hirwaun to provide the furnace at Brecon with additional iron ore. A furnace was also built at Hirwaun and this is thought to be the first coke furnace to operate in South Wales. The successful operation of the Hirwaun Ironworks meant that the furnace at Brecon soon fell out of use.[13] The building of this small coke fired iron furnace at Hirwaun in 1757 was to be the beginning of the large scale development of the South Wales Coalfield by the expanding iron industry.

References.

1. John van Laun, *The Clydach Gorge: Industrial Archaeology Trails in a North Gwent Valley*, 1979, p.18.
2. BRL, B&W, List of Ironworks, 1794, taken from the papers of the late Mr. Wilkinson.
3. William Rees, *Industry Before the Industrial Revolution*, Cardiff, 1968, p.304.
4. BRL, B&W, List of Ironworks, 1794.
5. Harry Scrivenor, *History of the Iron Trade*, 1854, pp.95-96.
6. BRL, B&W, List of Ironworks, 1794.
7. Harry Green, Melinycwrt Furnace: Earth, Air, Fire and Water, *Transactions of the Neath Antiquarian Society*, 1980-81, pp.43-76.
8. Arthur Raistrick, *Quakers in Science and Industry*, Newton Abbot, 1968, p.305.
9. Harry Green, op. cit., p.62.
10. William Rees, op. cit. pp.309-312.
11. Harry Scrivenor, op. cit., pp.95-96.
12. H.W. Paar and D.G. Tucker, The Old Wireworks and Ironworks of the Angidy Valley at Tintern, Gwent, *Journal of the Historical Metallurgy Society*, Vol.9, No.1, 1975, pp.1-14.
    John Pickin, Excavations at Abbey Tintern Furnace, *Journal of the Historical Metallurgy Society*, Vol.16, No.1, 1982, pp.1-21.
13. John Lloyd, *The Early History of the Old South Wales Iron Works 1760-1840*, 1906, pp.1-10.
    William Rees, op. cit., pp.308-309.

Figure Seven — The Glamorganshire Ironworks

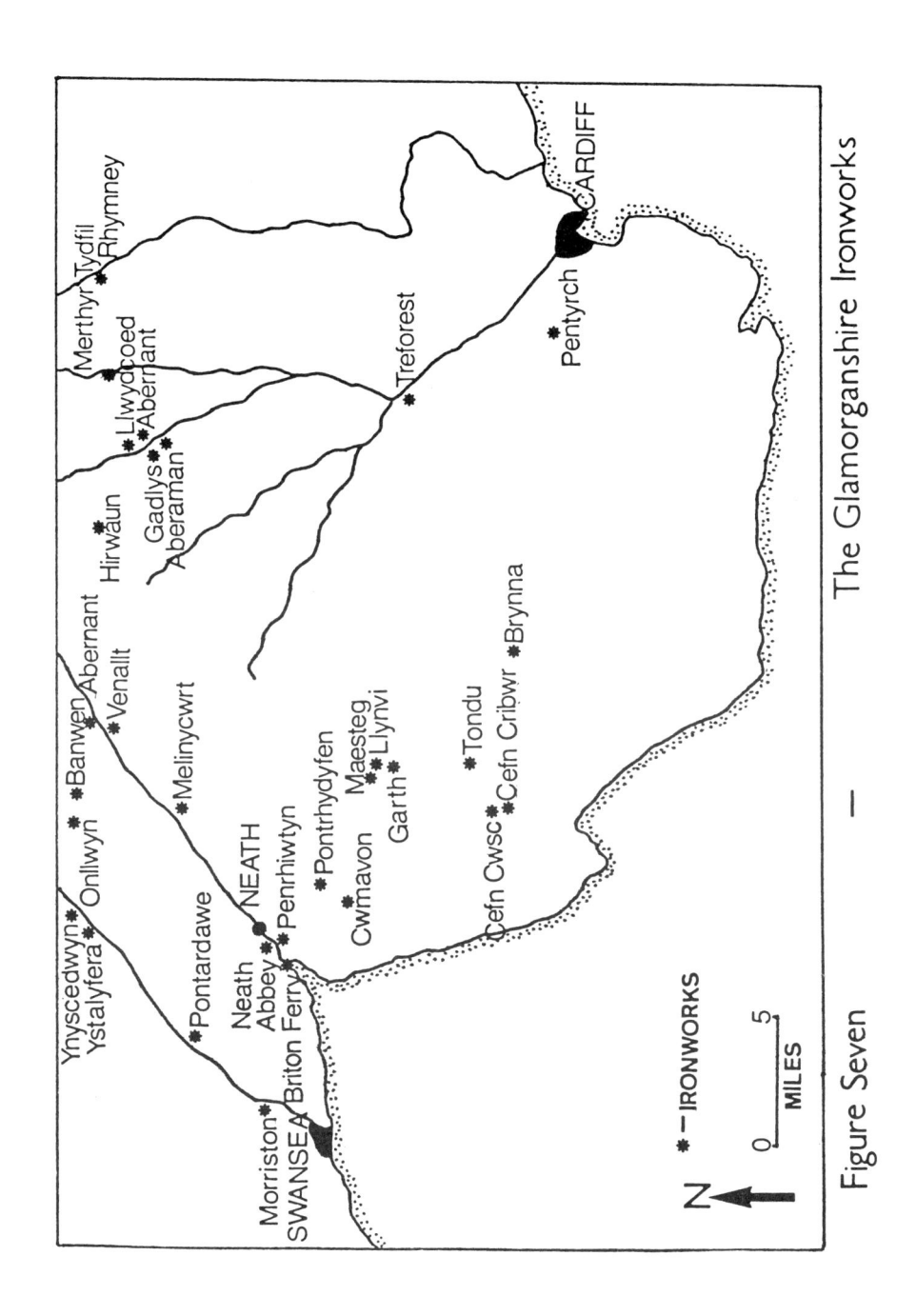

Chapter Five.

The Iron Industry of Aberdare and the Cynon Valley.

It is fitting that in this opening chapter on the coke iron industry we deal with the history of what was probably the first coke fired iron furnace in South Wales, namely Hirwaun. This enterprise dates back to 1757 when John Maybery leased land at Hirwaun which gave him the right to erect a furnace and also permission to take 200 dozen horse loads of iron ore to his furnace at Brecon. The furnace at Hirwaun was constructed on a site just outside Bute land but a new lease in 1760 incorporated the land on which the single furnace stood, the partners at this time being John Wilkins, John Maybery and Mary Maybery. These partners, in 1775, disposed of the Hirwaun Ironworks to John Wasse of Stafford and William King, a Bristol glassmaker. Their lease was to run for fourteen years and this new partnership agreed to repair the waterwheel and cylinders that blew the furnace. Another condition of the lease was that 300 tons of dark grey pig iron had to be supplied to the old partnership at £4 per ton. However, King died insolvent and the works had not supplied this iron so a distress was initiated through the courts. When this happened Bowzer, the agent and clerk at Hirwaun who was not highly thought of, removed pig iron from the yard at night and sent it to Bristol. This resulted in the termination of the lease in 1777.

The next period in the history of the Hirwaun Ironworks opens in 1780 with the concern being leased to Anthony Bacon of Cyfarthfa at a cost of £133. 6s. 8d. yearly.[1] It has been suggested that the Hirwaun Furnace was charcoal fired and Bacon converted it to coke.[2] This idea comes from the writings of Theophilus Jones who in 1809 stated that Hirwaun "was used for the purpose of smelting ore with charcoal for many years, and afterwards with pit or mineral coal, being supplied by blast by means of a water wheel". The 1757 lease allowed for the construction of a furnace and the local correspondent for *The Engineer* mentions an early furnace operating at Hirwaun from the 1660s onwards. In 1775 the new owners were required by the lease to repair the waterwheel and cylinders that provided the blast at the furnace. This blowing machinery was obviously of some age and cylinders were mainly associated with coke smelting.[3] It seems that Jones was describing an ancient charcoal furnace which operated at Hirwaun which was later replaced by Maybery's coke furnace.

Bacon put the works in repair and continued the production of iron on the site until his death in 1786. Hirwaun was then left to his natural sons Anthony and Thomas Bacon and as they were minors the property was placed under the custody of the Court of Chancery. The court granted the lease of the Hirwaun Ironworks to Samuel Glover of Abercarn who was allowed to carry on ironmaking at the site during the minority of Bacon's sons. Although the ironworks was assessed as producing 1,050 tons of iron in 1796, production seems to have seldom risen to over 10 tons per week.[4] When the brothers came of age they showed little interest in the iron trade and soon Anthony sold his share to Thomas for £3,000.

Thomas Bacon, even as sole owner, showed little liking for the business and in 1803 demised the property to Francis William Bowzer of Highwood, Hendon, Middlesex, Simon Oliver of Bristol, linen merchant, Lionel Oliver of Bristol, linen merchant and Jeremiah Homfray of Llandaff, ironmaster. Within a few years Homfray had retired from the partnership and his place was taken by George Overton. In 1805 there was still only one furnace at Hirwaun and during that year it produced 450 tons of iron.[5] After this date the partnership seems to have considerably developed the site for in 1813 when the Hirwaun Ironworks was put up for sale it consisted of two well constructed furnaces each 40ft. high, two cast houses, one 45ft. by 40, the other 36 by 33ft, an air furnace and two fineries, a blast engine on Boulton & Watt's principle 38in. x 6ft. 8in. with a 78in. blowing cylinder working through a water regulator, a forge 157ft. by 44ft. at one end and 34ft. at the other with ten puddling furnaces and five balling furnaces and a Trevithick steam engine working with a 6ft. stroke, two pairs of puddling and a pair of finishing rollers capable of rolling 80 to 100 tons weekly, (this engine was obviously put in during Homfray's involvement with the works as he and Birch were building Trevithick type engines for sale at their Abernant Ironworks, Aberdare). Other property in the sale included a counting house, a further forge, pattern room, drying sheds, carpenters' and smiths' workshops, a waterwheel for turning a lathe for the rollers and grinding clay, a brick kiln, four calcining kilns, mineral yard, coke banks, two counting houses, three limekilns, four collieries, iron ore levels, cottages and tenements.[6] The iron trade was in deep depression at this time and a sale was not concluded with the result that in the following year the partnership went bankrupt.

The ironworks remained unoccupied until William Crawshay of Cyfarthfa took over the lease in 1819. In the following year the two furnaces were rebuilt and a powerful 52½ in. beam blowing engine was constructed at the works by the Neath Abbey Iron Company.[7] Crawshay improved output at Hirwaun with 4,160 tons of iron being produced in 1823 and a year later two more furnaces were built.[8] Output continued to rise with 7,020 tons of iron being produced in 1826[9] and 9,370 tons in 1830.[10] The Hirwaun Ironworks was at first managed by William Crawshay's son Henry and after his departure to the Forest of Dean by Francis, another son. The Crawshay brothers appear to have been willing to experiment at Hirwaun for in 1830 a Gurney locomotive was tested on the tramroads serving the works.

The four furnaces continued in blast during the 1830s and 1840s with much of the iron produced at Hirwaun being sent to another Crawshay works at Treforest where it was made into bars and tinplate. It is possible that a second Neath Abbey 52½in. blowing engine was installed in 1839 and certainly a 24in. x 1ft. high pressure engine was purchased by the Hirwaun Ironworks from Neath Abbey in 1849.[11] Transport on the large network of tramroads around the works was improved with the purchase in around 1846 of locomotives built by the Neath Abbey Iron Company.[12]

Hirwaun was never a very profitable concern for any of its owners. During the 1850s the performance of the Hirwaun Ironworks under the management of Francis Crawshay gave the family grave concern. Also at this time relations between the Marquis of Bute, who owned part of the site, and Francis Crawshay worsened. The blast furnaces and mills were on Bute property with the furnace yard and limekiln on Crawshay property. From the mid 1850s onwards the Crawshays made plans to open blast furnaces at Treforest with the intent of abandoning Hirwaun. At that time it would appear that only one beam blowing engine was present at the works. This was a Neath Abbey low pressure condensing engine with a 52½in. steam cylinder and a 104in. blowing cylinder. The stroke of the engine was 7ft. 3in. and when making 16 strokes per minute it produced 13,688 cubic feet of air per minute at a pressure of 3 psi. The engine working the puddling rolls was also of a low pressure type with a 30in. x 6ft. cylinder working at 20 strokes per minute.[13]

The furnaces were in blast for the first six months of 1859 and then the Crawshays abandoned the site.[14]. The works reverted to the landowner who was the Marquis of Bute. His mineral agents managed to let the concern in 1864 when the Hirwaun Ironworks was leased by Handel Cossham and Thomas Challender Hinde who put two furnaces into blast.[15] In the following year the other two furnaces were repaired and in 1866 the works was controlled by the Hirwaun Iron and Coal Company headed by Handel Cossham.[16] However, the two furnaces only remained in blast for the first three months of that year. During this period two locomotives were purchased to aid the transportation of coal and iron ore on the Hirwaun tramroads. The first arrived in 1865 and was *Dewrance*, a rebuilt saddle tank with 14in. x 20in. cylinders purchased from Isaac Watt Boulton for £600. A second rebuilt saddle tank locomotive arrived in the next year from the same source and was called *Moon*. It had 12in. x 18in. cylinders and cost £800.[17] Operations at the ironworks were not a success and in 1867 the word iron was dropped from the title of the company.[18] The Hirwaun Ironworks was advertised for sale in 1870 and was described as having four furnaces with a powerful blast engine, arrangements for utilising waste gases, hot air stoves, a spacious forge and mills with powerful engine, trains of rolls, nineteen puddling furnaces, forges and steam hammers.[19] No interested parties came forward and the Hirwaun Coal Company was wound up.[20]

The ironworks site remained unoccupied until 1880 when the Stuart Iron, Steel and Tin Plate Company took it over.[21] The Hirwaun Ironworks was renamed the Stuart Ironworks and some work was carried out on the furnaces. These were altered to make them 54ft. high and 16ft. in diameter across the boshes with six tuyères.[22] It was thought that the efficiency of a furnace could be improved if the volume of air thrown into the structure could be increased, hence the multiplication of the tuyères. However, the result of adding more tuyères at Hirwaun is not known as little production of iron took place and the works later degenerated into a general foundry.

The development of the iron industry at neighbouring Aberdare began in 1800 with the formation of the partnership that was to lease land and build the Llwydcoed Ironworks (also known as the Aberdare Ironworks). In that year a lease for land at

Aberdare was transferred from Samuel Glover to John Thompson of Lye Hall, Quatt, Shropshire, John Hodgett of Gothersley, Kinver, Staffordshire and George and John Scale of Handsworth, Birmingham.[23] The lease was to run for seventy years with a payment of £1,000 per annum. This partnership contained a lot of practical iron making experience. John Thompson had operated forges in 1796/1797 at Hampton Loade and Eardington in Shropshire and John Hodgett was one of the principal slitters of iron in the Stour Valley.[24] Two furnaces were built, each 40ft. high with a diameter across the boshes of 14ft. The furnaces were waterwheel blown, the machinery constructed by Hazeldines's Foundry at Bridgnorth for £12 a ton.[25] In 1805 the two furnaces produced 3,586 tons of iron.[26] The partnership consisted in 1811 of William Thompson whose share included 3/16 purchased from Elizabeth Hodgett in that year, George Scale, John Scale, Samuel Homfray and William Forman.[27] The company expanded considerably when, in 1819, they purchased the neighbouring Abernant Ironworks.

The Abernant property had been leased in 1801 for 99 years to Jeremiah Homfray of Llandaff and James Birch of Aberdare.[28] Birch had previously been a manager at the Penydarren Ironworks which was owned by the Homfray family. The lease of Abernant stipulated that coal could be raised on the land for a payment of 6d. a ton and iron ore could be mined at a premium of 1s. per ton. A condition of the lease was that a furnace had to be built within two years and a second furnace completed within five years. In fact, three furnaces had been built by 1807. Birch and Homfray financed this expansion by enticing fresh money into the concern for in 1802 James Tappenden of Faversham, Kent, James Tappenden of Stourmouth, Kent and Francis Tappenden of Foster Lane, London joined the partnership. During the early years there seems to have been an attempt to develop engineering at the works for in 1804 the Abernant Ironworks was advertising the production of steam engines on Trevithick's and Boulton & Watt's plan.[29] The connection with Trevithick is easily traced for Jeremiah Homfray's brother Samuel was a partner with Trevithick in his patent for high pressure steam engines. Certainly, several Trevithick type stationary steam engines were constructed at this time by the Abernant Iron Company.[30]

Homfray and Birch retired from the company in around 1807 after a disagreement with the Tappendens. The Tappendens had built a tramroad from the differing industrial concerns in Aberdare to the Neath Canal and a dispute broke out between the partners over the running of the tramroad as a separate venture. Birch and Homfray were bought out of the company after Richard Fothergill acted as mediator. The Tappendens, who were bankers at Faversham, also became involved in a costly court action brought against them by the Neath Canal Company. On losing this action in 1814 they and their bank were forced into bankruptcy. The Abernant Ironworks was later sold to the Aberdare Iron Company in 1819.

In 1823 the company was operating three furnaces at each site and produced 5,676 tons of iron which had risen to 11,440 tons in 1826 and 12,571 tons in 1830.[31] The following year saw the Aberdare Iron Company consist of William Thompson, Thomas Fothergill, George Scale, Rebecca Scale and Thomas Forman.[32] John Scale had died in 1820 at the age of 53 and George Scale was to die in 1833 aged 50.[33] The enterprise continued to expand with two steam engines operating at Llwydcoed in 1837 and at the same time Abernant operated five engines. At the end of the 1830s the Aberdare Iron Company was producing 350 to 400 tons of iron per week from two furnaces using hot blast and four using cold blast.[34]

By 1844 the Aberdare Iron Company had been converted into a joint stock company with a capital of £100,000. However, within a few years of this event a dispute concerning the running of the company broke out. A disagreement arose between Henry and Mary Scale on one side and Rowland Fothergill on the other. The Court of Chancery decided in 1846 to settle the differences by selling the company. At that time Llwydcoed was described as having three blast furnaces, two engines and two large waterwheels for blowing, mine kilns and suitable workshops. Abernant had three blast furnaces, two blowing engines, a foundry, brick stove and kiln and a waterwheel for grinding clay and working lathes. Also at the Abernant site were fineries with a blowing engine.[35] Obviously the company had not yet entered the wrought iron trade but this was changed when the two ironworks were purchased by a new company headed by the Fothergills. The Aberdare Iron Company was managed by Rowland Fothergill (1794-1871) and later by his nephew Richard Fothergill (1822-1903).[36] Puddling furnaces were added and under Richard Fothergill both works were modernised.

Fothergill chose as his chief engineer Thomas Hosgood who had been trained at the engineering works of the Neath Abbey Iron Company. It is no wonder that part of the development of the works included the installation of Neath Abbey engines for in 1852 Neath Abbey supplied the Aberdare Iron Company with two 12in. horizontal engines and one 9½in. inverted vertical engine.[37] From 1854 to 1860 the Aberdare Iron Company, also known as Fothergill, Brown and Company, held the furnaces at Venallt in the Neath Valley although this proved an unsuccessful venture with little iron produced at this site.[38] In 1860 the puddling furnaces, which were at Abernant, were increased in number.[39] The Llwydcoed Ironworks at that time consisted of three blast furnaces, twenty hot blast stoves, fifty six coke ovens, six mine kilns, three limekilns, three blowing engines and two waterwheels of 40ft. diameter and 4ft. breadth.[40] The principal partners of the company in the early 1860s were Fothergill, Hankey and Bateman and after 1866 the partners were Fothergill, Hankey and Lewis.[41] Hankey and Bateman were London bankers and through their influence much 'blind capital' was attracted for investment in the Aberdare Iron Company. This money was used to purchase the Penydarren and Plymouth Ironworks in Merthyr Tydfil.

Expansion continued at Aberdare with a very large furnace being put into blast in 1861 although in the following year the Abernant Ironworks was only operating two furnaces.[42] At this time the production of iron by the company's furnaces was at about the 800 tons per week mark. Some production figures are available for the early 1860s and from these we find that No.1 furnace at Abernant produced 349½ tons of iron in the week ending November 7th 1862 while during the same period No.2 furnace at Abernant turned out 278 tons.[43] These furnaces served seventy puddling furnaces, a large rolling mill and two smaller mills. Another of the com-

pany's works at Treforest was at this time turning out 1,100 tons of rails each week. In the week ending 4th July 1863 the production figures of the company's furnaces were,
    Aberdare No.1 - 287 tons.
    Aberdare No.2 - 300 tons.
    Aberdare No.3 - 214 tons.
    Abernant No.1 - 287 tons.
    Abernant No.2 - 343 tons.
    Total - 1,431 tons[44]

Output was again improved in 1865 when a new blowing engine and blast furnace were put into operation at Llwydcoed.[45] Investment in this joint stock company was continuing to finance expansion with the concern becoming one of the largest suppliers to the wrought iron rail trade. A full picture of the extent of the Aberdare Iron Company is revealed in a description of its works published in 1869.[46] At that time Llwydcoed had three blast furnaces each 42ft. high with a diameter of 18ft. across the boshes. Two of these furnaces were in blast and were charged with ¼ Welsh mine with the remaining proportion being made up of Cumberland and Northampton ore. The coking of the coal for Abernant and Llwydcoed was achieved using 168 coke ovens. The blast at Llwydcoed was heated to 850-900°F. and was partly supplied by two waterwheels of 40ft. diameter and 5ft. wide positioned one above the other and working two 54in. blowing cylinders. It is probable that these were the waterwheels built by Hazeldine's Foundry at the commencement of the works. There were also four beam blowing engines providing the blast, one engine with an 84in. x 6ft. blowing cylinder, one with a 64in. x 7ft. blowing cylinder, one with a 78in. x 7ft. blowing cylinder and one engine having two blowing cylinders each 54in. x 6ft. All the engines blew into one large blast pipe. At Llwydcoed the iron was processed in three double refineries but all the puddling took place at Abernant. A railway connected the two works and was used to transport ore, coal and iron. The railway was built to a gauge of 2ft. 9in. and in 1864 two locomotives were used, namely a saddle tank with 8in. x 15in. cylinders built by Fletcher, Jennings and Company of the Lowca Engine Works, near Whitehaven and a saddle tank with 8in. x 16in. cylinders built by the Neath Abbey Iron Company. Two further Neath Abbey locomotives were also ordered in that year.[47] The average weekly production of the two furnaces at Llwydcoed and the one at Abernant was 1,105 tons of iron.

The furnace in blast at Abernant in 1869 was 40ft. high and 19ft. in diameter across the boshes, another furnace ready to be lit was 52ft. high and 18ft. in diameter across the boshes. The furnaces were closed with bell and hoppers and were blown with a hot blast at 850°F. The blast was supplied by five beam blowing engines, one engine with a 78in. x 7ft. blowing cylinder, one with a 68in. x 6ft. blowing cylinder, one with a 52in. x 5ft. blowing cylinder and two engines working four 30in. x 2ft. blowing cylinders.

The forges and mills at Abernant covered a very large area with the buildings consisting of iron roofing carried on cast iron columns. There were seventy eight puddling furnaces at Abernant supplying four trains of 19in. puddle bar rolls driven by four steam engines. The puddling furnaces received their draught from eight 48in. Lloyd's patent noiseless fans driven by two 10in. engines. There were also twenty seven balling furnaces and twenty one of these received a draught from six 48in. Lloyd's fans. The mills included two large rail mills and others for blooming fishplates and Russian chair plates; these mills were driven by three engines. There were also thirteen engines for driving saws, presses and punches including two 10in. engines for driving fans. One pair of shears was actuated by a single cylinder engine making 150 strokes per minute and was used to cut cold bars for the top and bottom of rail piles. Fifteen boilers provided steam for the engines at the mills and forges. There was also present a Lilleshall double acting steam hammer used for special orders and another was being made for the company. The forges produced 1,200 to 1,300 tons of puddled bars per week which supplied the mills at Abernant and Treforest. These mills were capable of producing 1,150 tons of railway iron per week. Also at Abernant were extensive foundries, smiths', carpenters' and fitting shops with the capability of making steam engines up to sixty horse power. The Aberdare Iron Company operated mills at Treforest which were served in 1869 by twenty four balling furnaces and two 48 in. Lloyd's fans. Additional power was achieved at Treforest with the purchase in 1871 of a 20in. x 2ft. vertical engine from the Neath Abbey Iron Company.[48]

There seems to have been some contraction in the capacity of the company in the early 1870s for in 1872 the Aberdare Iron Company was operating fifty five puddling furnaces and five rolling mills.[49] However, the company was still playing a large part in the export of wrought iron rails. In 1872 the Aberdare Iron Company was supplying rails to New Orleans, City Point (New York), Montreal and Pacasmayo and in 1874 large orders were supplied to Alexandria and France.[50] However, the collapse of the wrought iron rail trade extinguished Richard Fothergill's financial empire closing the ironworks at Abernant, Llwydcoed, Penydarren, Plymouth and Treforest during 1875. Many felt that Fothergill's dealings had not always been ethical. An industrial correspondent in 1875 held the opinion that the Plymouth and Aberdare Iron Companies had been virtually bankrupt for 25 years.[51] No doubt 'blind' investment through the joint stock system had kept the companies afloat. Perhaps the last word can be left to William Crawshay of Cyfarthfa who had made large sales of bars and slabs to Fothergill in the early 1860s and when the Aberdare Iron Company took a Spanish rail contract for 15,000 tons at £5 a ton he commented, 'What can they be at, selling rails at £5 a ton and giving us £5. 2s. 6d. for what they make them of.'[52]

Fothergill's companies were liquidated by arrangement and the debts capitalised. The assets were valued at £1,200,000 and it was decided that the works could be carried on by a committee of control. This consisted of seven men, five representing the largest creditors, the sixth representing the mortgage debt and the seventh representing the working capital subscribed. A dividend of one shilling in the pound was paid out from the sale of some iron left at the works' sites.[53] Some of the collieries were worked but the iron making side of the business was never reopened and Richard Fothergill retired from the company in 1877.

The third ironworks to be built in the Aberdare area was at Gadlys in 1827. The partners in this single furnace ironworks were George Rowland Morgan, Edward Morgan Williams and Matthew Wayne.[54] Wayne had been a furnace manager at the Cyfarthfa Ironworks and then was involved in the development of the Nantyglo Ironworks. The furnace was first put into blast in 1828 and was blown by a 34 in. beam blowing engine supplied by the Neath Abbey Iron Company.[55] The works was advertised for sale in 1835 and consisted of 350 acres of mineral property with an ironworks employing 150 people. The single furnace was described as being able to make 1,700 to 2,000 tons of iron annually, blown by an engine which also supplied the blast to a refinery. Other property on the site included a cast house, stove room, turning room, cupola, smiths' shop, weighing machine, bridge house, carpenters' shop, office, punching machine and turning lathe. There were also three calcining kilns for burning off the impurities in the iron ore. The iron produced at Gadlys was praised for its strength in castings and for engine parts. No less than 5,600 yards of tram plates weighing 200 tons were present in 1835 in and about the works. A coal pit was situated close to the works and was drained by two 8in. pumps, one worked by a 24ft. diameter waterwheel and the other by a high pressure steam engine.[56] A sale of the ironworks does not appear to have been negotiated for the concern remained in the hands of a company headed by Matthew Wayne (1780-1853) and after his death Gadlys was managed by his son, Thomas Wayne (1810-1867).

In 1845 a 24in. beam engine was supplied to Gadlys by the Neath Abbey Iron Company and this was followed two years later by the supply of a 12in. engine from the same source.[57] This must have been part of a general development of the works for in 1850 there were three furnaces in blast and a further engine with a 30in. cylinder was supplied by the Neath Abbey Iron Company.[58] The number of furnaces at Gadlys had risen to four by 1854 but in that year only two were in blast.[59] The Gadlys Iron Company concentrated on producing cold blast iron for tinplate bars or ductile armour iron.[60] Production was diversified when, in 1861, a small rail mill was built which could roll merchant bars or rails.[61] One of the furnaces at Gadlys was rebuilt in 1869 and a further rail mill was constructed giving the works the capacity to produce 500 to 600 tons of rails per week.[62] The Gadlys Ironworks was listed in 1872 as operating fifteen puddling furnaces and two rolling mills and in that year the owners reorganised under the title of the Gadlys Coal and Iron Company Limited which was later changed to Wayne's Merthyr Steam Coal and Iron Works Limited.[63] The ironworks continued to produce cold blast iron until its closure in 1876 and in the following year it was put up for sale at £60,000 although there was a £120,000 mortgage on the property.[64] No prospective purchasers came forward and the furnaces were never put into blast again although the associated collieries continued to be worked.

A later development in the iron industry of the Cynon Valley occurred when the rich mineral estate of Aberaman was purchased in 1837 by Crawshay Bailey.[65] Bailey was a cousin of the Crawshays of Cyfarthfa and had successfully operated the Nantyglo and Beaufort Ironworks making himself a considerable fortune. Bailey did not exploit his Aberaman investment until 1845 when he constructed three furnaces on the property.[66] A 44in. x 9ft. beam blowing engine with a massive 122in. blowing cylinder was purchased from the Neath Abbey Iron company to provide the blast.[67] Although the furnaces were out of blast in 1854 they were continually at work from 1855 until 1866.[68] There was an attempted sale of the works in 1862 for £250,000 and there was another reported sale in 1864 when a £100,000 deposit was paid and the Aberaman Iron Company floated.[69] This attempt at taking over the Aberaman Ironworks appears to have turned into a shambles for the company's advertisements stated that they were to use the local iron ore which had an iron content of 60 to 70%![70] The affairs of the Aberaman Iron Company were wound up by the Court of Chancery in 1867 and in that year the ironworks was taken over by the Powell Duffryn Steam Coal Company.[71] At that time the works consisted of four furnaces, seventeen puddling furnaces, a small forge and a mill.[72] Although there were reports in 1868 of the alteration of the buildings into a tinworks and reports in 1872 of repairs to the works, it would appear that the works remained abandoned.[73] It would seem that the Aberaman Ironworks was acquired for its valuable mineral ground which continued to be exploited while the works remained unoccupied.

It will also be expedient in this chapter to deal with the industrial developments at Treforest which is in the main Taff Valley. The Treforest area had a strong commercial link with the Cynon Valley for the Aberdare Iron Company had rolling mills there and also bar iron was transported from Hirwaun to the Crawshay's tinplate works at Treforest. The deterioration of relations between Francis Crawshay and the Marquis of Bute over operations at Hirwaun prompted the Crawshays to develop a site near their tinplate works at Treforest. Two furnaces were completed in 1859 and another was two thirds finished.[74] However, a dispute broke out between Francis Crawshay and his father and the furnaces remained out of blast. They were described as three of the finest blast furnaces in Wales with a powerful blast engine which cost £6,500.[75] The furnaces continued to be kept out of blast and by 1869 only two furnaces were operable. The Treforest Ironworks was saved from ruin when it and 60 acres of mineral ground were purchased in late 1871 by the Forest Iron and Steel Company (Limited).[76] The partners in this enterprise were Sir William T. Lewis of Aberdare, William Menelaus, Edward Williams of Bolckow, Vaughan and Company, Sir Isaac Lowthian Bell, G.T. Clark, and some London bankers.[77] Three furnaces were in blast during 1873 producing Bessemer pig iron using imported haematite ores.[78] At this time iron made using Welsh ore was unsuitable for conversion into steel using the Bessemer process. Imported ores which were low in phosphorus had to be used to make a suitable iron for conversion through the Bessemer process. Output at Treforest in 1876 was 250 tons weekly for each of the two furnaces in blast and in 1880 a furnace was constructed on the Middlesbrough pattern which produced 80 tons daily.[79] Ironmaking at Treforest continued until 1900 when exhaustion of coal at the works' collieries forced a closure.[80]

References.

1. John Lloyd, *The Early History of the Old South Wales Iron Works 1760-1840*, 1906, pp.11-18.

2. For a discussion of this see, Philip Riden, *A Gazetteer of Charcoal-fired Blast Furnaces in Great Britain in use since 1660*, Cardiff, 1987,p.3.
3. Laurence Ince, Water Power and Cylinder Blowing in early South Wales Coke Ironworks, *Historical Metallurgy*, Vol.23, No.2, 1989, pp.108-111.
4. BRL, B&W, Journal of a Visit to Ironworks in South Wales, James Watt Junior, c.1800.
5. BRL, B&W, List of Furnaces in Great Britain, 1806, giving statistics for 1805.
6. D. Morgan Rees, *Mines, Mills and Furnaces*, 1969, pp.74-75.
7. Glamorgan Record Office (G.R.O.), Cardiff and Swansea, Neath Abbey Ironworks Collection (NAI), D/D N.A.I., M/108/4-M/108/5, Drawings for a 52½in. engine for Hirwaun Ironworks, 1820. Laurence Ince, *The Neath Abbey Iron Company*, Eindhoven, 1984, p.104.
8. Harry Scrivenor, *History of the Iron Trade*, 1854, p.134.
9. Harry Scrivenor, op. cit., p.134.
10. *The Engineer*, February 3rd 1860, p.82.
11. GRO, NAI, D/D N.A.I., M/108/1-M/108/3, Drawings for engines for Hirwaun Ironworks.
12. GRO, NAI, D/D. N.A.I., L/9/2.
    Laurence Ince, *The Neath Abbey Iron Company*, p.117.
13. William Truran, *The Iron Manufacture of Great Britain*, 1863, p.228 & 272.
14. Robert Hunt, *Memoirs of the Geological Survey of Great Britain and the Museum of Practical Geology, Mining Records. Mineral Statistics of the United Kingdom of Great Britain and Ireland, 1859*.
15. *Mining Journal*, January 14th 1864, p.44.
16. Robert Hunt, *Mineral Statistics, 1865-1866*.
17. Alfred Rosling Bennett, *The Chronicles of Boulton's Siding*, 1971, p.61 & p.64.
18. Robert Hunt, *Mineral Statistics, 1867*.
19. *Mining Journal*, July 2nd 1870, p.561.
20. *The Engineer*, December 23rd. 1870, p.438.
21. Robert Hunt, MIMineral Statistics, 1880.
    The Engineer, March 12th 1880, April 9th 1880 p.274, and April 23rd 1880, p.310.
22. *The Engineer*, April 32rd 1880, p.310.
23. John Lloyd, op. cit., pp.113-116.
24. Barrie Trinder, *The Industrial Revolution in Shropshire*, Chichester, 1973, p.75.
25. BRL, B&W, Journal of a Visit to Ironworks in South Wales - James Watt Jnr. c.1800.
26. BRL, B&W, List of Furnaces in Great Britain, 1806.
27. Charles Wilkins, *The History of the Iron, Steel, Tinplate and Other Trades of South Wales*, Merthyr Tydfil, 1903, p.163.
28. John Lloyd, op. cit., pp.116-126.
29. *The Cambrian*, August 11th 1804.
30. Laurence Ince, Richard Trevithick's Patent Steam Engine, *Stationary Power*, Vol.1, 1984, pp.67-73.
31. Harry Scrivenor, op. cit., p.134.
    The Engineer, February 3rd 1860, p.82.
32. John Lloyd, op. cit., pp.116-126.
33. Charles Wilkins, op. cit., p.164.
34. R. Meade, *Coal and Iron Industries of the United Kingdom*, 1882, p.618.
35. Cardiff Central Library, Sale Details of the Aberdare Iron Company, June 11th 1846.
36. *Dictionary of Welsh Biography*, 1959, pp.266-267.
37. GRO, NAI, D/D. N.A.I., M/5/1.
    Laurence Ince, *The Neath Abbey Iron Company*, p.108.
38. Robert Hunt, *Mineral Statistics, 1854-1860*.
39. *Mining Journal*, June 2nd 1860, p.376.
40. *Mining Journal*, October 20th 1860, p.718.
41. Robert Hunt, *Mineral Statistics, 1860-1870*.
    The Engineer, June 1st 1866, p.406.
42. *Mining Journal*, August 24th 1861, p.552.
    Robert Hunt, *Mineral Statistics, 1862*.
43. *Mining Journal*, January 3rd 1863, p.12.
44. John Percy, *Metallurgy, Iron and Steel*, 1864, p.556.

45. *The Engineer*, October 13th 1865, p.243 and December 15th 1865, p.397.
46. *Mining Journal*, October 6th 1869, p.762.
47. Dean Forester, Mr. Keeling Buys a Locomotive, *The Industrial Railway Record*, Vol.1, pp.58-64. Keeling records the gauge of the railway as 2ft. 9in. while the report in the 1869 Mining Journal indicates that the railway was 2ft. 8in. gauge.
48. GRO, NAI, D/D. N.A.I., M/161.
    Laurence Ince, *The Neath Abbey Iron Company*, p.110.
49. Robert Hunt, *Mineral Statistics, 1872*.
50. *The Engineer*, April 19th 1872, May 3rd 1872, p.322, January 9th 1874, p.16 and October 16th 1872, p.332.
51. *Iron and Coal Trades Review*, June 4th 1875, p.679.
52. J.P. Addis, *The Crawshay Dynasty - A Study in Industrial Organisation and Development*, Cardiff, 1957, p.121.
53. *The Engineer*, December 17th 1875, p.438.
54. *Dictionary of Welsh Biography*, 1959, entry for Matthew Wayne.
55. GRO, NAI, D/D. N.A.I., M/200/2-M/200/3. Drawings for Blowing Engine for Wayne, Williams and Company, 1827.
    Laurence Ince, *The Neath Abbey Iron Company*, p.105.
56. John Lloyd, op. cit., pp.127-128.
57. GRO, NAI, D/D. N.A.I., W/3/2, Inventory of Works, 1847.
58. GRO, NAI, D/D. N.A.I., M/87/3, 30 inch engine for Waynes, Gadlys.
59. Robert Hunt, *Mineral Statistics, 1854*.
60. *The Engineer*, September 24th 1875, p.226.
61. *Mining Journal*, July 6th 1861, p.440.
62. *The Engineer*, February 12th 1869, p.113 and September 2nd 1870 p.164.
63. Robert Hunt, *Mineral Statistics, 1872-1875*.
64. *The Engineer*, April 20th 1877, p.280.
65. R. Ivor Parry, Aberdare and the Industrial Revolution, *Glamorgan Historian*, Vol.4, 1967, p.196.
66. John Lloyd, op. cit., pp.111-112.
67. GRO, NAI, D/D. N.A.I., M/193/5.
    Laurence Ince, *The Neath Abbey Iron Company*, p.107.
68. Robert Hunt, *Mineral Statistics, 1854-1866*.
69. *Mining Journal*, July 16th 1864, p.516 and August 20th 1864, p.597.
70. *Mining Journal*, September 3rd 1864, p.632.
71. *The Engineer*, January 4th 1867, p.23.
    Robert Hunt, *Mineral Statistics, 1867*.
72. Robert Hunt, *Mineral Statistics, 1872*.
73. *The Engineer*, April 24th 1868, p.308 and March 1st 1872.
74. Robert Hunt, *Mineral Statistics, 1859*.
75. &
76. *The Engineer*, November 24th 1871, p.372.
77. John Lloyd, op. cit., p.111.
78. Robert Hunt, *Mineral Statistics, 1873*.
79. *The Engineer*, October 15th 1880, p.293.
80. John Lloyd, op. cit., p.111.

Plate Two   The remains of the furnaces at the Hirwaun Ironworks.

Plate Three   The Llwydcoed Ironworks photographed shortly after closure. This picture clearly shows how the furnaces were partly blown by a waterwheel which was constructed in 1800 when the works was founded. (Courtesy Welsh Industrial & Maritime Museum, Cardiff)

Plate Four   *Crawshay Bailey, 1789-1872.*

Chapter Six.

Merthyr Tydfil: The Iron Town.

No less than four great ironworks were founded at Merthyr Tydfil in the second half of the eighteenth century. These works were to grow into great concerns with Merthyr Tydfil in the nineteenth century not only becoming the centre of the South Wales iron industry but also the focal point of the British iron trade. In 1858 there were no less than 46 furnaces existing at Merthyr with 43 of them in blast. The area around Merthyr had abundant supplies of coal, limestone and iron ore and this coupled with the early adoption of Cort's puddling process produced the right conditions for Merthyr to become the iron making capital of South Wales.

The first and longest lived ironworks constructed at Merthyr Tydfil was situated at Dowlais. The partnership which built the Dowlais Furnace in 1759 consisted of Thomas Lewis of Newhouse, Llanishan, Monmouthshire, Thomas Price of Watford, Glamorgan, Richard Jenkins of Cardiff, a Mercer, Thomas Harris of Bristol, John Curtis of Bristol, Nathaniel Webb of Bristol, John Jones of Bristol, Ironmaster, Isaac Wilkinson of Plas Gronow, Denbigh and Edward Blakeway of Shrewsbury.[1] The partners' capital consisted of a joint investment of £4,000. Several of the partners had experience of the iron trade and these included Wilkinson and John Jones who owned an iron foundry in Cheese Lane, Bristol. The other Bristol partners were very experienced traders in several fields. Webb was a gentleman of independent means, Curtis owned a china and earthenware warehouse and Harris was an alderman and merchant.[2] The coke fired furnace at Dowlais was soon in blast and produced 18 tons of iron weekly during 1760.[3] At this time the furnace was blown by cylinders and pistons worked by a waterwheel. In 1767 John Guest of Broseley was appointed manager. By this time Blakeway had dropped out of the company having not paid his share of the initial capital. His shares were taken over by Thomas Harris who had also purchased Curtis' shares. Harris' 6/16 investment in the company was purchased in 1782 by John Guest. During that year there was two furnaces in blast at Dowlais. In 1786 the partnership consisted of William Lewis of Pentyrch, Joseph Cowles, John Guest, John Jones and aitt, WilliamWilliam Taitt.[4] The partnership was to be changed in the following year when John Guest died leaving 3/16 of the concern to his son Thomas and 3/16 to the rest of his family. The management of the Dowlais Ironworks was now entrusted to Thomas Guest and his brother-in-law William Taitt. Thomas Guest disposed of 1/16 of the company to Joseph Cowles who later sold it to Robert Thompson who was manager at Dowlais during the early 1790s. Output of iron at Dowlais had risen from 500 tons in 1760 to 1,000 tons during 1763 and 2,800 tons for 1796.[5] Dowlais in the early 1790s were operating three furnaces but was falling behind the advances made by some of the other Merthyr ironworks. Unlike some ironworks in the locality Dowlais was not producing wrought iron. Pig iron produced by Dowlais was often sold to other ironworks for manufacturing into wrought iron as in 1796 when an agreement was signed with the Cyfarthfa partners for Dowlais to supply them yearly with 2,000 tons of iron.[6] This agreement was to last for five years.

Changes in ownership continued when Taitt increased his interest in the works by purchasing Thompson's 1/16 share for £3,817.[7] In 1801 Taitt held eight shares in the company with Thomas Guest having two and William Lewis holding six. It was in that year that the important decision was made at Dowlais to manufacture wrought iron using Cort's puddling process. In order to increase production the company had invested in a Boulton and Watt beam blowing engine. This engine was built at Dowlais in 1798 and had a 40in. x 8ft. steam cylinder with a 90in. x 7ft. blowing cylinder.[8] The engine certainly seems to have had the desired effect for in 1805 the three furnaces at Dowlais produced 6,800 tons of iron with 8,148 tons produced in the following year.[9] To aid the manufacture of wrought iron the company was also operating rolling mills powered by Boulton and Watt engines. The first of these engines was built in 1803 and was a 36½in. x 8ft. beam engine. The second engine was installed in 1808 and was a 31½in. x 7ft. beam engine which had an 18ft. flywheel working at 17½ r.p.m.[10]

Although Thomas Guest died in 1807 and was succeeded as manager by his son Josiah John Guest, the company's early faith in steam power continued. A fourth furnace was put into blast in 1810 and a 50in. x 8ft. beam blowing engine with an 84in. x 8ft. blowing cylinder was purchased from Boulton and Watt.[11] The following year saw new nozzles and working gear being installed on the 1798 beam blowing engine.

In 1808 a fourth blast furnace was built at Dowlais. This furnace was capable of producing 50 tons of per week. At that time the works also consisted of four refineries, twenty puddling furnaces and ten balling furnaces. A fifth furnace was added in 1815 with the Dowlais Ironworks being able to produce 15,600 tons of iron per year. In that year the partnership received a set back with the death of William Taitt which left Josiah John Guest as managing partner. By 1819 the company consisted of Josiah John Guest, Wyndham Lewis, William Price Lewis and Thomas Revel Guest. The works suffered in the general trade depression which accompanied the end of European hostilities in 1815. However, this set back was to be of a fairly short duration for in 1817 three further blast furnaces were built at Dowlais. A beam blowing engine was also constructed in that year. This engine was probably built by the company itself and had a 50in. x 7ft. 6in. steam cylinder and a 100in. blowing cylinder. It was a low pressure condensing engine without a flywheel and during the 1840s it worked making twenty strokes per minute and produced 16,350 cubic feet of air per minute.[12] Additional furnaces were put into blast and by 1823 the Dowlais Ironworks possessed ten furnaces which made in that year 22,287 tons of iron.[13] In the following year another beam blowing engine was constructed at the works. This condensing engine had a 54½in. x 7ft. 6in. steam cylinder with a 108in. blowing cylinder. This engine was still working in the 1840s making 17 strokes per minute and producing 16,218cu. ft. of air per minute.[14] A further blast furnace was added in 1828 together with a fifth blowing engine.[15] This was a non-condensing, high pressure beam blowing engine with a 54in. x 9ft. 3in. steam cylinder which was working in the 1840s with a 144in. blowing cylinder making 13 strokes per minute and blowing 27,476cu. ft. of air per minute.[16] This was the first of Dowlais' beam blowing engines to be supplied with a flywheel which was 15ft. in diameter. During 1830 the Dowlais Ironworks had twelve furnaces in blast which produced 32,611 tons of iron.[17] Certainly, by this date, Dowlais had become the largest of the South Wales ironworks.

The expansion of the works was partly due to Dowlais' successful entry in the late 1820s into the wrought iron rail trade. To cater for the production of rails the rolling capacity of the works was improved with the opening of the Big Mill in 1830.[18] After this event output of rails steadily rose reaching 20,000 tons for 1835. To help with the transportation of finished products the Dowlais Ironworks purchased six locomotives from the Neath Abbey Iron Company during the period 1832-1838.[19] These locomotives were used on the Penydarren Tramroad and also on the internal works' line. The Penydarren Tramroad was constructed because of a quarrel between Richard Crawshay of Cyfarthfa and the neighbouring ironmasters. Crawshay possessed a controlling interest in the Glamorganshire Canal Company and received preferential treatment with regards to the carriage of his products. The other Merthyr Ironmasters decided to build a tramroad that bypassed the upper and most inconvenient stretch of the canal. Dowlais and Penydarren each owned five shares in the tramroad with the Plymouth Ironworks holding four. Work on the tramroad began in 1800 and the 9½ mile track was completed in 1802. The gauge of the tramroad was 4ft. 2in. inside the plate flanges or 4ft. 4in. over them.

The Dowlais Ironworks continued to expand during the 1830s when two further blast furnaces were constructed and an additional beam blowing engine was installed in 1838. This engine was a high pressure example with a 40in. x 8ft. steam cylinder and a 122in. blowing cylinder. This engine was built for the Dowlais Ironworks by the Neath Abbey Iron Company at a cost of £3,894.[20] In the 1840s this beam blowing engine was making 16 strokes per minute and discharging 20,687 cu. ft. of air per minute. Like beam blowing engine No.5 this engine was provided with a flywheel which was 16ft. in diameter. Further expansion was undertaken by the company but not at Dowlais for a subsidiary concern called the Ivor Ironworks was built at Merthyr. The Ivor Ironworks consisted of four furnaces, forges, fitting shops and a foundry and was completed in 1839. The furnaces received their blast from a high pressure beam blowing engine with a 53in. x 9ft. steam cylinder and a 144in. blowing cylinder. This engine had a 22ft. 6in. flywheel and worked at 14 strokes per minute discharging 28,476 cu. ft. of air during the same period.[21] Except for the 144in. blowing cylinder, the engine was constructed by the engineers at Dowlais. The blowing cylinder was supplied by the Copperhouse Foundry, Hayle, Cornwall.[22] Several other Cornish engines were purchased at this time, this perhaps being prompted by William Truran, a Cornishman who was the works' engineer at Dowlais. In 1839 Harvey and Company of Hayle, Cornwall supplied Dowlais with two 24in. beam engines costing each £675 and this was followed by the delivery in the same year from Harveys of an 80in. x 10ft. beam engine costing £2,370.[23] This was probably used to drain water on the Dowlais property. The period of expansion was completed in 1840 when the Little Mill was opened with its two rail rolling mills.[24]

Dowlais was now the largest ironworks in the world and in 1845 its eighteen furnaces produced 74,880 tons of iron with 7,300 people being employed. The Big Mill alone turned out 400 tons of rails per week and in total the mills produced monthly 2,000 tons of rails and 2,000 tons of bars.[25] The Dowlais Ironworks was now pre-eminent in the wrought iron rail trade and had also built up an extensive export trade in this product. Large foreign orders were common as in 1844 when the works won a contract for 50,000 tons of rails for Russia.[26]

The works experienced some difficulties during the late 1840s when the problem of the renewal of the Dowlais lease faced the Guest family. At one time it looked as though the family would quit the industry but the negotiations were brought to a successful conclusion when in 1848 the lease was renewed. During the final years of the Dowlais lease investment and modernisation of the plant had been neglected. The renewal of the lease prompted a new period of expansion with the modernisation of the blowing engines undertaken. Two of the old beam blowing engines were sold off in 1849 in preparation for the building of a new large blowing engine. The engines sold off were probably the 1798 Boulton and Watt engine and the 1817 engine.[27]

New rolling capacity was added by the company in 1850 with the opening of a 12in. merchant bar mill at the Ivor works.[28] Also in that year Sir Josiah John Guest bought Wyndham Lewis' share of the works for £200,000 which brought his holding to fourteen shares with his nephew holding two shares. In the following year the two blowing engines that had been sold off were replaced by the mighty Merthyr Guest engine. This was designed by Samuel Truran, the works' engineer, with all the component parts being made at Dowlais except for the cylinders which were supplied by the Perran Foundry, Falmouth. This 55in. x 13ft. beam engine had a blowing cylinder of 144in. diameter working with a 12ft. stroke. Each minute the engine made twenty strokes producing 44,000 cu. ft. of air at a pressure of 3¼ psi. The air blast was discharged into a 5ft. diameter pipe which was 140 yards long and acted as a regulator. This non-condensing engine was worked up to 650h.p. with a steam pressure of 60 psi at one third cut off. The beam was 40ft. 1in. long and cast in two parts, each part weighing 16½ tons. The 22ft. diameter flywheel weighed 35 tons and there was a further 75 tons of cast iron framing under the steam cylinder. For a period this powerful blowing engine supplied the blast to eight furnaces but later it was used with three other blowing engines to provide the blast for twelve furnaces.[29] At that time some of the Dowlais furnaces were making 235 tons of forge iron per week.

The one great wish of Josiah John Guest was to gain complete control of the Dowlais Ironworks and this was achieved in 1851 when he bought out Edward Hutchins for £58,000. However, the enjoyment of being sole owner of this giant concern did not last for long for in the following year Sir Josiah John Guest died. The management of the works fell on the shoulders of his widow Lady Charlotte Guest with trustees being appointed when Lady Charlotte remarried in 1855. The trustees employed William Menelaus to act as works' manager. At that time the enormous size of the Dowlais Ironworks can be gauged by the number of steam engines on the site for they included four pumping engines draining collieries, iron ore workings and supplying the works with surface water, sixteen engines winding at coal and iron ore pits, fourteen engines working inclined planes, eleven locomotives, two engines driving clay and pug mills, five blowing engines, ten forge and mill engines and two engines driving lathes and shearing cold iron. These engines gave a total of 7,308 h.p.[30] Details of the puddling mill engines in the early 1850s are known and these engines consisted of:-

No.1 - 45in. x 7ft. low pressure condensing beam engine working at 22 strokes per minute.

No.2 - 36in. x 7ft. low pressure condensing beam engine working at 22 strokes per minute.

No.3 - 42in. x 6ft. high pressure beam engine working at 20 strokes per minute.

No.4 - 37in. x 7ft. high pressure horizontal engine working at 23 strokes per minute.

No.5 - 26in. x 4ft. high pressure vertical engine working at 30 strokes per minute.[31]

In 1856 sixteen furnaces out of Dowlais' eighteen were in blast with the works continuing to dominate Britain's wrought iron rail trade[32]. To enable Dowlais to continue in its pre-eminent position in the rail trade the building of a new mill was started in 1857.[33] This was to be the legendary Goat Mill. The mills inside this building were powered by a pair of 45in. x 10ft. coupled high pressure beam engines. They worked at 24 strokes per minute with a one third cut off with six Cornish boilers 44ft. long and 7ft. diameter supplying the steam. The two beams were supported upon eight columns and each beam was constructed in two parts and weighed 37 tons. The flywheel was 21ft. in diameter and weighed 30 tons. These engines were capable of driving one rail mill turning out 1,000 per week, another mill capable of turning out 700 tons of rails or roughed down iron per week and one bar or roughing down mill capable of making 200 tons per week. Two blooming mills and two hammers were also worked by the same engines. The roof of the Goat Mill was 240ft. by 210ft. and was supported by lattice girders of an average length of 45ft. The covering of the roof was made up of corrugated iron plates and the floor of the mill was constructed of one inch cast iron plates.[34]

Within two years the Goat Mill was in full production and it was probably in this building that special bars were rolled for the 1862 exhibition. The Dowlais Ironworks sent three exhibits to London consisting of a bar 31½ft. long and 15in. wide with a 5½in. measurement in the horns and a ⅛in. measurement in the stem, weighing 1½ tons, a bar 48ft. by 8½in. by 4in. weighing 1 ton and a bar 53ft. long by 10in. by 5in. weighing 40lbs per foot.[35] In 1865 the weekly production at Dowlais was 1,400 tons of rails and 600 tons of bars, plates, angles and girders.[36] At this time two 5 ton Bessemer converters were being put into commission with four others approaching completion. This development allowed Dowlais to manufacture steel rails and steel headed rails. The blowing machinery for the steel plant was manufactured by Hick and Son of Bolton. Ores being used at Dowlais in the mid 1860s were from Wales,

Whitehaven, Barrow, Cornwall, Forest of Dean, Northampton and Spain. When the Dowlais Ironworks was inspected in 1865 it was operating seventy balling furnaces and one hundred and fifty puddling furnaces with all the steam in the works being generated by waste gases. To aid transportation of materials at this time there were thirteen locomotives and six to seven hundred horses at the works. The weekly wage bill amounted to £7,000 and the works employed no less than 8,000 people.

A detailed description of the Dowlais Ironworks was made in 1869 when sixteen out of the seventeen furnaces were in blast.[37] All the furnaces were fed with raw coal and were blown at a pressure of 3-3¼ psi. The works employed 9,000 people and produced yearly 150,000 tons of iron. Each furnace had evolved into the characteristic shape of being square at the base and taking a cylindrical shape at half its height. Output from each furnace was 180 tons weekly with tapping taking place three times in twenty four hours. The furnaces were blown by six beam engines namely (a) the Merthyr Guest engine, (b) the Ivor works' engine with a 144in. blowing cylinder, (c) an engine with a 80in. x 6 ft. blowing cylinder, and (d) three engines with 120in. x 8ft. blowing cylinders. There were six forges at the old works and three at the Ivor works with the puddling furnaces receiving their draught from eighteen Lloyd's fans driven in groups of two or three by independent engines. Dowlais had seven mills consisting of a 24in. steel mill, a four roll 21in. girder mill, two 20in. rail mills and three 18in. bar mills with the Ivor Ironworks possessing six mills consisting of a 24in. plate train, an 18in. rail mill, two 12in. trains and two 8in. guide mills. In the steel department there were six 5 ton converters blown by vertical 36in. Hick engines with 54in. x 5ft. blowing cylinders although more blowing capacity was to be added with installation of a pair of beam blowing engines. For hammering steel ingots the works had recently installed a duplex steam hammer. In 1869 there were just under one hundred steam engines working at Dowlais and Ivor including six blowing engines, twenty seven mill engines, four large pumping engines and thirty winding and underground engines.

Even through the difficult years of the 1870s Dowlais continued to be fairly well employed with the company still dominating the rail market. However, there was a change of emphasis as greater amounts of foreign ore arrived at Dowlais and as the steel making capacity of the works was expanded. Dowlais built its first Siemens steel furnace in 1871 and also during that year a new cogging mill was opened.[38] This mill was designed for rolling down steel ingots and was driven by a pair of 30in. horizontal engines without flywheels. The mill engines and additional small engines for working the rollers were built by Kitson and Company of Leeds with the rolling machinery being designed and built by the ironworks itself.[39] During this period the works had sixteen furnaces in blast and possessed one hundred and fifty puddling furnaces serving fourteen rolling mills. To improve the steel making capacity at the works a new furnace was put into blast in 1874 which was 55ft. high with an 18ft. diameter across the boshes. This furnace was capable of turning out three hundred tons of Bessemer pig iron per week. It had a closed top and was blown with hot blast at 1,200°F. The materials were raised to the furnace top by means of a water balance.[40]

By this date the Dowlais Iron Company was operating four regenerative gas furnaces on the Siemens-Martin steel process and six Bessemer converters.

The Dowlais Iron Company continued to experiment and improve its plant for in 1876 tests were being made in bringing molten iron from the furnaces directly to the converters and by 1881 fuel economy was such that 22cwt. of coal was being used as fuel to produce a ton of iron.[41] The works also increased its steel making capacity by enlarging their Bessemer converters in 1881 so that they possessed four 8 ton converters and two 6 ton converters. The mills also received new investment during the mid 1880s for in 1884 a new set of reversing mill plant was installed. This mill was powered by a pair of 60in. x 5ft. horizontal engines made by Kitson and Company. These were piston valve engines driving on one shaft and they produced 120 revolutions per minute.[42] In the following year two new foundries were constructed, one in the upper works for moulding steel and one in the lower works for ingot moulds. A new cogging mill was also built at this time on the site of the old centre Goat Mill.[43]

Although Dowlais continued to produce iron and steel for many more years the management had realised that the future development of the iron industry would be on coastal sites where richer ores could be easily imported. In 1888 construction started on a new works situated at Cardiff. Production of iron at the new site commenced in 1891 and the two works continued to work in tandem until iron making ceased at Dowlais in 1930.[44]

The second ironworks to be constructed at Merthyr Tydfil owes its origin to a lease of land in 1763 from the Earl of Plymouth. The land was leased by Isaac Wilkinson of Plas Gronow, Wrexham and John Guest of Broseley, Shropshire. The deed stated that they intended to build 'ffurnaces, fforges, mills, pothouses or other works for the making and manufacturing of iron.'[45] Wilkinson and Guest needed extra money to exploit their investment and so sold shares in the concern to John White and Company, Edward Blakeway, Francis Evans, William Perritt and Sarah Guest. The enterprise did not prosper although it was calculated that the furnace could produce 14 tons of pig iron per week. For each ton of iron produced it was calculated that it would take 5 tons of coal and 3.5 tons of ironstone.[46] In 1766 the Plymouth Ironworks was sold to Anthony Bacon who used it mainly to supply his Cyfarthfa ventures with pig iron. Anthony Bacon died in 1788 and the Plymouth Ironworks was left to his son Thomas, who was then under age. The Court of Chancery intervened to look after his interests and the lease of the works was granted to Richard Hill who had been employed by Bacon at the Plymouth Furnace and was also a trusted friend. There were also family links for Hill had married Mrs. Bacon's sister in 1772. When Hill took over the works it consisted of a small furnace blown by bellows and a waterwheel. Hill purchased the furnace and stock for £490. 12s. 0d. and also paid an annual rent of £650 to Thomas Bacon for the lease of the land on which the works stood. A further £268. 7s. 0d. was paid yearly to Anthony Bacon for the lease of adjoining land.[47]

By the mid 1790s the furnace at the Plymouth Ironworks could produce about 2,200 tons of iron in a year with most of this being sold to the Cyfarthfa Ironworks.[48]

Richard Hill was able to consolidate his hold on the venture when Bacon came of age in 1799. The landowner granted a further lease to Hill on a yearly payment of £815 with Hill also paying Bacon £1,262 for the first 2,000 tons of pig iron produced at Plymouth, plus 5s. a ton for every additional ton made annually.[49] Hill now needed to find more capital for expansion and so he took John Nathaniel Miers and Amos Struttle into partnership in 1803. Miers, who was married to Hill's daughter Mary, was one of the partners of John Miers and Company who operated furnaces, forges and tinplate works in West Glamorgan. Struttle was a Bristol merchant. The two new partners each provided an investment of £5,000. This money was used to build a subsidiary works to the south of Plymouth at Pentrebach where puddling furnaces and a rolling mill were erected. The main works was also enlarged for in 1805 there were three furnaces at the Plymouth Ironworks which produced 5,789 tons of iron during the year and 5,928 tons in the following year.[50]

In 1806 Richard Hill died and his share of the partnership was divided between his three sons, Richard, John and Anthony. Soon Struttle and Miers retired from the venture leaving the works in the hands of the Hill brothers. Richard Hill soon moved to Llandaff and concerned himself with the selling side of the business while John and Anthony ran the works. Although the furnaces remained waterwheel blown, output at Plymouth was pushed up to 7,800 tons of iron in 1815.[51] This was in part due to Anthony Hill who had become deeply interested in the technology of iron making and had widely studied geology, chemistry and metallurgy. The differing approaches adopted by the two brothers in running the works are illustrated by a story circulating in the 1860s. Each morning the brothers would separately visit the furnaces, John Hill would approach the manager and ask, 'What is the sow worth?' Anthony, when he came to the furnaces, would always ask, 'What is the quality of the iron?' It was to be Anthony Hill's interests that guaranteed the high quality of Plymouth iron.[52]

Plymouth iron was always in demand and so additional furnaces were built at a subsidiary site which came to be known as the Dyffryn Ironworks. The Hill brothers now had three separate works positioned along the River Taff. Water was extracted from the river and then through a feeder taken to each works. The water was thus able to power waterwheels at each of the sites. This efficient use of water allowed Anthony Hill to postpone the adoption of steam power at his main works. However, when the first of the Dyffryn furnaces was built in 1819, Hill purchased a 52½in. beam engine from the Neath Abbey Iron Company to provide the blast.[53] Soon after this event Anthony Hill became the managing partner. In 1823 the three Plymouth furnaces produced 6,387 tons of iron.[54] An additional furnace was built at the Plymouth Ironworks in 1825 and in 1826 the four furnaces produced 11,440 tons of iron with the two furnaces at Dyffryn producing 5,460 tons.[55] An increase in production after 1825 was helped by a lucky speculation by the two brothers. The two younger Hill brothers had travelled to Cumberland to trace a customer and while there leased 600 acres of rich mineral ground. This land, by 1849, was sustaining four iron ore mines which produced 20,000 tons of rich ore yearly.[56] This speculation ensured increased production with a third furnace being built at Dyffryn in 1827.

The seven furnaces at Plymouth and Dyffryn were able to produce 18,852 tons of iron in 1830.[57]

John Hill sold his share in the works to his brothers in 1826 and for some unexplained reason Richard and Anthony attempted to sell the whole concern in 1834. This move did not meet with success and the works remained in the hands of the Hill brothers. The sale document for the works gives us a detailed description of the Hill undertakings. The property included seven furnaces, four at Plymouth and three at Dyffryn, these being capable of producing 500 tons of iron per week. At Plymouth the blast was provided by two waterwheels about 8ft. wide with a 28ft. head of water from the Taff. The Dyffryn furnaces received their blast from a 14ft. wide waterwheel with a 24ft. head of water and also a double acting 52½in. x 8ft. beam blowing engine with a 122in. blowing cylinder. These sites also boasted thirteen running out fineries, a foundry with air furnaces, a cupola, stoves, a crane, a carpenters' shop, a smiths' shop, a lathe and two hundred workmen's houses. The brothers also owned a rolling mill and puddling forges worked by two waterwheels of 10ft. and 6ft. widths with a 24ft. fall of water and capable of producing three hundred tons of finished bars per week.[58]

Expansion continued with a fourth furnace being built at Dyffryn during 1839.[59] The furnaces at Dyffryn were a great attraction to visitors as they were some of the largest at work in South Wales. They were each 40ft. high with an 18ft. diameter in the boshes and a capacity of 7,000cu. ft. Each of these furnaces and the Plymouth examples were capable of producing 120 tons of iron per week. The Plymouth product was expensive but readily found a market because of the high quality of the iron manufactured by the Hills. Much of the iron produced was sold to chain and cable manufactures. The Plymouth Ironworks also produced large amounts of rail with no less than 40,000 tons being completed in 1846.[60]

The reputation and successful marketing of the products from the Hill concerns allowed the partners to undertake a programme of expansion during the 1850s. In the early part of the decade two blowing engines were purchased. These engines were certainly needed, for too long had the management relied on water power for the major part of the blast for the furnaces. The engines purchased were rather unusual for they were two horizontal blowing engines. They had been built by the Soho Foundry, Birmingham as vacuum engines for the abortive atmospheric London, Croydon and Epsom Railway. The engines were converted for blowing by the Soho Foundry and they had 45in. x 7ft. steam cylinders and 90in. blowing cylinders.[61] These were two out of only four horizontal engines used for furnace blowing in South Wales. Additional furnaces were also built, for the two works were operating nine furnaces by 1854, ten in 1856 and eleven in 1862.[62] At this time the works were producing 40,000 tons of iron yearly.

Anthony Hill died in 1862 and in the following year the works were sold to Fothergill, Hankey and Bateman for £250,000.[63] These gentlemen were the principal partners of the Aberdare Iron Company. The Plymouth Ironworks and its subsidiaries were linked with Fothergill's Aberdare works. By 1865 Fothergill had modernised some of the plant at the works, although the furnaces continued to be blown by cold blast. Fothergill had reduced the number of furnaces in blast to ten, increased the number of puddling furnaces by eight, added more steam power, increased the speed of the blowing engines and purchased two steam hammers for the works. Locomotives had also been introduced to the 2ft. 8in. railway line that served the three works and the associated coal pits.[64] In 1864 only one locomotive was used on the works' railway, this was a product of Hawthorn and Company of Leith and had 8in. x 15in. cylinders. The success of this locomotive prompted the ordering of four more during the same year. Two were 0-4-0 saddle tanks built by Fletcher, Jennings and Company of Lowca and the other two were 0-4-0 saddle tank locomotives with 8in. x 16in. cylinders built by the Neath Abbey Iron Company.[65] In 1865 the works employed 4,000 people and 360 horses. There were four forges and nine mills at the three sites capable of turning out bar iron of a diameter from 3/16 to 6in. Nearly the whole of the mineral ground was drained by an engine which was built in around 1852. This was an 85in. x 11ft. Cornish beam engine built by the Perran Foundry which in 1865 was working at 25 psi making 3 to 6 strokes per minute while raising 134 gallons each minute.

There was some reduction in output during the late 1860s for in 1867 only seven out of the ten furnaces were in blast.[66] The extent of the Plymouth undertakings can be gauged from a description of the works written in 1869.[67] Six locomotives conveyed materials at high level from the pits to the works while on the lower level six tank engines on a 4ft. 8½in. gauge line transported materials to the Taff Vale Railway siding. All the Plymouth Company's furnaces were about 40 to 50ft. high with 16ft. being the greatest diameter in the boshes. Weekly pig iron production was 90 to 110 tons per furnace using Welsh mine and haematite. The iron ore was calcined in kilns behind the furnace tops while the coal was coked in open clamps. At the Plymouth Ironworks there were five furnaces with three of them in blast. The furnaces were blown with a cold blast provided by two waterwheels working four 66in. blowing cylinders, a 45in. horizontal engine with a 90in. blowing cylinder and a 52½in. beam engine with a 122in. blowing cylinder. There was no blast regulator as the blast was equalised by the number and size of the blast pipes. At Pentrebach there were seventy four puddling furnaces, four forges and seven rolling mills. Power at the forges was provided by a 20ft. diameter waterwheel which was 16ft. wide and a pair of 22in. steam engines were used for auxiliary power when water was short. Also the forges possessed a 27in. engine driving direct to rolls and a 60in. x 8ft. engine driving two pairs of forge rolls and two bar mills. There were present three steam hammers for beating the puddle balls, one being of Condie's patent design and also a squeezer. Two more hammers were in the course of erection. The seven rolling mills at Pentrebach were capable of producing 850 tons of finished iron per week. These included a rail and bar mill driven by a 27ft. diameter waterwheel. When water was scarce these mills were powered by a pair of 20in. x 2ft. inverted vertical engines installed and built by the Neath Abbey Iron Company in 1865.[68] A 16in. engine powered a slitting mill and an 18in. x 2ft. engine powered bar mills. Two small mills were powered by a 23in. oscillating engine and there were several small engines for driving saws, presses, punches and shears.

At the Dyffryn Ironworks were five blast furnaces and two refineries. The furnaces received a cold blast from two waterwheels, a 45in. horizontal engine with a 90in. blowing cylinder and a 52½in. beam blowing engine with a 122in. blowing cylinder (the Eolus engine).

During the early 1870s the furnaces were modified for hot blast, this modernisation took Fothergill's expenditure on the works to over £100,000. Rail orders continued to be placed at the Plymouth Ironworks with large contracts being completed in 1872 for India, Canada and the Great Western Railway.[69] However, the number of furnaces in blast was reduced to four and by 1874 only two furnaces were being worked.[70] In 1875 the Aberdare and Plymouth Ironworks Company collapsed with the ironworks side of the business never to be reopened. Immediately the heaps of Welsh and Spanish ore at the works were purchased by the Dowlais Ironworks and some of the plant was sold off in 1877.[71] So depressed was the iron trade that the Creswick beam blowing engine which was named after the works' engineer was sold off for £150 after costing £1,100 to construct. The works were put up for sale in 1882 but no purchaser was found and in the following year the dismantling of the buildings commenced.[72]

A second of the Merthyr Tydfil ironworks was also to come under the ownership of Richard Fothergill's company. This was the Penydarren Ironworks whose foundation dates from 1784. In that year land was leased for the works by Samuel and Jeremiah Homfray who were the sons of Francis Homfray of Broadwaters, Worcestershire and Stourton.[73] This family had considerable interests in the iron trade of Worcestershire, Staffordshire and Shropshire. The setting up of the Penydarren Ironworks was partly financed by Richard Forman of the Tower of London who advanced two sums of money to the concern, namely £2,500 in 1784 and £8,666. 13s. 4d. in 1786.[74] By this later date the partners in the company consisted of Jeremiah Homfray of Penydarren, Thomas Homfray of Franch, Kidderminster, Samuel Homfray of Penydarren and Richard Forman of the Tower of London.[75] More members of the Forman family were attracted to the enterprise for in 1796 the partnership consisted of the three Homfray brothers, William Forman of the Tower of London and Henry Forman of Woolwich, Kent.[76] The Forman family had extensive business interests in London including participation in the ordnance trade. In 1794 there was one furnace at Penydarren which was blown by cylinders and pistons. The works also consisted of two chaferies, three melting fineries and four balling furnaces.[77] Two years later the company was operating two furnaces which produced 4,100 tons of iron in the year.[78]

The managing partner appears to have been Samuel Homfray who was keenly interested in the technology of iron making. Certainly the Penydarren Ironworks experimented with puddling at an early date and the management were pioneers in the use of an intermediate refinery stage. Svedenstierna noted in 1802 that there were three blast furnaces operating at Penydarren coupled with three refineries and twenty five puddling furnaces producing about 8,000 tons of iron yearly.[79] Samuel Homfray also developed an interest in steam power and in 1798 two Boulton & Watt engines were constructed at Penydarren. One was a 40in. x 8ft. beam blowing engine with an 84in. blowing cylinder and this engine was notable as being one of the first Boulton & Watt engines to be built with an iron beam, no doubt Homfray had a part to play in the adoption of this innovation.[80] The second engine was a double acting 33$\frac{1}{3}$in. x 7ft. beam engine to power rolling and slitting mills.[81] Samuel Homfray already had a wealth of experience with steam power as he had already operated several Newcomen engines on the Penydarren property. Homfray's interest in steam power led him in 1803 to become a partner with Richard Trevithick in the development of his compact high pressure steam engine. Several Trevithick engines were built at Penydarren including the world's first steam locomotive which made successful journeys along the Penydarren Tramroad in 1804. Another Trevithick engine was used at Penydarren to provide a blast, probably for the refineries.[82]

Samuel Homfray appears to have left the Penydarren Iron Company in around 1813 to switch his resources to the development of the Tredegar Ironworks in Monmouthshire. In 1819 the partners operating the Penydarren Ironworks were William Forman and William Thompson of London. Alderman Thompson was a member of a family much involved in the Welsh iron industry. His uncle, another William Thompson was an iron merchant and co-partner with William Forman, Samuel Homfray and others in the Tredegar Ironworks. Alderman Thompson was twice made Lord Mayor of London and was married to one of Samuel Homfray's daughters.

There was a period of expansion at the Penydarren Ironworks during the early 1820s. A 52$\frac{1}{2}$in. beam blowing engine was purchased from the Neath Abbey Iron Company in 1819 and after this date additional furnaces were constructed.[83] By 1823 there were five furnaces in blast and during that year they produced 15,547 tons of iron.[84] One important customer for Penydarren iron was Robert Stephenson and Company who purchased £1,252 of iron during the period 1826-30. Some of the engineering products of Stephenson's works were purchased by the Penydarren Iron Company possibly in part payment for the iron. A 10 h.p. stationary engine without boilers and flywheel was purchased from Stephenson for £280 in 1827.[85] This was followed by the acquisition of an 0-6-0 locomotive in 1829. This Stephenson product had 7in. x 20in. cylinders and spent two years hauling trams on the Penydarren works' line before being returned to Stephenson for conversion to 4ft. 6in. gauge as an 0-4-0 locomotive. It was then used on the Penydarren Tramroad and received the name Eclipse.[86]

The Penydarren Ironworks was one of the earliest concerns to enter the wrought iron rail trade for in 1830 they produced rails for the Liverpool and Manchester Railway. In that year the works produced 17,025 tons of iron.[87] Further expansion of the Penydarren Ironworks took place in the late 1830s. A 38$\frac{1}{2}$in. Neath Abbey beam blowing engine was installed in 1837 and by 1839 the company had six furnaces in blast.[88] In 1845 the number of furnaces in blast at Penydarren had risen to seven which in that year produced 25,600 tons of iron.[89] However, the death of Alderman Thompson in 1854 seems to have debilitated the company and in 1859 William Forman attempted to sell the concern. The Dowlais Iron Company showed a serious interest in the works but decided only to purchase the mineral ground. At that time

the Dowlais engineers made a detailed inventory of the Penydarren ironworks.[90] The works consisted, in 1859, of the following:
Cinders Incline - a pair of 14in. x 2ft. high pressure engines with two boilers.
Rail Shed - four presses, two punches plus one small punch, a new 21in. engine nearly ready with a boiler.
Brick Yard
New Mill - a 33in. x 6ft. 6in. high pressure beam engine with three boilers, twenty four heating furnaces for this and old mill.
Old Mill - a 30in. x 6ft. 6in. high pressure beam engine with three boilers.
New Puddling - a 36in. x 6ft. 9in. high pressure beam engine with three boilers and thirty one puddling furnaces.
Roll Lathes - a 24in. x 4ft.6 in. engine, one boiler, five roll lathes, new machine for cutting rail ends (cost £70) and stock of rolls.
Fitting-Up-Shop - a 10in. x 1ft. 7in. engine with one small boiler, five lathes, two screwing machines, one drilling machine, one old boring mill and one old chuck lathe.
Blast Engines - an old low pressure beam engine with 50in. steam cylinder and 96in. blowing cylinder, working 14 stokes per minute (in bad repair), a high pressure beam engine, 38½in. x 8ft. with 122in. blowing cylinder working at 17 strokes per minute.
Blast Furnaces - six in blast, 45ft. high, 16ft. in boshes, one out of blast for repairs, six hot blast stoves and six refineries.
Smiths' Shop - eleven fires, two fires for chain makers, one fire for boiler makers and one furnace for heating plates.
Foundry - two old wood cranes, one small cupola, one small foundry with an air furnace, one small furnace for brass and one old wood crane.
Also a new engine not yet erected, 36in. x 6ft. 9in., a stable engine, 10in. x 1ft. 7in., two donkey engines, 10in. x 10in. and one donkey engine, 7½in. x 7½in.
Estimated value of plant - £18,140.

The Penydarren Ironworks remained unoccupied until 1863 when the enterprise was taken over by Davies, Williams and Phillips.[91] In the following year this partnership was working a blast furnace, a rolling mill and a puddling furnace.[92] However, the production of iron turned out to be a most expensive venture because the partners did not own any mineral ground. This led to the sale of the ironworks to the Aberdare Iron Company in 1865. This sale was to result in a long court case for Richard Fothergill brought an action against the previous partners. Fothergill claimed that between the time he had initially inspected the works and when his company occupied it some demolition had taken place which damaged buildings and machinery.

When the case was resolved Fothergill began to rehabilitate the works. Puddling commenced in 1869 and in 1870 repairs were undertaken and refineries put to work.[93] Fothergill fully intended to put some of the Penydarren furnaces into blast for the Neath Abbey Iron Company was called in during 1871 to repair the 122in. blowing cylinder of No.1 engine.[94] At this time the company was operating thirteen puddling furnaces but no rolling mills were listed as being on the site.[95] Presumably the rolling mills had been removed at an earlier date. However, conditions in the iron trade worsened and the furnaces were never relit.

In 1873 a steam hammer was erected in the forges but the little activity that took place on the site ended with the collapse of the Fothergill undertakings in 1875.[96] The Penydarren Ironworks remained in a derelict state until 1883 when the remaining plant was sold off. At the sale the Cyfarthfa Ironworks purchased the steam hammer which had originally cost £1,500 and had been used only three times.[97]

At the same time that the plant at the Penydarren Ironworks was being sold off the Cyfarthfa Ironworks was entering on its second lease of life. The foundation of the Cyfarthfa Ironworks dates from a lease granted in 1765 to Anthony Bacon of Throgmorton Street, London and William Brownrigg of Whitehaven, Cumberland.[98] Bacon, who was one of the founding fathers of the South Wales iron industry, originally came from Cumberland and had amassed a considerable fortune as a merchant in the City of London. A furnace was completed in 1767, this being 50ft. high and 38ft. square. A forge was also erected at Cyfarthfa to make wrought iron using the stamping and potting process. There was also a boring mill at Cyfarthfa which was used for making cannon and so successful was this venture that it had to be supplied with iron from Bacon's other furnaces.

In 1777 the original partnership was dissolved with Brownrigg retiring from the company and receiving £1,500 15s. 5d. for his share of the works. An important development occurred in 1782 when Bacon leased part of the Cyfarthfa Ironworks to Francis Homfray of Stourton, Staffordshire. Homfray was granted the mill for boring cannon and a foundry. It is probable that the land leased by Homfray included the forge. This agreement was nominally for a period of fifty years with a payment of £20 per annum to Bacon.[99] However, Homfray did not occupy the property for long and in 1784 the forge and mill were taken over by David Tanner. Also associated with this venture were James Cockshutt, Thomas Treharne and Francis William Bowzer.[100] Thomas Treharne acted as manager along with Cockshutt until 1786 when the property was sold to Richard Crawshay and Company. In the same year Bacon died and a lease of the furnace at Cyfarthfa was granted by the Court of Chancery for nine years to Richard Crawshay, William Stevens and James Cockshutt. The new owners of the furnace now enlarged their forge and mill and an additional furnace was built. These improvements cost the partnership no less than £50,000. Cockshutt, Stevens and Crawshay operated the Cyfarthfa Ironworks for five years before the partnership was dissolved with Richard Crawshay and Watkin George taking over the works from 1792 onwards.[101] In 1794 Crawshay and George were able to gain a full lease of the Cyfarthfa property and purchase the ironworks.

Under Crawshay's direction the Cyfarthfa Ironworks expanded to become the largest of the Merthyr works during the early years of the nineteenth century. Richard Crawshay was born in Normanton, Yorkshire but left his home at the age of fifteen to seek his fortune in London. He found a job in a warehouse in York Yard, Thames Street, ultimately rising to the ownership of the concern. The connection with Cyfarthfa and Bacon began when Crawshay became a partner in the sale of some cannon made at Cyfarthfa.[102] Crawshay became interested in the ordnance trade and entered into it when he leased Bacon's cannon boring mill. The production of cannon proved to be so successful that the boring mill had to be supplied with iron not only from the Cyfarthfa furnaces but also from the Dowlais and Plymouth furnaces. It is no wonder that Richard Crawshay chose as a crest a mastiff dog (symbolizing the name Cyfarthfa) standing over a pyramid of cannon balls.[103]

Although Richard Crawshay made a good profit from cast iron cannon he was a wise enough businessman to take an early interest in the bulk production of wrought iron. The Cyfarthfa Ironworks was one of the first concerns to make wrought iron using Cort's puddling process which was adopted by Crawshay in 1787.[104] Cort visited the Cyfarthfa Ironworks and supervised the installation of eight of his puddling furnaces. However, puddling at Cyfarthfa was not an immediate success and to make the process successful it took some changes in the design of the plant and its operation.[105] It was not until the use of a preliminary refining stage that the true advantage of puddling was demonstrated over other methods. On the 3rd of March 1791 Crawshay could describe Cyfarthfa in the following terms,

> We work all with Fossel coal - my Blast Furnaces are 60 feet high, blow with a steam Engine, each furnace produces about 1400 tons per annum - we make use of Air Furnaces instead of Finerys, when the metal is brought into nature, instead of hammers, we put it between a pair of Rolls, & crush it like a paste about ¾in. thick - then break it into small pieces, pile up 60 to 80lbs weight on a Cake of baked Clay, heat 20 of those piles at a time in another Air Furnace, then shingle them under a Hammer of 1200lbs weight fixed in an Iron helve of 2 Tons weight. The blooms thus finished is again heated in an Air Furnace and brought into a very handsome Bar by Grooved Rollers......to make 'em straight & handsome, we planish 'em under a lighter Hammer.[106]

Later, in June 1791, Crawshay recorded that at Cyfarthfa it took 3 tons of raw coal to make a dozen of coke which could make a ton of iron at the blast furnace. Other raw materials needed to make a ton of iron were one ton of limestone and 3 tons 10cwt of ironstone. In the forge twelve tons of pig iron were consumed in each refinery every week. The wastage in making finers metal ranged from 20 to 23cwt. In puddling it took 25cwt. of finers metal to make a ton of blooms.[107] Even with the initial problems, the early adoption of puddling gave Cyfarthfa an advantage in the wrought iron trade and this financed further expansion within the works. In 1794 the Cyfarthfa Ironworks consisted of two coke furnaces, eight puddling furnaces, three refineries, three balling furnaces and a rolling mill driven by a 20ft. diameter waterwheel.[108] Soon Crawshay was spending money on additions to the forge and a new furnace. The three furnaces were able to produce 7,204 tons of iron in 1796 and a fourth furnace was added in 1797.[109] Not only was money being invested in furnaces but Crawshay was able to invest heavily in the development of his forges and mills. The expansion of the works during the 1790s can be gauged from the following description of the Cyfarthfa plant made in 1798:[110]

Upper Works.
Great waterwheel, 56ft. diameter, 6ft. wide working four blowing cylinders 52in. diameter, 5ft. stroke blows two furnaces with 1¾lb with 4in. pipes and four double refineries with 2in. pipes. Waterwheel 25ft. diameter, 3 ft. wide works four pairs of rolls, a pair for roughing down blooms, a pair for bars, a pair for rolling balls into blooms and a pair for planishing. Rolls working at 40 revs. per minute. A waterwheel 20ft. diameter and 6ft. wide works a shingling hammer, a waterwheel 38ft. diameter and 4ft. wide for turning rolls, a steam engine 50in. cylinder, 9ft. stroke for blowing in case of scarcity of water.
Lower Works.
A 20ft diameter, 7ft. 5in. wide waterwheel working two pairs of rolls, 35 to 40 turns per minute, a 20ft. diameter, 6ft. wide waterwheel works a shingling hammer and a second 20ft. waterwheel works a planishing hammer.

It is obvious from this description that the two old furnaces at Cyfarthfa had been decommissioned and demolished. Svedenstierna only saw two furnaces at the main Cyfarthfa site in 1803 and these were blown by the great waterwheel coupled to a 70-80h.p. steam engine.[111] The Swedish tourist noted that the wheel was 52ft. in diameter and 7ft. wide and another observer put the cost of this waterwheel at £4,000.[112]

The success of Crawshay's undertakings allowed further expansion during the early 1800s. A subsidiary ironworks was built at Ynysfach and two furnaces put into blast there in 1801. In 1805 the four furnaces were in blast and produced 10,460 tons of iron for the year.[113] Expansion continued for in 1807 there were six furnaces at the two sites, two rolling mills and four steam engines (50h.p., 40h.p., 12h.p. and 7h.p.).[114] Cyfarthfa was now the largest of the Merthyr Ironworks and by all accounts the largest ironworks in the world. Much of the necessary engineering expertise for the development of the Cyfarthfa Ironworks was supplied by Crawshay's partner Watkin George. Certainly the design of the great waterwheel and the steam blowing engine was his contribution to the rise and dominance of the Cyfarthfa Ironworks in the iron trade. However, George left Cyfarthfa in about 1807 to become a partner with C.H. Leigh in the Pontypool Ironworks leaving Crawshay as sole owner. The works was to remain in Crawshay family hands from this date until the early years of the twentieth century. When Crawshay died in 1810 he left ⅜ of the Cyfarthfa Ironworks to his son William, ⅜ to his son-in-law Benjamin Hall and ⅖ to his nephew Joseph Bailey.[115] The stormy relationship that existed between Richard and William Crawshay ensured that the eldest son did not inherit the complete Cyfarthfa property. There appears to have been a long standing disagreement in the family on how much control the main London Crawshay merchant house should have in the management of iron making at Cyfarthfa. Bailey soon sold his share to William Crawshay leaving only two partners in the venture.

The slackness in the iron trade at the end of the Napoleonic Wars affected Cyfarthfa like all the other British ironworks. Yearly production for 1814 was only 9,600 tons and at times during the year only three furnaces were in blast.[116] Conditions gradually improved and in 1817 Cyfarthfa produced 14,191 tons of iron.[117] It was also in that year that William Crawshay was able to buy out Hall and obtain sole ownership of the Cyfarthfa Ironworks. Expansion continued during the 1820s commencing with the purchase of a 52½in. beam blowing engine from the Neath Abbey Iron Company in 1820. By 1823 there were eight furnaces in blast and in that year they produced 24,200 tons of iron. A ninth furnace was added in 1824 and in 1830 the nine furnaces produced 29,000 tons of iron.[118]

A pair of high pressure beam engines were purchased from the Neath Abbey Ironworks in 1833 but instead of being used directly to drive rolling mills they were used to return water for the mills' waterwheels.[119] This adherence to water power was to continue at Cyfarthfa up to the 1870s by which time the works was clearly lagging behind the modern practices of ironworks such as Dowlais. However, further steam power was added when the works purchased in 1835 an 18in. high pressure beam engine from the Neath Abbey Iron Company.[120] At Ynysfach the construction of two more furnaces commenced in 1839 and in 1840 a 52½in. beam blowing engine was bought from the Neath Abbey Ironworks to provide the blast.[121] At the same time an old beam blowing engine at the main works was replaced by an example built by the Cyfarthfa engineers themselves.[122]

The water powered mills at Cyfarthfa were at a serious disadvantage because they were unable to produce the heavier type rails. This problem was partly solved in the mid 1840s by the building of a large rail mill which was steam powered. The mill was built at a total cost of £25,000 and was powered by a condensing beam engine built by Maudslay, Sons and Field of Lambeth.[123]

During the 1850s the Cyfarthfa Ironworks was fully employed making a variety of products. In the period 1856-61 all eleven of the Crawshay furnaces were in blast and in 1857 a new mill was constructed.[124] Output reached a yearly total of 50,000 tons in 1864 and in the following year a detailed description of the works was published.[125] At that time a fifty year old beam blowing engine made at Cyfarthfa was being replaced by a new engine of greater power. The hot blast was being applied to five out of the eleven furnaces with waste gas being used for the generation of steam. The forges and mills which were powered by five waterwheels and several steam engines were able to produce 1,200 tons of puddled bars per week. For moving materials around the works four hundred horses and four locomotives were employed. A further locomotive was purchased from the Neath Abbey Iron Company in 1871. It was an 0-4-0 saddle tank with 8½in. x 16in. cylinders for use on a 3ft. plateway.[126] In 1865 the works employed 5,000.

The production at Cyfarthfa seems to have been divided between rails and merchant bar iron. Much of this was exported for the Crawshays had built up important trade links with Eastern Europe, particularly Greece, Turkey and Russia. In 1872 the works was operating seventy two puddling furnaces and seven mills but still the Crawshays relied heavily on water power.[127] The members of the Institution of Mechanical Engineers visited Merthyr in 1874 and at Cyfarthfa they saw seven furnaces available for iron production although only four were in blast during the year. The furnaces were 52½ft. high with 14½ft. diameters across the boshes. Five of the furnaces could be blown by cold blast and two with hot blast. All except one had closed tops with bell and hoppers. The puddling mills were driven by two waterwheels and two non-condensing engines. The bar mills were driven by two condensing beam engines and an oscillating non-condensing engine. The power produced by the waterwheels could be aided by a 30in. x 8ft. non-condensing beam engine which pumped water from the river back to the mills.[128]

Problems with the unions, the decline of the wrought iron trade and the old fashioned nature of the works prompted Robert Thompson Crawshay to close down Cyfarthfa. The works was slowly run down during 1874 and one furnace was in blast during the first three months of 1875 before complete closure took place.[129] This closure sparked off much controversy within the Crawshay family. The death of Robert Crawshay in 1879 allowed his sons to reopen the Cyfarthfa Ironworks and in the following year 900 tons of iron was being produced weekly.[130] However, owners and managers realised that the works had to be modernised. The Cyfarthfa Ironworks was again closed in 1881 but this time the closure took place to carry out a complete rebuild of the furnaces and for the installation of a steel works. The work was completed during 1884 with the first batch of steel being produced in February 1885.[131]

The steel works was designed by Edward Williams of Middlesbrough. During 1884 three plate encased furnaces were erected and the foundations of a fourth laid. The blast was provided by three vertical engines built by J.C. Stevenson of Preston with 33in. steam cylinders and 72in. blowing cylinders both with 4ft. 5in. strokes. These engines worked at 25 to 30 strokes per minute producing a blast at 5-6 psi. Later the blowing capacity was increased by the addition of three 44in. x 5ft. Davy vertical blowing engines with 96in. blowing cylinders. The blast was heated up to 1,400°F by seven Cowper stoves. Steel was manufactured in two 8 ton Bessemer converters which could be worked up to 10 tons. The converters received their blast from vertical compound blowing engines with 42in. high pressure cylinders, 78in. low pressure cylinders and 55in. blowing cylinders, all working to a 5ft. stroke. Also at this time two new reversing cogging mill engines with 40in. cylinders were installed together with a pair of Davy reversing mill engines with 50in. cylinders. The Bessemer machinery was constructed by Tannett, Walker and Company.[132] Such was the expense of the modernisation that the Crawshays were forced to change the structure of the business into a limited liability company.

The Cyfarthfa Iron and Steel Works under the title of Crawshay Brothers, Cyfarthfa, Limited continued in operation until 1902 when it was bought out by Guest, Keen and Nettlefold of the Dowlais works. The Cyfarthfa works continued in production until closure in 1910. The works was reopened in 1915 but final closure came in 1919.[133]

References.

1. John Lloyd, *The Early History of the Old South Wales Iron Works, 1760-1840*, 1906, pp.19-47.
2. Edgar Jones, *A History of GKN, Vol.1, 1759-1918*, 1987, p.12.
3. John A. Owen, Chronological Date Sequence of Events for the Dowlais Ironworks, *Merthyr Historian*, Vol.1, 1976, p.7.

4. John Lloyd, op. cit., pp.19-47.
5. Harry Scrivenor, *History of the Iron Trade*, 1854, p.96.
6. John Lloyd, op. cit., pp.19-47.
7. John A. Owen, op. cit., p.9.
8. Birmingham Reference Library (BRL), Boulton & Watt Collection (B&W), Portfolio No. 704, Drawings for engine for Lewis, Taitt and Company, 1798.
9. BRL, B&W, List of Furnaces in Great Britain, 1806.
The Engineer, November 3rd 1865, p.298.
10. BRL, B&W, Portfolio No. 339, Drawings for engine for Dowlais, 1803, Portfolio No. 406, Drawings for engine for Dowlais, 1808.
11. BRL, B&W, Portfolio No. 678, Drawings for engine for William Taitt and Company, 1810.
12. William Truran, *The Iron Manufacture of Great Britain*, 1863, p.228.
13. Harry Scrivenor, op. cit., p.134.
14. William Truran, op. cit., p.228.
15. Harry Scrivenor, op. cit., p.134.
16. William Truran, op. cit., p.228.
17. Harry Scrivenor, op. cit., p.134.
18. John A. Owen, op. cit., p.10.
19. M.J.T. Lewis, Steam on the Penydarren, *Industrial Railway Record*, No.59, 1975, pp.18-32.
Laurence Ince, *The Neath Abbey Iron Company*, Eindhoven, 1984, p.116.
20. Laurence Ince, op. cit., p.106.
William Truran, op. cit., p.228.
John A. Owen, op. cit, p.11.
21. William Truran, op. cit., p.228.
22. W.H. Pascoe, *The History of the Cornish Copper Company*, Redruth, p.96
23. D.B. Barton, *The Cornish Beam Engine*, Truro 1969, p.280.
24. John A. Owen, op. cit., p.11.
25. *The Engineer*, November 3rd 1865, p.278.
26. John A. Owen, op. cit., p.11.
27. *Mining Journal*, March 31st 1849, p.149.
28. John A. Owen, op. cit., p.12.
29. William Menelaus, Description of Large Blowing Engine and New Rolling Mill at Dowlais Ironworks, *Proceedings of the Institution of Mechanical Engineers*, 1857, pp.112-118.
30. William Truran, *The Iron Manufacture of Great Britain*, 1855, p.168.
31. William Truran, op. cit., p.272.
32. Robert Hunt, *Mineral Statistics, 1856*.
33. *Mining Journal*, July 18th 1857, p.516.
34. William Menelaus, op. cit., pp.112-118.
35. *Mining Journal*, April 5th 1862, p.231.
36. *The Engineer*, November 3rd 1865, p.278.
37. Ferdinand Kohn, *Iron and Steel Manufacture*, 1869, pp.86-91.
38. John A. Owen, op. cit., p.13.
39. *Journal of the Iron and Steel Institute*, 1871, p.80.
40. *Proceedings of the Institution of Mechanical Engineers*, 1874, pp.239-241.
41. *The Engineer*, May 12th 1876, p.369
The Engineer, May 27th 1881, p.396.
42. *The Engineer*, August 22nd 1884, p.136.
Journal of the Iron and Steel Institute, 1885, p.217.
43. *The Engineer*, February 20th 1885, p.157.
44. John A. Owen, op. cit., p.15.
45. John Lloyd, op. cit., p.72-85.
46. Edgar Jones, op. cit., pp.8-11.
47. Margaret S. Taylor, The Plymouth Ironworks, *Glamorgan Historian*, Vol.5, Cowbridge, 1968, p.187.
48. Harry Scrivenor, op. cit., p.96.
49. John Lloyd, op. cit., p.72-85.

50. BRL, B&W, List of Furnaces in Great Britain, 1806.
    The Engineer, November 24th 1865, pp.330-331.
51. *The Engineer*, November 24th 1865, pp.330-331.
52. *The Engineer*, January 1st 1869.
53. GRO, NAI, D/D. N.A.I., M/107.
    Laurence Ince, op. cit., p.104.
54. Harry Scrivenor, op. cit., p.134.
55. *The Engineer*, February 3rd 1860, p.82.
56. Margaret S. Taylor, op. cit., pp.189-190.
57. Harry Scrivenor, op. cit, p.134.
58. John Lloyd, op. cit., pp.72-85.
59. David Mushet, *Papers on Iron and Steel*, 1840, pp.414-415.
60. Alan Birch, *The Economic History of the British Iron and Steel Industry*, 1784-1879, 1967, p.221.
61. BRL, B&W, Portfolio No. 674, Engines for Plymouth Ironworks, 1848-1850.
62. Robert Hunt, *Mineral Statistics, 1854, 1856 & 1862*.
63. Robert Hunt, *Mineral Statistics, 1863*.
    Margaret S. Taylor, op. cit., 191.
64. *The Engineer*, November 24th 1865, pp.330-331.
65. Dean Forester, Mr. Keeling Buys a Locomotive, *The Industrial Railway Record*, Vol.1, pp.58-64.
    Laurence Ince, op. cit., p.117.
66. Robert Hunt, *Mineral Statistics, 1867*.
67. *Mining Journal*, October 2nd 1869, pp.742-743.
68. GRO, NAI, D/D N.A.I., M/161, Drawing for two 20 inch engines for the Plymouth Iron Company, 1865.
    Laurence Ince, op. cit., p.109.
69. *The Engineer*, April 26th 1872.
70. Robert Hunt, *Mineral Statistics, 1874*.
71. *The Engineer*, November 12th 1875, p.348 & November 23rd 1877, p.382.
72. Glamorgan Record Office, Sale Catalogue of Plymouth Collieries and Ironworks, 16th August 1882, D/D xdk 22.
    The Engineer, October 12th 1883, p.290.
73. John Lloyd, op. cit., pp.86-91.
74. Margaret S. Taylor, The Penydarren Ironworks, 1784-1859, *Glamorgan Historian*, Vol.3, Cowbridge, 1966, p.84.
75. Glamorgan Record Office, Penllyn Castle Papers, Nos. 1 & 2, Lease of 1786.
76. Margaret S. Taylor, op. cit., p.84.
77. BRL, B&W, List of Ironworks, 1794.
78. Harry Scrivenor, op. cit., p.86.
79. *Svedenstierna's Tour of Great Britain, 1802-3*, Newton Abbot, 1973, pp.54-55.
80. BRL, B&W, Portfolio No. 705, Drawings for Engine for J. Homfrey, Penydarren Ironworks, 1798.
81. BRL, B&W, Agreement between J. Homfray & Co. and Boulton & Watt for purchase of engine, cost £1,129.
82. Laurence Ince, Richard Trevithick's Patent Steam Engine, *Stationary Power*, Vol.1, 1984, pp.67-75.
83. GRO, NAI, D/D. N.A.I. M/157/5-157/6, Drawings for 52½in. engine for Penydarren, 1819.
    Laurence Ince, *The Neath Abbey Iron Company*, Eindhoven, 1984, p.104.
84. Harry Scrivenor, op. cit., p.134.
85. Michael R. Bailey, Robert Stephenson and Company, 1823-1829, *Transactions of the Newcomen Society*, Vol.50, 1978-79, pp.128-132.
86. M.J.T. Lewis, Steam on the Penydarren, *Industrial Railway Record*, No. 59, April 1975, pp.15-18.
87. Harry Scrivenor, op. cit., p.134.
88. GRO, NAI, D/D. N.A.I. M/157/4. Drawing for a 38½in. engine for Penydarren, 1837.
    Laurence Ince, *The Neath Abbey Iron Company*, Eindhoven, 1984, p.106.
89. *The Engineer*, November 24th 1865, pp.330-331.
90. GRO, Dowlais Iron Company, D/DG Section E, Box 8, Penydarren Valuation, March 1859.
91. Robert Hunt, *Mineral Statistics, 1863*.

92. *The Engineer*, December 10th 1869, p.392.
93. *The Engineer*, June 24th 1870, p.404.
94. GRO, NAI, D/D. N.A.I., M/157/8-157/10, Repairs for No.1 blast engine, 1871.
95. Robert Hunt, *Mineral Statistics, 1872*.
96. *The Engineer*, April 4th 1873, p.212.
97. *The Engineer*, February 9th 1885, p.114 and April 13th 1883, p.295.
98. John Lloyd, op. cit., pp.48-71.
99. John Lloyd,op. cit., pp.48-71.
100. John P. Addis, *The Crawshay Dynasty - A Study in Industrial Organisation and Development, 1765-1867*, 1957, Cardiff, pp.10-11.
101. John P. Addis, op. cit., pp.12-13.
102. Margaret S. Taylor, *The Crawshays of Cyfarthfa Castle*, 1967, pp.19-21.
103. Margaret S. Taylor, op. cit., p.24.
104. R.A. Mott, *Henry Cort: The Great Finer*, 1983, pp.51-56.
105. *The Letterbook of Richard Crawshay 1788-1797*, Cardiff, 1990.
106. *The Letterbook of Richard Crawshay 1788-1797*, Cardiff, 1990, pp.95-96.
107. *The Letterbook of Richard Crawshay 1788-1797*, Cardiff, 1990, p.107.
108. BRL, B&W, List of Ironworks, 1794. Alan Birch, op. cit., p.78.
109. Harry Scrivenor, op. cit., p.96.
    Alan Birch, op. cit., p.77.
110. BRL, B&W, Description of Cyfarthfa Ironworks, 18th September 1798.
111. Svedenstierna, op. cit., pp.56-57.
112. *The Engineer*, November 10th 1865, p.298.
113. BRL, B&W, List of Ironworks, 1806.
114. John Lloyd, op. cit., pp.92-96.
115. Margaret S. Taylor, op. cit., p.27.
116. John P. Addis, op. cit., p.59.
117. *The Engineer*, November 10th 1865, p.198.
118. Harry Scrivenor, op. cit., p.134.
119. Laurence Ince, *The Neath Abbey Iron Company*, Eindhoven, 1984, p.105.
120. Laurence Ince, *The Neath Abbey Iron Company*, p.105.
121. GRO, NAI, D/D. N.A.I., M/56/2. Drawing for a 52½in. engine for Cyfarthfa, 1840.
122. *The Engineer*, November 10th 1865, p.298.
123. Alan Birch, op. cit., p.168.
    The Engineer, November 10th 1865, p.298.
124. *Mining Journal*, July 18th 1857, p.516.
125. *The Engineer*, November 10th 1865, p.298.
126. GRO, NAI, D/D. N.A.I., L/9/1. 8½in. cylinder locomotive for Robert Crawshay, 1871.
    Laurence Ince, *The Neath Abbey Iron Company*, Eindhoven, 1984, p.118.
127. Robert Hunt, *Mineral Statistics, 1872*.
128. *Proceedings of the Institution of Mechanical Engineers*, 1874, p.239.
129. Robert Hunt, *Mineral Statistics, 1875*.
130. *The Engineer*, January 2nd 1880, p.20 & February 13th 1880, p.134.
131. *The Engineer*, February 13th 1885, p.137.
132. *Journal of the Iron and Steel Institute*, 1884, pp.199-200.
133. John A. Owen, op. cit., pp.14-15.

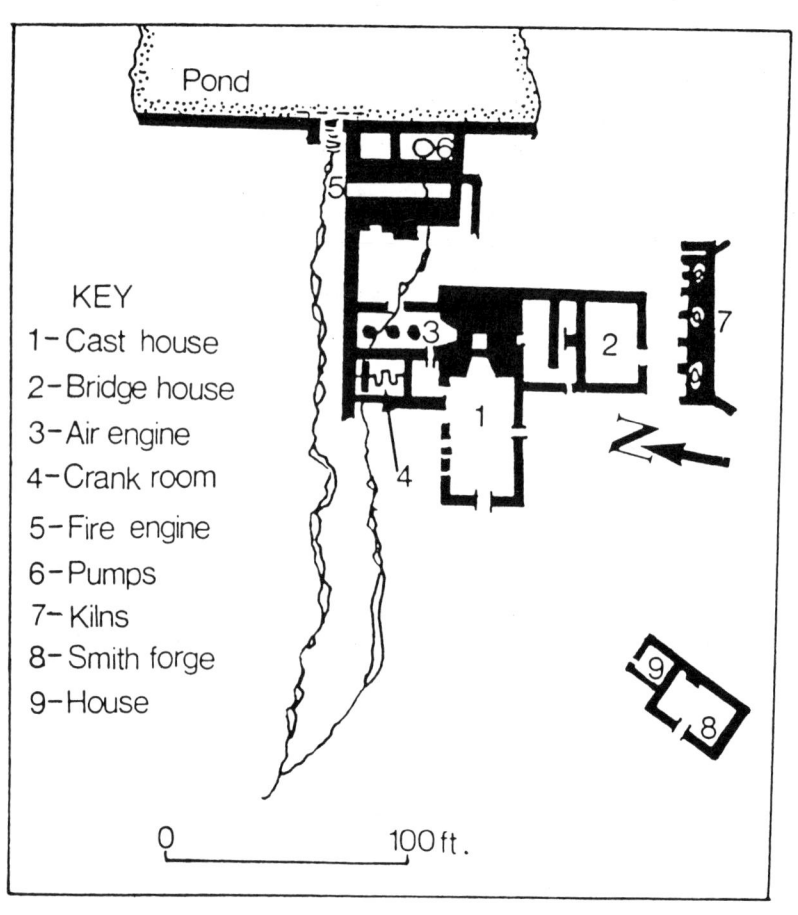

KEY
1 – Cast house
2 – Bridge house
3 – Air engine
4 – Crank room
5 – Fire engine
6 – Pumps
7 – Kilns
8 – Smith forge
9 – House

Figure Eight   —   Dowlais Furnace 1763

Plate Five   Josiah John Guest, 1785-1852. (Courtesy National Library of Wales)

Plate Six   *Richard Crawshay, 1739-1810. (Courtesy Sir William Crawshay)*

Plate Seven — The ruined casting houses and blowing engine house of the Ynysfach Ironworks. This photograph was taken in the early 1900s.

Plate Eight *William Crawshay II, 1788-1867.*

Chapter Seven.

The Homfrays of Penydarren and Tredegar.

For the moment we leave the cataloguing and describing of the South Wales ironworks to concentrate on a case study of one of the great families of Welsh ironmasters. The ironmasters are the Homfrays who are important because their story illustrates the main features of the adoption of coal using technology in the South Wales iron industry. Furthermore, their story is an example of the migration of skills from the West Midlands and also it clearly demonstrates the rise of steam power in the British iron industry.

The Homfray family in the seventeenth century was based at Wales near Rotherham, Yorkshire. Some writers have described the family as having gentry origins but there appears to be no direct evidence for this. The first reference to a member of the family being involved in the iron trade is 1702. This was Francis Homfray (1674-1737) who had moved from Wales to Old Swinford near Stourbridge. In 1702 Francis Homfray had just given notice of leaving his employment to his employer Ambrose Crowley III. Homfray was nail-keeper at Stourbridge in the large Crowley iron making and merchanting business.[1] His presence at Stourbridge does not nullify the gentry claim as several sons of gentlemen were apprentices to the Crowleys and Homfray's position was that of a manager. Homfray left the Crowleys to set himself up in business as a dealer in iron goods and later a slitter of wrought iron. By the late 1720s he was buying wrought iron from the Knight family who owned furnaces and forges in the West Midlands centred around the Stour Valley. Homfray's business was probably based at two sites. These were the Gothersley Slitting Mill and the Swindon (Swin) Forge. Gothersley Mill had been an old blade mill which was rebuilt by Francis Homfray in the 1730s.[2] Unlike many of the Stour slitters the Homfrays seem to have manufactured their own nail rods as well as slitting to hire for others. The slitting mills turned wrought iron bars into thin rods ready for nail manufacture. Although Francis Homfray died in 1737 the business continued under the management of his second wife Mary (née Jeston). The burden of managing the family concern was taken off her shoulders when her sons came of age. It is quite probable that in the 1750s the family converted a corn mill near Kidderminster into a forge. This was the Broadwaters Middle Forge which had previously been a fulling mill and a corn mill.[3] This mill was converted to serve the iron trade in 1753 by John Homfray of Wollaston Hall (1731-1760). However, during this period it has been impossible to discover if members of the family acted together or as separate entities.

Of the second generation of Homfray ironmakers it was to be Francis Homfray of Broadwaters and Stourton Castle (1725-1798) who was to achieve fame in the iron trade of the Midlands. He continued to operate his father's concerns at Gothersley and Swinford but also greatly expanded the family's involvement in the iron trade. By 1794 the Homfray family were highly involved in the industrial life of the Stour Valley and held the following forges and mills:

(1) Lower Broadwaters Forge. This had been a blade mill which operated during the Civil War making weapons for the Royalists. In 1774 the premises were for sale as a slitting and plating works. The works was described in 1794 as consisting of a chafery and a balling furnace. Lower Broadwaters was at this time held by John Homfray of Wollaston Hall (1759-1827). Later he assumed the surname Addenbrooke. This was his mother's maiden name for she was Mary, daughter of Jeremiah Addenbrooke of Wollaston Hall. He presumably did this to carry on the Addenbrooke name and inherit the family money. He was active in the iron industry in the Stour Valley and elsewhere in the Midlands and later became High Sheriff of Worcestershire. In 1822 Edward Addenbrooke owned the forge and three years later the property was on the market. It consisted of two parts, the first being a finer's forge with two cast iron waterwheels, one working a stamping hammer and the other driving machinery to blow three fineries and occasionally to work a corn mill. The other part consisted of a hammerman's forge with a cast iron waterwheel driving machinery for working a shingling hammer and a train of rolls for rolling bar iron.[4]

(2) Broadwaters Middle Forge. This was a fulling mill which had been converted in 1746 into a corn mill and in 1753 into a forge. In 1794 it was held by Homfray & Co. and consisted of a single chafery and a balling furnace.[5]

(3) Broadwaters Upper Forge. This forge in 1794 consisted of a chafery and a balling furnace held by Jeston Homfray (1752-1816) who was the eldest son of Francis Homfray of Broadwaters and Stourton. In 1812 the forge was unoccupied and was being sold by the Addenbrookes.[6]

These properties were all on the Wannerton Brook which was a Stour tributary meeting the main river at Kidderminster. The other Homfray ironworks consisted of:

(4) Gothersley Mill. This was a slitting mill held by the Homfrays since the 1730s. Originally this had been a blade mill. In 1788 John Hodgetts leased it to Francis Homfray of Broadwaters and Stourton and his sons Francis and Jeston. The mill came out of Homfray hands in 1798 when it was leased to John Hodgetts.[7]

(5) Stourton Mill. This was originally three corn mills altered to a forge and then modified to become a slitting mill in 1698. Francis Homfray of Broadwaters and Stourton took a twenty year lease of the mill in 1783. In 1792 the slitting mill was altered to become a rolling mill with some of the surplus machinery being sent to Gothersley. Stourton Mill operated with a head of water of 6ft. 10in. and a 3ft. fall. Jeston Homfray succeeded his father as owner of Stourton and after his death in 1816 his executors continued to pay the rent until 1828.[8]

(6) Hyde Mill. This was a very early slitting mill. From 1736 Jeremiah Caswell was the tenant and on his death in 1769 the mill was operated by his daughter Eleanor. She married the Reverend Paul White and soon after his death entered into a partnership to run the mill with Francis Homfray the son of Francis Homfray of Broadwaters and Stourton. The mill was converted into a rolling mill during the

1780s and in 1793 Francis Homfray of the Hyde took complete control. On his death in 1809 he was succeeded by his son Jeremiah. In 1810 Jeremiah Homfray offered the works for sale. It consisted of a steam engine, a forge, rolling and slitting mills and twelve workmen's cottages as well as the eighteenth century Hyde House. The purchaser was his uncle Thomas Homfray who moved to the Hyde and was still living there in 1818. He was declared bankrupt in 1819 and in 1821 the mill was sold out of the family's hands.[9]

(7) One of the most important assets of the Homfray family was the Swin or Swindon Forge on the Smestow Brook. This had been in the hands of the Homfray family certainly since the 1730s. However, in 1794 the freehold was held by Francis Homfray but the forge, which consisted of a finery, a chafery and a balling furnace was being worked by a Mr. Finch. The forge was being worked by the third Francis Homfray at the time of his death in 1809 and two years later it was advertised for auction. In 1816 it was stated that the forge was lately occupied by Thomas Homfray and then it was later owned by P. Homfray and R. Shinton who dissolved their partnership in 1820.[10]

(8) In 1794 Jeston Homfray held the freehold of Stourbridge Forge with its single chafery and single balling furnace. However, it was not being worked by a Homfray but by G. Briscoe.[11]

These industrial undertakings show clearly the wealth of experience the Homfray family had built up in forging, slitting and the marketing of iron goods. Of the family the most experienced in the iron trade was Francis Homfray of Broadwaters and Stourton Castle. Francis Homfray not only continued the family interest in the Stour Valley but expanded his iron making empire into Shropshire. By 1787 Francis Homfray and John Homfray (later Addenbrooke) owned the Lightmoor Ironworks in Shropshire. After Francis' death his son, also Francis, became a partner in the Lightmoor Ironworks. By 1796 there were three blast furnaces at Lightmoor and a visitor in 1802 found three blast furnaces at the works with a few refineries and a balling furnace.[12] Most of the iron produced at Lightmoor was sent to the Stour Valley to be worked into plate, bar and rods at the other Homfray forges and mills. In 1800 a 44in. x 8ft. beam blowing engine was supplied to the works by Boulton and Watt. It had a 84in. blowing cylinder which fed two 100in. regulating cylinders. The beam of this engine was made of wood and was 26½ft. long.[13]

The Lightmoor investment was an important feature in the Homfray family's involvement in the iron trade but a further incursion by Francis Homfray of Broadwaters and Stourton was to have repercussions for the later career of the family in the British iron industry. In 1778 we find Francis Homfray as a partner in the Calcutts Ironworks.[14] This ironworks was situated near Brosely in Shropshire and Homfray's partner in the concern was George Matthews who had founded the ironworks. Although the evidence points to only a short Homfray involvement in the works it was during an important time for the concern. For here was being made cannon for the American war and so Francis Homfray gained experience of yet another branch of the iron trade. Later in February 1786, when Matthews as sole owner had died, the Calcutts Ironworks was advertised for sale. It included two blast furnaces capable of making 40 tons of iron a week, air furnaces, two forges for making bar iron, three steam engines, a water corn mill, a brick kiln, twelve coke and tar ovens and 96 acres 'abounding' with coal, rich iron ore and brick earth. The sale notice also pointed out that during the last war the Calcutts Ironworks had supplied cannon, 'of the best quality which can be justified by the proof book at Woolwich Warren.'[15]

So by the early 1780s Francis Homfray had gained experience in slitting, the manufacture of nails, selling iron and iron goods, operating forges, working blast furnaces and the boring of cannon. It is no wonder that Anthony Bacon turned to Francis Homfray when his iron making business in and around Merthyr Tydfil faced a crisis. Anthony Bacon was a successful merchant who was the founding father of the Merthyr Tydfil iron industry. In 1765 Bacon and his partner William Brownrigg leased land at Cyfarthfa where they erected a furnace and forge. Expansion at Cyfarthfa took place in 1773 when a mill for boring cannon was added. So successful was the manufacture of cannon at Cyfarthfa that the mill depended not only on supplies of iron from its own furnace but supplies from several neighbouring furnaces including Hirwaun which was also owned by Bacon. However, Bacon was also the M.P. for Aylesbury and in 1782 Clerke's Act was passed which forbade government contractors from sitting in the House of Commons. Bacon could continue making iron but could not manufacture cannon for sale to the government. The way around the problem was for Bacon to sub-let the cannon boring mill and the forge to another operator but continue to sell the pig iron he made to the mill. So Bacon turned to Francis Homfray who had all the necessary experience to work both the forge and mill at Cyfarthfa. It was quite likely that Bacon knew Homfray from the time Homfray was a partner at the cannon manufacturing Calcutt Ironworks. Francis Homfray already had some experience of the South Wales iron industry for his first wife was Hannah Popkin a member of a well known family in the Welsh iron trade.

To guarantee profits from the manufacture of cannon at Cyfarthfa the mill and forge was leased by Bacon to Homfray in 1782 with rather all embracing terms. The lease was to run for 50 years at a yearly payment of £20. The terms for the lease were:

(1) Homfray was not to erect blast furnaces in Glamorgan without the consent of Bacon.

(2) Homfray was to supply Bacon with all castings in iron for the works at Cyfarthfa at cost price.

(3) Bacon was to supply all the dark grey metal made at his furnaces at Cyfarthfa and Plymouth at £5 per ton.

(4) At the end of the war Cyfarthfa and other furnaces were to supply iron at the rate of £4 10s 0d. per ton.

(5) Homfray was not to purchase iron from other sources.[16]

Francis Homfray worked the Cyfarthfa Forge and Mill until March 1786. While at Cyfarthfa he seems to have improved the manufacture of wrought iron at the forge. Wrought iron was made at Cyfarthfa using the stamping and potting process and Francis Homfray's portrait records that, 'He was the first who brought to perfection the art of making bar iron with pit coal in Wales and which he established at Cyfarthfa Forge in the parish of Merthyr co. Glamorgan in the year 1783.' Although successful in some aspects it is quite clear that the terms of the lease all but tied Homfray's hands in his commercial dealings in Wales. During periods of high demand Francis Homfray was unable to buy in any additional iron for the mill or forge in order to accrue extra profits. During times of low demand Homfray had to buy in all the iron produced by the Cyfarthfa Furnace. This produced a serious problem when few orders for cannon were coming in for the forge could not handle any extra iron. This forced Francis Homfray to sell the surplus iron on the open market. In 1783-84 Homfray was selling pig iron to the Knight family for processing into wrought iron at their Stour Valley forges. This pig iron was sold at £5. 12s. 6d. per ton.[17] The Treaty of Versailles ending hostilities was not signed until September 1783 so it was quite possible that Homfray was buying in the iron at £5 and then having to sell it on for a small profit. After a disagreement with Bacon over the supply of iron Homfray gave up the lease of the Cyfarthfa property in March 1786 when he was replaced by David Tanner.

Although disappointed by his experiences at Cyfarthfa Francis Homfray had realised the great potential of the South Wales Coalfield for iron making. As early as February 12th 1784 a 99 year lease had been taken out by the Homfrays in a dingle called Penydarren (the head of a steep bank or rocks). The lease was between John Rees of Merthyr Tydfil, gentleman and two of Francis Homfray's sons, Jeremiah and Samuel.[18] This mineral lease was to become the basis of the foundation of the Penydarren Ironworks. However, there was a shortage of coal on the Penydarren property and further veins had to be leased from the neighbouring Dowlais holding. The problem with raw materials was later to restrict the development of the Penydarren Ironworks and also generate a number of lawsuits. The furnace and other buildings at Penydarren were built by attracting additional capital into the company. This new blood consisted of Thomas Homfray, the brother of the other Homfray partners, and Richard, William and Henry Forman. William Forman was an ordnance agent at the Tower of London and acquainted with the Homfrays through cannon manufacture.[19] Richard Forman seems to have been very active in helping to get the Penydarren Ironworks established. In May 1788 he wrote to Jeremiah Homfray concerning the furnace in the following terms:

> I beg leave to return you and Mrs. Homfray my best Thanks for your care and attention and kindness to me while at your Plant. I own I am anxious to hear how the tuyère in the Furnis remains as it appears something dangerous in my Ideas and may cause the inside of the Furnis to fall in which will be a great damp to our expectations, and as this may probably happen it would be right to have everything got as forward as possible to put her into blast again. - The Hearth Stones should be got to Pendarran and the proper Person employed to shape and bed them ready to be laid when necessity required, and as this is a matter of Consequence, I recommend your employing the Person who laid the hearth before that we may run no hazards of its being improperly done.[20]

There existed a close co-operation at this time between the Penydarren and Cyfarthfa Ironworks and Richard Forman was able to liaise with Richard Crawshay who was residing in London.[21]

Soon a forge was constructed at Penydarren and Richard Crawshay encouraged the Homfrays into experimenting with Cort's puddling process. The Homfrays had taken an early interest in Cort's methods but had built their forge to use the stamping and potting method. The final part of Cort's puddling process involved a rolling of the wrought iron through a set of grooved rolls. As early as 1784 the Homfrays had arranged a trial of Cort's rolling process at Hyde Mill.[22] However, the Homfrays seem to have had grave doubts concerning Cort's ideas and for the time remained faithful to stamping and potting. Samuel Homfray was keenly interested in the technology of iron making and at Richard Crawshay's bidding was soon using and trying to improve Cort's methods at Penydarren. This was necessary for the initial results of puddling at Cyfarthfa were disappointing. Richard Crawshay could write to Samuel Homfray on May 3rd 1788 concerning the arrival of a consignment of Penydarren wrought iron describing it as, 'the worst British iron we have seen lately, faces hollow, edges rough - we can do nothing with it here.'[23] However, improvements to the puddling furnace made by Crawshay and the introduction of a preliminary refinery stage, probably the idea of Samuel Homfray, solved the problems and by December 1791 good puddled iron was being produced at Merthyr Tydfil.

Although Homfray was experimenting with puddling he seems to have continued to make wrought iron by stamping and potting at Penydarren. As early as 1787 Samuel Homfray seems to have been loathe to adopt puddling because of the patent payment involved. On October 25th Henry Cort wrote to Richard Crawshay concerning his reception at Penydarren:

> I called on Tuesday at Penydarron Forge with Mr. Cockshutt the hammers work well and saw some very good iron but it happened as we went in that the Bar Iron then drawing dropped in pieces at the red short heat and there had been drawn that morning some others of that quality. We asked from whose pig it had been made and Mr. Homfray said it was Plymouth Pig made in the stamped way-he had worked a few tons but would work no more, that he would not give anything for them, that he had been informed Mr. Crawshay had contracted for a large quantity on moderate terms (1000 tons per annum at £4). We brought with us a piece of the Bar and had it tried but it was so rotten it could not be worked into anything. He said he would write to you about it & which might be unpleasantly received. I was determined to have some Plymouth Pigs brought from the same heap Mr. Homfray received his. I have worked them by my process better Iron cannot be made, very tough, a strong body intirely free from red short quality, which you will have confirmed from this house, when they have occasion to write to you. Mr.Homfray acknowledged he never expected my process brought to what it is. Mr. Homfray said he could make his Iron by my method forty shillings per ton cheaper than by the method he

now pursued but whilst others kept on stamping he should-if others altered their method he should do so too and at the same time was ungenerous to say he would not pay me any thing if he went into it. What I felt is not to be expressed - however my ardour is not to be stated.[24]

In 1794 no mention was made of any puddling furnaces at Penydarren but by Ladyday 1796 there were two furnaces at Penydarren producing 84 tons 5 cwt. of iron per week and the forge was making 65 tons of wrought iron weekly all of which was puddled iron.[25] By this time patent payments were not being collected because of Cort's bankruptcy, and also doubts concerning the validity of the patent had surfaced.

The progress of the Penydarren Ironworks was interrupted by a dispute between Jeremiah and Samuel Homfray. This seems to have taken place before 1796 and resulted in Jeremiah Homfray withdrawing from the active management of the concern on the payment of £1,000 per year. Jeremiah Homfray still kept an interest in the partnership for on the August 4th 1796 he wrote to his solicitors regarding Samuel's running of the concern in the following terms:

> Some curious discriminations are made by him upon the Arbitration clauses, etc., etc., and we are all sett at defiance, and as he says without any possible remedy. He insists he has a right without our knowledge or consent to lay out our money in whatever he pleases to think is for the benefit of the concern - say in Peach Houses, Fishponds, Mortgages, Turnpikes ....Some remedy to check his unbound ambition, misapplication of that power and money he is entrusted with, and procuring a certain income without being obliged to beg it from him, is what I aim at ...[26]

This simmering dispute came to a head later in that year when Samuel Homfray refused to pay to Jeremiah the quarterly payment of £250 in the Autumn.[27] This payment was resumed later at a yearly payment of £1,200 to Jeremiah Homfray and his descendants while the Penydarren Ironworks was in production. Soon after this event Jeremiah Homfray seems to have withdrawn completely from the partnership to concentrate his talents on founding other ironworks in South Wales. This left Samuel Homfray as the undisputed managing partner. He was now able to fully follow an interest in steam power. By 1798 he possessed a wealth of experience in the operation of Newcomen engines as demonstrated in this letter to Boulton & Watt in January 1798:

> We are at this time erecting an engine of 50 inches diameter cylinder to work a rolling mill and a hammer at the same time and being informed your patent has but two years to run and that the saving of coals is considerable I am inclined to think it may be in our mutual interest to stop our hands and adopt one on your plan. The engine house is nearly built and the boiler made and in its place. It's of 19ft. diameter. Most of the castings for the engine are made, but its no great object to us to break them and melt them down in our fineries. I will

therefore thank you to inform me what the cost of an engine of your plan, to do the same work as ours of 50 inches diameter in the cylinder allowing ours to raise 8 pounds on the inch and the daily saving of coals, and if you would undertake to put it to work for a certain sum, finding such parts and things for the engine as you may enumerate, or if you would send a man down now to direct the castings etc. to be made and to inspect the putting of them together. We have every convenience for making castings etc. here and have five fire engines now at work of different dimensions and it may probably be worth your while to agree with us for altering them to your plan before your patent expires. The price of our coal is from 3 shillings to 4 shillings per ton.[28]

Impressed by the savings achieved by the Boulton & Watt engine Samuel Homfray had erected two examples at Penydarren in 1798. One was a blowing engine while the other was an engine to power rolling and slitting mills. The blowing engine could well have been the first Boulton & Watt engine built with an iron beam. Homfray's interest in steam power is also shown by the visits of Carl Friedrich Buckling to Britain. Buckling wanted to erect a steam engine in Prussia. On his second visit in 1786 he purchased a cast iron cylinder from the Penydarren Ironworks and also there secured the services of an engineer called George Richards.[29]

Samuel Homfray's interest in steam engines brought him into contact with Richard Trevithick in May 1803. The result of this meeting was that Samuel Homfray bought a ¼ share in Trevithick's high pressure steam engine patent. Together, these strong willed men promoted the advantages of high pressure steam to the industrial community. Manufacturers were allowed to construct Trevithick high pressure engines on the payment of a premium.[30] Richard Trevithick wrote in 1805 that there were seventeen or eighteen foundries producing these high pressure engines. One of these engines was constructed at Penydarren in 1804 as a tramroad locomotive. This locomotive is acknowledged as the world's first steam locomotive and it made several trips along the Penydarren Tramroad before being converted to stationary use.

Samuel Homfray like many of his family exhibited a rather restless nature and in around 1813 quit the Penydarren Iron Company to concentrate his resources on developing the Tredegar Ironworks in Monmouthshire. Also up to this date Jeremiah Homfray had been active in the development of other Welsh ironworks. This can be demonstrated by the following chronology:

1790 - Jeremiah Homfray was one of the original partners who set up the Ebbw Vale Ironworks. In 1791 Jeremiah Homfray became the sole owner and in 1792 Harford, Partridge & Co. became partners, later buying out Homfray in 1796.

1801 - Jeremiah Homfray and James Birch were partners in the setting up of the Abernant Ironworks.

1803 - A new partnership took over the Hirwaun Ironworks. Jeremiah Homfray was one of these partners but left after a few years.

Jeremiah Homfray seems to have made a profitable career in setting up iron-works and then selling them as going concerns. In 1807 Birch and Jeremiah Homfray were bought out of the Abernant Ironworks by the Tappenden Brothers and the deal included a £100 payment yearly to Homfray.[31] This echoes the deal struck at Penydarren where at first a yearly payment of £1000 was due to Jeremiah Homfray. However, the other business interests of Jeremiah Homfray were not so successful and when he died in 1833 he had spent the last twenty years of his life abroad trying to escape his creditors.

After leaving Penydarren Samuel Homfray's ambitions rested with the development of the Tredegar Ironworks. Samuel Homfray had married the widowed daughter of Sir Charles Gould Morgan and in 1800 leased from him a large area of land at Bedwellty Common near Tredegar. His partners in this venture were Richard Fothergill, Matthew Monkhouse, William Thompson and William Forman. By 1805 there were two furnaces in blast and in 1823 the works had five furnaces which were producing over 16,000 tons of iron per year. Samuel Homfray's success as an ironmaster in Monmouthshire led him to become High Sheriff of the county in 1813 and the M.P. for Stafford in 1818. He died in 1822 and was buried in Bassaleg Church.

Samuel Homfray's sons continued to take an active role in the running of the Tredegar Ironworks, particularly Samuel Homfray and Watkin Homfray. The Homfray family continued to have the largest holding in the Tredegar Ironworks and in 1834 the partnership was known as Samuel and Watkin Homfray & Co.[32] Samuel Homfray's interest in steam power was passed on to his sons with the result that several interesting steam locomotives were built by the Tredegar Ironworks for their own use during the period 1832-1853. By 1867 the structure of the Tredegar partnership had changed with the Forman family becoming the dominant faction and in the following year the Homfray shares were purchased by the Fothergill and Forman families. In this later period the Homfray shares seem to have been held by Samuel George Homfray, Lorenzo Homfray and the Reverend Watkin Homfray.[33] Samuel George Homfray continued to live at Glen Usk, near Newport but the family's connection with the iron industry of South Wales had come to a close.

References.

1. M.W. Flinn, *Men of Iron - The Crowleys in the Early Iron Industry*, Edinburgh, 1962, p.234.
2. *Victoria County History of Staffordshire*, Vol.20, p.146.
   S.M & M.V. Cooksley, Watermills and Water-powered Works on the River Stour, Worcestershire and Staffordshire, Part 5, The Smestow Brook, *Wind and Water Mills* (The Occasional Journal of the Midland Wind and Water Mill Group), No.7, 1986, p.13.
3. H.W. Gwilliam, Mills and Forges on the Wannerton Brook, *Wind and Water Mills*, No.2, 1981, p.28.
4. H.W Gwilliam, op. cit., pp.28-29.
5. Birmingham Reference Library (BRL), Boulton & Watt Collection (B&W), List of Ironworks, 1794.
6. H.W Gwilliam, op. cit., p.28
7. *Victoria County History of Staffordshire*, Vol.20, p.146.
8. *Victoria County History of Staffordshire*, Vol.20, pp.145-146.
   M.V. Cooksley, Watermills and Water-powered Works on the River Stour, Part Two, Wolverley and Kinver, *Wind and Water Mills*, Vol.5, 1984, p.14.
9. M.V. Cooksley, op. cit., p.146.
   Victoria County History of Staffordshire, Vol.20, p.146.

10. *Victoria County History of Staffordshire*, Vol.20, pp.213-214.
    S.M. & M.V. Cooksley, op. cit., pp.19-20.
    BRL, B&W, List of Ironworks, 1794.
11. BRL, B&W, List of Ironworks, 1794.
12. Barrie Trinder, *The Industrial Revolution in Shropshire*, Chichester, 1973, p.71.
13. BRL, B&W, Portfolio No. 683, Drawings for Lightmoor Engine, 1800.
14. Laurence Ince, *The Knight Family and the British Iron Industry*, Solihull, 1991, p.119.
15. Barrie Trinder, op. cit., p.63.
16. National Library of Wales, Aberystwyth, Maybery Papers, Lease dated 27th of September 1782.
17. Laurence Ince, *The Knight Family and the British Iron Industry*, Solihull, 1991, p.119.
18. M.S. Taylor, The Penydarren Ironworks, 1784-1859, *Glamorgan Historian*, Vol.3, Cowbridge, 1966, pp.75-76.
19. M.S. Taylor, op. cit., pp.83-84.
20. National Library of Wales, Aberystwyth, Homfray Accounts and Papers, 15593, letter 20th May 1788.
21. NLW, Homfray, Letter from Richard Forman to Jeremiah Homfray & Co., 25th October 1787.
22. R.A. Mott (Ed. P. Singer), *Henry Cort, the Great Finer*, 1983, p.51.
23. NLW, Homfray, R. Crawshay to Jeremiah Homfray & Co., 3rd May 1788.
24. R.A. Mott, op. cit., pp.54-55.
25. Kidderminster Public Library, Homfray Notebook.
26. M.S. Taylor, op. cit., p.77.
27. NLW, Maybery Papers, 2776-2779.
28. BRL, B&W, Letter Samuel Homfray to Boulton & Watt, 8th January 1798.
29. W.O. Henderson, *Britain and Industrial Europe 1750-1870*, Leicester, 1965, p.149.
30. Laurence Ince, Richard Trevithick's Patent Steam Engine, *Stationary Power*, Vol.1, 1984, pp.67-75.
31. NLW, Maybery Papers, 1920-1921.
32. *Historical Metallurgy Group Bulletin*, No.5, 1965, p.30.
33. Gwent Record Office, Cwmbran, D. 917.325, Assignment of Shares, June 2nd 1862.

Plate Nine   The Penydarren Ironworks in 1813.

Plate Ten

Francis Homfray of Wales and Old Swinford, 1674-1737.

Plate Eleven

Francis Homfray of Broadwaters and Stourton Castle, 1725-1798.

Plate Twelve Sir Jeremiah Homfray of Llandaff, 1759-1833.

Plate Thirteen   *Samuel Homfray of Penydarren, 1762-1822. The young Homfray is pictured in front of the Cyfarthfa Furnace and Forge, c1784.*

Plate Fourteen   *Watkin Homfray, 1796-1837.*

Plate Fifteen   *Samuel Homfray of Glen Usk, 1795-1882.*

Plate Sixteen Glen Usk, the Monmouthshire home of the Homfrays.

Plate Seventeen — *A Homfray wedding party at Glen Usk, c1880. Samuel Homfray is seated on the left and next to him are probably his sons, Samuel George Homfray and Lorenzo Augustus Homfray.*

Chapter Eight.

The Iron Industry of the Neath Valley.

The large scale development of the iron industry in the Neath Valley dates from the early 1790s. Two ironworks were built at this time although one of these was to have a very short life. A furnace was built at Penrhiwtyn in 1792 but little, if any, iron seems to have been produced. The land on which the works stood was leased to Alexander Raby, Herbert Evans and others. Raby was a forgemaster from the Weald who was attempting to shift his operations to South Wales. At that time Raby was also developing a second ironworks at Llanelli, Carmarthenshire. A further lease was granted at Penrhiwtyn in 1796 but Raby was then the sole owner.[1] There appears to have been little activity on the site with Raby later becoming bankrupt in the early part of the nineteenth century.

The second ironworks founded at this time was certainly a more successful venture. This was the building of the Neath Abbey Ironworks in 1792 by a Cornish partnership.[2] With regard to industry Cornwall and the Neath Valley had been linked for many years. The early copper industry had flourished in the Neath area attracting ships bringing Cornish copper ore and returning to Cornwall with cargoes of coal. Amongst the copper ore shippers was the Fox family of Falmouth who in 1791 expanded their business interests by building a foundry at Perran Wharf close to their home town. In 1792 they took over an ancient industrial site at Neath Abbey and constructed two furnaces on the property. It was the intention of the partners to produce pig iron at Neath Abbey for use at their Perran Wharf Foundry. There, they would manufacture machinery and machine parts for the Cornish mines. The founding partners were George Croker Fox, Robert Were Fox, Thomas Were Fox, Mary Fox, George Fox, Thomas Fox, Edward Fox, Peter Price, Samuel Tregelles, Thomas Wilson of Truro (Copper Smelter), John Gould of Truro (Dr. of Physic) and William Wood of Swansea (Ironmaster). The majority of these partners were Quakers and members of the inter-related Fox, Price and Tregelles families.

The Neath Abbey Ironworks had an advantage not possessed by the works founded along the northern outcrop of the coalfield. This advantage was the work's situation close to the tidal reaches of the Rivers Clydach and Neath which allowed easy shipment of raw materials and products. The position of the Neath Abbey Ironworks facilitated the importation of richer ores from such areas as Lancashire. The production of pig iron at Neath Abbey seems to have commenced with the use of a mixture of native and imported ores.

The Neath Abbey Iron Company had not been able to lease any coal ground and so an efficient steam engine was built to blow the two Neath Abbey furnaces. This engine was a 40in. x 8ft. Boulton & Watt beam blowing engine with a 70in. blowing cylinder. The blowing engine was completed in 1793 and was praised as being the most powerful beam blowing engine then operating in Britain. The Neath Abbey partners paid an annual premium of £120 to Boulton & Watt for the use of this engine. The furnaces were blown at 2¾ psi and when working at full capacity they were able to produce from 60 to 80 tons of iron per week. The first ironmaster at Neath Abbey was William Wood who was replaced by Peter Price in 1801. Price was by far the most experienced of the partners with regards to the iron industry. He was born in Madeley, Shropshire in 1739 and was trained as a moulder in the Coalbrookdale Ironworks. In 1759 Price was recruited by Dr. John Roebuck for his Carron Ironworks, Falkirk where he rose to become foreman of the boring mill. After ten years at Carron he left for America where he spent five years putting up blast furnaces in Pennsylvania, Maryland, North Carolina and Virginia. On the outbreak of the War of Independence he returned to Britain. For a period Price was agent to the Dale or Ketley Company in London, then a corn factor in Stourport before moving to Cornwall to become involved with fellow Quakers in the setting up of the Perran Wharf Foundry.

It was soon realised that it would be more economical to build some machine parts at Neath Abbey rather than transport the pig iron to Perran Wharf. The Cornish connection helped the Neath Abbey Ironworks graduate from the building of machine parts to producing complete engines. The first steam engines built at Neath Abbey were of the Trevithick high pressure type. Soon the partners were building beam engines for their own coal mines having taken over the lease of the Dyffryn estate minerals in 1806. The engineering side of the business continued to expand until the works was put up for sale in 1817. This sale was probably connected to the fall in demand for iron at the end of the Napoleonic War. Another factor was that several of the original partners had died and their shares were then held in the hands of several executors. At the time of the sale the ironworks was described as consisting of two blast furnaces, a very extensive foundry, a powerful boring mill worked by water, an excellent site for a rolling mill, an extensive smithery and commodious buildings now employed making steam engines on the most approved plan, being furnished with an excellent steam engine, turning lathes and all the necessary apparatus.

The lease and works were in fact taken over in March 1818 by a new Fox/Price partnership consisting of Joseph Tregelles Price, Henry Habberly Price, Alfred Fox and Thomas Were Fox. Joseph T. Price acted as managing partner and under his direction the works won renown for its precision engineering. The building of marine steam engines commenced in the early 1820s, railway locomotives in 1829 and iron ships in 1842. The Neath Abbey Iron Company was an important component in the development of the South Wales iron industry for the works was the main supplier of steam engines to the industry. Beam blowing engines were one of the Neath Abbey Ironworks' most popular products with examples being built up to the 1870s. The works appears to have constructed their first beam blowing engine in 1819 which was a 52½in. x 8ft. engine. This became a standard design and could be supplied with 105in., 112in. or 122in. blowing cylinders. The 122in. cylinders were the largest to be cast in one piece in Britain until Harvey and Company of Hayle cast a 144in. cylinder in 1843. The Neath Abbey Ironworks produced condensing beam blowing engines as well as high pressure non-condensing engines. The high pressure non-condensing engines were favoured by some engineers who felt that the fewer moving parts in this type would mean fewer break downs.

As well as beam blowing engines the Neath Abbey Iron Company also built beam engines for driving rolling mills and from the late 1840s onwards horizontal and inverted vertical engines were turned out. In the late 1830s the partners at Neath Abbey began to experiment with making iron with anthracite coal as the fuel. The use of anthracite as a fuel at Neath Abbey continued during the 1840s. However, output of iron was low and the Neath Abbey furnaces were put out of blast in the late 1840s. At this time the partners had already opened another ironworks at Abernant, Glynneath which was situated in the proximity of their iron ore mines. The Neath Abbey Iron Company suffered a severe setback with the death of Joseph Tregelles Price in 1854. However, the works was to continue under the ownership of the Fox and Price families for a further twenty years. Decline in orders from the local markets and an increase in the rent for the land on which the works stood forced a closure in 1874. The Neath Abbey Ironworks remained closed for only a short period and was reopened by a partnership of local men consisting of Edward Davies, Henry Jones and John Howell. The new owners made a grave error in trying to produce the complete range of Neath Abbey products namely iron ships, marine steam engines, locomotives and stationary steam engines and the works was forced to close in around 1885-86.

The Fox-Price partnership's second works had a fairly short life when compared with the Neath Abbey Ironworks. The Abernant Ironworks was built in 1845 and consisted of two furnaces and refineries. The fuel used in the Abernant blast furnaces was anthracite for the Neath Valley is situated on the boundary between bituminous and anthracite and possesses both types. The partners had been producing iron with anthracite at Neath Abbey but it was hoped that a purpose built anthracite ironworks would be more successful.

The two furnaces at Abernant were blown by a 40in. x 8ft. Neath Abbey beam blowing engine (60 h.p.). The refineries received their blast from a 12in. table engine. A third furnace was added in 1851. During the period 1856-57 all three furnaces were in blast but there appears to have been no iron production in 1858. The period 1859-61 saw only one furnace in blast and it would seem that the works, like the majority of anthracite ironworks, was a commercial failure. The Abernant Ironworks was put up for sale in 1862 when the property consisted of 127 acres of mineral ground, three blast furnaces capable of making 250 tons of iron per week, a cupola, two refineries, hot blast stoves, calcining kilns, workshops, cast houses and twenty one cottages.[3] No interested parties came forward and the works was dismantled in around 1868.

The three other anthracite ironworks founded in the Neath Valley also had limited life spans. The oldest of these concerns was the Venallt Ironworks which was built in 1839.[4] It was constructed as a two furnace ironworks by Arthur & Company but by 1846 it was owned by Jevons and Wood.[5] In 1849 the works was up for sale and consisted of 3,000 acres of coal and ironstone, two blast furnaces, hot blast stoves, casting houses, a foundry, a finery and a blowing engine house built for a pair of engines but containing a single 50 h.p. high pressure beam blowing engine.[6]

For a time during the 1850s the Venallt Ironworks was owned by the Aberdare Iron Company but little production of iron seems to have taken place.[7] In 1860 the site was in the hands of N.V.E. Vaughan who allowed the works to stand idle while he used his resources to exploit the rich mineral ground.[8] The Neath Abbey Iron Company was in possession of the works during 1869-70 but probably this was solely for the dismantling of the machinery.[9] The following year saw the furnaces in the hands of W. Gregory who had taken over the property to exploit the coal and iron ore reserves.[10]

Two further anthracite ironworks were built in the valley of the tributary Dulais in the early 1840s. The Onllwyn Ironworks with its two furnaces was at work in 1844 when the Neath Abbey Ironworks repaired a 21½in. engine at the site.[11] A 24in. high pressure engine was also supplied to the Onllwyn Ironworks by Neath Abbey in 1846.[12] In 1854 there was one furnace in blast with the works having been recently purchased by W. Llewellyn & Son who had interests in coal mining and tinplate works in the Neath Valley.[13] The Onllwyn Ironworks was taken over by William Parsons in 1859 with one furnace remaining in blast.[14] So unsuccessful was production of iron with anthracite coal that the furnaces were modified to burn with bituminous coal from 1861 onwards.[15] During the period 1862-64 the two furnaces were in blast and on the death of William Parsons in 1864 the works was taken over by the Onllwyn Iron and Coal Company.[16] The two furnaces remained in blast until the financial collapse of the company in 1866. In that year Lewis, the manager of the ironworks, sued for wrongful dismissal and this was closely followed by a petition issued for the winding up of the company.[17] A new company with the same name was formed to buy up the old company but the furnaces were never put in blast again.

The Banwen Ironworks, founded in the early 1840s by a joint stock London company, also had a disappointing commercial career. The company was formed in 1845 with some of the directors having South Wales connections.[18] In 1849 the Banwen Iron Company was wound up with little production of iron having taken place. An unsuccessful attempt was made to sell the concern through the Chancery Court in 1850.[19] It was stated that the two furnaces could produce 90 tons of iron per week.[20] Later the works was purchased by James Henty in 1852 but again little or no iron was produced and the Banwen Ironworks was again offered for sale in 1854. The furnaces were described as being blown by a 19½in. x 5ft. 6in. high pressure beam blowing engine with a 60in. blowing cylinder. The works remained unoccupied until 1861 when taken over by Llewellyn & Son who put both furnaces into blast.[21] The following year saw no iron production at Banwen and the two furnaces remained out of blast until disappearing from the Mineral Statistics after 1871.

A far longer lived venture was the Briton Ferry Ironworks which owes its origin to the formation of a partnership in 1846. Although its early history was fraught with commercial difficulties, the enterprise had one great advantage and that was its position close to the mouth of the River Neath. The original partnership consisted of Joel Lean, Joseph and George Davey and Edward Willet.[22] A rolling mill was constructed and a 60in. x 7ft. Neath Abbey beam engine with a 20ft. flywheel was purchased.[23] It was envisaged that the works would buy in pig iron and convert it into rails. Production commenced in 1847 with twelve puddling furnaces, twelve balling furnaces, a forge train and a rolling mill. The total cost of equipping the works was put at £40,000 and before the year was out a clay mill was built for the company by the Neath Abbey Ironworks.

In 1849 the Briton Ferry Iron Company experienced serious financial problems and a new company was formed with Henry Scale as a major shareholder. New capital was injected into the works with the puddling furnaces being increased to forty. A second forge train was built at this time and the rolling capacity of the works was increased by the addition of a merchant bar mill, a plate mill and a guide mill. However, this expansion did not prove to be a success and the company went bankrupt in 1854. Almost immediately a new company was formed which included Thomas Jenkins as chief shareholder along with James Evans and Evan Roberts. A decision was made to produce pig iron at Briton Ferry and two blast furnaces with six hot blast stoves were constructed. The furnaces had closed tops and were fitted with bell and hopper mechanisms built by the Neath Abbey Ironworks. The furnaces were charged by means of a vertical lift powered by a Neath Abbey engine. The blast was provided by a second hand beam blowing engine, probably purchased from the Garth Ironworks, Maesteg. The first Briton Ferry furnace was put into blast in 1855 and the second furnace commenced operations in 1856. The coastal site of the Briton Ferry Ironworks allowed easy importation of iron ores and this was to be the key to its long commercial life. Both furnaces were put out of blast for a period in 1857 when a new 96in. blowing cylinder, supplied by Jonah and George Davies of Tipton, was fitted. Output after this repair can be gauged from the figures for the week ending June 6th 1857 when No.1 furnace made 123 tons of iron and No.2 produced 100 tons using Lancashire, Brixham and Llantrisant ore.

In 1863 the two furnaces at Briton Ferry were being operated by Willett and Davey with the works continuing under this partnership until purchased in 1870 by Townshend Wood and Company.[24] There was some new investment by this owner for a 30in. condensing beam engine was purchased from the Neath Abbey Ironworks for Briton Ferry. On the death of Townshend Wood in 1871 the company became Biddulph, Wood, Jevons & Co. who continued to keep the two furnaces at Briton Ferry in blast. At this time the Briton Ferry Ironworks possessed forty four puddling furnaces and four mills. During the period 1879-81 the blast furnaces were rebuilt making them 50ft. high with 6ft. 6in. diameter hearths. The furnaces were also equipped with new bell and hoppers manufactured by the Neath Abbey Ironworks. This new investment appears to have severely strained the company for in 1881 the works was closed and in the following year the company failed.

A new operating company was formed in 1883 by G.H. Davey who had been general manager at the works and in 1884 production of iron recommenced. This was a short lived venture for the Briton Ferry Ironworks was again to close in 1886.

The works remained idle until 1889 when a resuscitation was completed by a new company consisting of G.H. Davey, M.G. Roberts, D.T. Sims, W.P. Struve, H.F. Taylor and Robert Roberts. The company met with far more success with the Briton Ferry Ironworks operating well into the twentieth century.

References.

1. Harry Green, Penrhiwtyn Ironworks and Eaglesbush Coal, *Transactions of the Neath Antiquarian Society*, 1978, pp.50-57.
2. For a comprehensive account of this venture with detailed references see, Laurence Ince, *The Neath Abbey Iron Company*, Eindhoven, 1984.
3. *Mining Journal*, March 15th 1862, p.14.
4. David Mushet, *Papers on Iron and Steel*, 1840, pp.414-415.
5. Harry Green, Cwmgwrach Iron and Resolven Coal, *Transactions of the Neath Antiquarian Society*, 1977, pp.48-52.
6. *Mining Journal*, January 6th 1849, p.1.
7. Robert Hunt, *Mineral Statistics, 1854-59*.
8. Robert Hunt, *Mineral Statistics, 1860*.
9. Robert Hunt, *Mineral Statistics, 1869-70*.
10. Robert Hunt, *Mineral Statistics, 1871*.
11. GRO, Neath Abbey Ironworks' Collection, D/D. N.A.I., M/149/1, Piston and Rod for 21½in. engine, Onllwyn Ironworks.
12. GRO, NAI, D/D. N.A.I., M/149/2, Drawing for a 24 inch engine, Onllwyn Ironworks, 1846.
13. Robert Hunt, *Mineral Statistics, 1854*.
14. Robert Hunt, *Mineral Statistics, 1859*.
15. Robert Hunt, *Mineral Statistics, 1861*.
16. Robert Hunt, *Mineral Statistics, 1864*.
17. *The Engineer*, April 6th 1866, pp.259-60 & November 9th 1866, p.371.
18. Stephen Hughes, *The Brecon Forest Tramroads*, Aberystwyth, 1990, pp.25-31.
19. *Mining Journal*, September 15th 1849. p.442.
20. *Mining Journal*, July 20th 1850, p.337.
21. Robert Hunt, *Mineral Statistics, 1861*.
22. For a complete account of this concern see, C.W. Roberts, *A Legacy from Victorian Enterprise, the Briton Ferry Ironworks and the Daughter Companies*, Gloucester, 1983.
23. GRO, NAI, D/D. N.A.I., M/30/3-M/30/4, Drawings for a 60 inch engine for the Briton Ferry Ironworks, 1846.
24. Robert Hunt, *Mineral Statistics, 1863-70*.

Plate Eighteen   The remains of the Neath Abbey Furnaces which were built in 1793.

Plate Nineteen   *Henry Habberly Price, 1794-1839.*

Plate Twenty   *Joseph Tregelles Price, 1784-1854.*

Plate Twenty One   *The works yard at the Neath Abbey Ironworks. Pictured in the yard is a typical product of the company, an 0-6-0 narrow gauge industrial tank locomotive.*

Plate Twenty Two The remains of the double blowing engine house at the Venallt Ironworks.

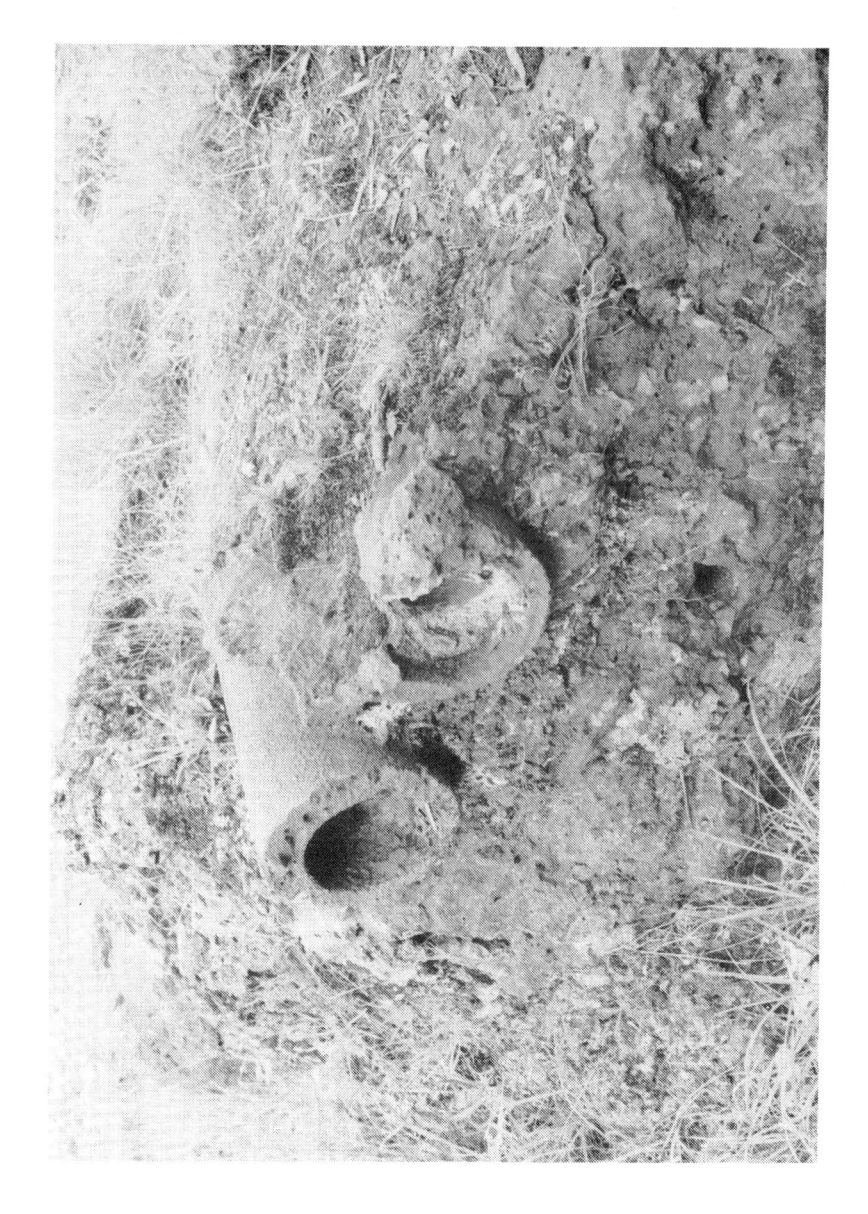

Plate Twenty Three   The remains of a double tuyère at the Venallt Ironworks site.

Plate Twenty Four   The remains of an anthracite blast furnace at the Banwen Ironworks.

Chapter Nine.

The Ebbw Vale Group of Ironworks.

An important role was played in the Welsh iron industry during the nineteenth century by the Ebbw Vale Iron Company. The Ebbw Vale Ironworks was a fairly large concern in itself but several other ironworks were taken over by the company as it expanded its interests in Monmouthshire. Much of the capital for this expansion was generated through the joint stock company system and it is a fairly easy task to discern similarities between the operation of the Aberdare Iron Company in Glamorgan and the Ebbw Vale Iron Company in Monmouthshire.

The first furnace at Ebbw Vale was built in 1790 with the partners in this venture being Charles Cracroft of Crickhowell, Walter Watkins and Jeremiah Homfray.[1] In 1791 the partnership was dissolved with Homfray becoming sole owner and in the following year Harford, Partridge and Company were admitted as partners in the Ebbw Vale Ironworks. In 1796 the Ebbw Vale Ironworks was able to produce 397 tons of iron in the year and at this time Homfray was bought out of the partnership.[2] The partners in the company at the end of the eighteenth century were John Partridge of Monmouth, Philip Crocker, Samuel Harford, James Harford and Richard John Tomlinson.[3] Crocker, Tomlinson and the Harfords were all natives of Bristol. This Quaker partnership was a rare example in South Wales of managerial transfer from the charcoal iron industry to the coke iron industry.

A second furnace was built at Ebbw Vale by 1805 although only one of the furnaces was in blast during the year producing 3,664 tons of iron.[4] The iron making operations at Ebbw Vale must have continued successfully for the partners increased their investment in the South Wales iron industry when they took over the Sirhowy Ironworks in 1818. However, the manoeuvre carried out to absorb Sirhowy did not pass without criticism from certain quarters. By 1823 the Ebbw Vale and Sirhowy Ironworks each possessed three furnaces which produced 20,425 tons of iron during the year.[5] Output rose to 26,020 tons in 1830 by which time the works were being operated by Harfords, Davies and Company.[6]

Transportation of raw materials and products at the Ebbw Vale Ironworks was improved by the purchase of railway locomotives from the Neath Abbey Iron Company. The first locomotive was built in 1831 and was an 0-6-0 with 10½in. x 24in. inverted vertical cylinders driving through bell cranks. In the following year a second 0-6-0 locomotive was supplied to Ebbw Vale. This example of Neath Abbey engineering was called Industry and had horizontal 10½in. cylinders mounted on the top of the boiler with rocking beam drive.[7] Money was also expended on improving output for a fourth furnace was being constructed at the Ebbw Vale Ironworks in 1839.[8] However, the growth of the Ebbw Vale concern was brought to a halt when the operating company went bankrupt in 1842 possibly because of problems with extensive investments in America.

The Ebbw Vale and Sirhowy Ironworks were operated for a short period by trustees before being put on the market in 1844.[9] The Ebbw Vale Ironworks was described in detail in the sale document and consisted of four blast furnaces of which three were at work each producing 90 to 100 tons of iron per week. The fourth furnace was new and was ready to be put into blast. The furnaces were furnished with hot blast apparatus, cast houses, bridge houses and six mine kilns. The blast was provided by two beam blowing engines, No.1 having a 52in. steam cylinder and No.2 having a 42in. steam cylinder. Also situated close to the furnaces were various yards, a clay mill with engine, a brick yard, a limekiln, four fineries, a boring mill, fitting up shops, lathes, a smith's shop (23 fires), a carpenters' shop and a pattern makers' shop. The rolling mill yard consisted of twenty eight puddling furnaces with mills for making rough bars, worked by a 42in. condensing engine with three boilers. Reheating was carried out in twenty eight balling furnaces which served rolling mills for finishing bars worked by two high pressure engines (28in. & 32in.) with eight boilers. Also present on the site were five annealing and other furnaces, saws and engines for cutting rails, punching engines, a 30ft. waterwheel erected two years previously with lathes for turning rolls, a mill for manufacturing small iron, a 26in. engine with hammer and plating rolls and a sand mill. The Ebbw Vale Ironworks, at this time, produced 26,000 tons of bar and railway iron yearly.[10] The Ebbw Vale and Sirhowy Ironworks were purchased by a partnership consisting of Abraham Darby, Alfred Darby, Henry Dickenson, Francis Tothill, Thomas Brown and Joseph Robinson.[11] The majority of these partners were Quakers who were experienced in operating within the iron trade. The Darby family, in particular, had been associated with the iron trade since the early eighteenth century. The new partnership was prepared to expand their iron making empire not only by building at Ebbw Vale but also by purchasing other ironworks. In 1849 the neighbouring Victoria Ironworks was bought and three years later the Abersychan Ironworks was taken over. The Pentwyn Ironworks was acquired in 1857 and by the end of the decade the Ebbw Vale Company had eighteen furnaces at their disposal and employed a work force of 12,000.[12]

The amount of investment injected into the Ebbw Vale site can be gauged from the following description made in 1863-1864 of the plant at the forges and mills.[13] This consisted of:

(1) A 43in. x 8ft. condensing beam engine, working twenty strokes per minute and driving three trains of puddle rolls at twenty revs. per min. This engine also powered three squeezers and was served by fifty puddling furnaces.

(2) A 26½in. x 5ft. high pressure condensing beam engine, working at twenty five strokes per minute and driving a train of rolls and powering a four ton helve hammer. The steam for the engine and a steam hammer was generated by the waste heat of sixteen puddling furnaces. The engine worked at a pressure of 40 psi at a ¼ cut off.

(3) A 32in. x 8ft. high pressure beam engine making thirty strokes per minute driving two trains of rolls at one hundred and two revs. per minute.

(4) A 33in. x 8ft. high pressure beam engine making 23 strokes per minute driving three trains of rolls at seventy eight revs. per min.

(5) An 18in. x 2ft. 4in. horizontal high pressure engine making fifty strokes per minute driving blooming rolls at sixteen revs. per minute.

(6) A 16in. x 3 ft. horizontal high pressure engine making fifty strokes per minute driving blooming rolls at sixteen revs. per minute.

(7) A 19in. x 3ft. horizontal high pressure engine making fifty strokes per minute driving blooming rolls at sixteen revs. per minute.

(8) Two engines for driving saws for sawing ends of rails.

(9) A pair of 24in. x 4ft. horizontal high pressure engines making thirty strokes per minute driving a train of rolls at twenty revs. per minute to flatten the crop end of rails.

(10) A 16in. x 3ft. high pressure horizontal engine powering presses and punches for straightening and punching rails.

(11) Two pairs of 10in. x 1ft. 6in. horizontal engines making eighty strokes per minute driving six 48in. Lloyd's fans.

(12) Four sets of shears for cutting up iron.

In 1864 the Ebbw Vale Iron Company Limited, with Abraham Darby as chairman, was formed with a nominal capital of £4,000,000.[14] The Ebbw Vale Iron Company held an important position in the South Wales iron industry and the new limited company was able to attract more investment which, however, was not wisely spent. The new company made the same mistakes that Richard Fothergill's company perpetrated at Aberdare and Merthyr Tydfil. Not content with holding five ironworks, a sixth, namely the Pontypool Ironworks, was acquired by the Ebbw Vale Ironworks in 1864.[15] At the same time some iron ore mines in the Brendon Hills in Somerset were expanded although these were worked at a loss between 1864 and 1867.[16]

One sound investment that was made during this period was in adopting the Bessemer process for making steel. A new rail mill was completed in 1865 for the manufacture of Bessemer rails and in 1867 a steel rail works was completed with engines built by Galloway and Sons of Manchester.[17] At this time the Ebbw Vale Iron Company was operating two 5 ton Bessemer converters and a 1½ ton converter. A further pair of converters were installed in 1869 and in the following year the company was operating seven 6 ton converters.[18]

The iron producing department also experienced some investment at the same time for in 1865 the massive Darby blowing engine was constructed at the Ebbw Vale Ironworks. The Darby engine was a 72in. x 12ft. beam blowing engine with a 144in. blowing cylinder. The engine was designed by Loam & Son and manufactured by the Perran Foundry, Falmouth. The beam was made of Pontypool cold blast iron and was 36ft. long with a 7ft. depth at the centre. The piston rod was made of Bessemer steel and the 31ft. 6in. connecting rod was an open forging filled with oak. The flywheel was 30ft. 4in. diameter but was replaced after a short period by a heavier example manufactured by the Millwall Iron Company. The new flywheel had 40 tons weight in the rim, 18 tons in the boss, 24 tons in the eight arms, 8½ tons in the shaft and a 4½ ton crank making 95 tons of revolving weight.[19]

Such was the growth of the company that in 1870 it had sixteen furnaces in blast and in 1872 it was operating 161 puddling furnaces and 12 mills.[20] In 1873 Darby retired and a new company, the Ebbw Vale Steel, Iron and Coal Company (Ltd.) was constituted. However, the managers of the concern continued to receive much criticism from the technical press with the company losing £160,000 on ironworking during the year ending March 1875.[21] The Ebbw Vale Ironworks was turning out weekly 1,200 tons of steel rails during 1878 with much of the original iron being made from Bilbao haematite. Steel was then being made in four 6 ton converters and two 8 ton converters.[22] A profit of £34,406. 15s. 1d. was made in the year ending March 31st 1881 and during this year the company kept from thirteen to fourteen furnaces in blast.[23] A detailed description of the Ebbw Vale Ironworks was written in 1884 by which time iron making had ceased at Sirhowy, Pentwyn and Abersychan.[24] The Ebbw Vale Ironworks then possessed four furnaces which were 60ft. high and topped with iron bands. There were three beam blowing engines at the works, namely the Darby engine and two 45in. x 6ft. condensing beam engines with 90in. blowing cylinders erected in about 1880 by the Coalbrookdale Iron Company. The Bessemer department was situated halfway between the Ebbw Vale and Victoria Ironworks. The blast for the converters was provided by two pairs of blowing engines. One pair were vertical 40in. x 5ft. engines with 54 inch blowing cylinders manufactured by Daniel Adamson and Company while the second pair were horizontal 36in. x 5ft. engines with 48in. blowing cylinders manufactured by Galloway and Sons. Situated close to the blowing engines were three pairs of 18in. x 2ft. horizontal hydraulic pumping engines for working the Bessemer converters and rail mills. A pair of 36in. x 4½ft. horizontal blooming engines by Galloway and Sons drove two trains of 36in. rolls. This mill and engine had only recently been completed and were capable of reducing steel ingots from 14½in. square to 6in. square. The feeding rollers were powered by a pair of 10in. x 1ft. 2in. vertical engines and the blooms were transported from the rolls to the shears by a train of live rollers driven by a pair of 6½in. x 10in. vertical engines. The shears operating with this mill were powered by a 12in. x 1ft. 4in. vertical engine.[25] Two engines provided the works with pumped water, namely a 60in. x 6½ft. Cornish beam engine and a 40in x 4ft. engine.

The sheer size and inertia of the Ebbw Vale undertakings saw the concern successfully into the twentieth century with the Ebbw Vale Ironworks being the last upland works to operate in South Wales. However, the decline in the South Wales iron industry in the late nineteenth century forced the closure of several of Ebbw Vale's subsidiary ironworks.

The first ironworks to become associated with Ebbw Vale was the Sirhowy Ironworks which was situated in an adjacent valley. This venture dates from 1778 when a lease for the land was taken out by John Sealy and Bolton Hudson of Threadneedle Street, London, grocers and teamen, Thomas Atkinson of Skipton, Yorks, merchant (late of South Carolina) and William Barrow of Newgate Street, London, grocer and teaman.[26] One water blown furnace was built with the managing partner being Thomas Atkinson.[27] In 1794 William Barrow and the Rev. Matthew Monkhouse were the owners of the Sirhowy ironworks and in that year Richard Fothergill was admitted into the partnership.[28] The single furnace at Sirhowy during this period was capable of producing about 2,000 tons of iron each year.[29]

The Sirhowy Ironworks was subject to a period of expansion in the late eighteenth and early nineteenth century. The first part of this development involved the building of a Boulton & Watt beam blowing engine in 1799. This was a most unusual engine. It had a 23¾in. x 5ft. beam blowing engine with a 52in. blowing cylinder. The steam end of the 18ft. beam was connected to an ancillary beam which worked a 20ft. flywheel. The blowing cylinder was connected to a 6ft. diameter regulator which also received a blast from one or more 87in. x 2ft. 3in. cylinders worked by a 38ft. diameter waterwheel.[30] This beam blowing engine provided the extra blast which was required when a second furnace was built in 1801-1802.[31]

Most of the iron made at Sirhowy in the early 1800s seems to have been sold to the Merthyr iron companies. However, in 1803 the Sirhowy Ironworks was building up stocks of pig iron for puddling at the newly developed Tredegar Ironworks in which Fothergill was a partner.[32] The output at Sirhowy in 1805 was 3,700 tons with most of this iron being sent for processing at the nearby Tredegar Ironworks.[33] This role for Sirhowy as being a producer of pig iron for Tredegar continued until 1818. In that year the Sirhowy lease was up for renewal and Fothergill confided this fact to James Harford. Harford was one of the partners in the Ebbw Vale Ironworks and the company acquired the Sirhowy property much to Fothergill's anger. In 1826 there were three furnaces at Sirhowy of which two were in blast producing 7,800 tons of iron during the year.[34] Although the ownership had changed, Sirhowy's role continued but now it produced pig iron for puddling at Ebbw Vale and not at Tredegar. By 1839 there were four furnaces at work at Sirhowy and during that year a 60in. high pressure beam blowing engine was purchased for the works from the Neath Abbey Iron Company.[35]

In 1844 when the Ebbw Vale Iron Company's assets were put up for sale the Sirhowy Ironworks consisted of five blast furnaces with four of them utilising hot blast. The furnaces were each capable of producing from ninety to one hundred tons of iron per week. Serving the furnaces were cast houses, bridge houses, four mine kilns, coke yards, two limekilns and a clay mill worked by a 22ft. waterwheel. The 60in. beam blowing engine and a 52in. pumping engine were worked together and provided with steam by nine boilers. The site included four refineries and two winding engines for raising mine and coal. No.1 winding engine had a 30in. cylinder while the second engine had just been constructed but not put into operation. The works also possessed a tunnel running to Ebbw Vale by which metal was conveyed to the rolling mills. A second tunnel was under construction and at the time of the sale was nearly complete.[36]

The purchase of the Ebbw Vale assets by the Darby inspired company saw the Sirhowy Ironworks continue as a pig iron producer. In the 1850s there were five furnaces in blast at Sirhowy but this had been reduced to three by the 1870s.[37] The worsening conditions in the iron trade saw all three furnaces closed down in 1879 with three hundred people being made unemployed.[38] The works reopened later for a short period but seems to have closed finally in 1882.

The second works bought by the Ebbw Vale Iron Company was the neighbouring Victoria Ironworks which was purchased in 1849 for £55,000 after the operating company went bankrupt.[39] The building of the Victoria Ironworks was started in 1837 by the Monmouthshire Iron and Coal Company whose chairman was Sir Thomas Buckler Lethbridge who owned the Brendon Hills estate. The works received its name because of the Queen's coronation coinciding with the construction work. Initially two furnaces were put into blast with two further furnaces being constructed in 1839.[40] The blast was provided by a 60in. x 8ft. beam blowing engine with a 122in. blowing cylinder purchased by the Neath Abbey Iron Company.[41] In 1849 when the Victoria Ironworks was put up for sale it consisted of four blast furnaces which were 45ft. high, 16ft. in diameter across the boshes and 8ft. in diameter across the tops. The blast was provided by the 60in. beam blowing engine with the 122in. blowing cylinder which produced 20,000cu. ft. of air per minute with the furnaces being blown through a 24ft. diameter air receiver. Also included in the sale were four bridge lofts, extensive kilns for roasting ironstone and a water balance for raising limestone to the furnace tops. The ironworks also possessed a large casting house, three double refineries, a single refinery, a bar iron forge, ten puddling furnaces and a rolling mill making rails or merchant iron from eight balling furnaces. The mill was powered by a 90 h.p. engine and was capable of turning out 10,000 tons of bar iron each year. The sale document also lists a foundry with an air furnace and cupola, a waterwheel for blowing the cupola and turning the bar iron rollers and for turning and boring in general, a smith's shop, a carpenters', pattern makers' and fitting up shop, a punching machine, a brass foundry, a brick yard with two kilns and drying stoves, several reservoirs, seven pits sunk on the property, a shop, houses and two residences for the managers. It was claimed that the works had cost £200,000 to build with outgoings of a rent of £300 per year plus mineral payments.[42]

The Victoria Ironworks was altered and extended but by 1870 only three furnaces remained on the site.[43] Two of these remaining furnaces were demolished in the late 1870s leaving only one furnace in blast.[44] This demolition was to make way for two new furnaces which were completed in 1883. Each furnace was 60ft. high and possessed seven tuyères. Also constructed at this time were six Cowper stoves. The furnaces were blown by two vertical blast engines built by Kitson and Company of Leeds with boilers by Adamson. It was envisaged that after these alterations the Victoria Ironworks would be able to turn out 700 tons of iron per week.[45]

In 1884 the Victoria Ironworks was visited by members of the Institution of the Mechanical Engineers. They saw two furnaces which were 60ft. high with 20ft. diameter boshes. The blast at 5 psi was provided by two vertical engines with 50in. x 5ft. steam cylinders and 100in. blowing cylinders. The mills inspected were a 12in. bar mill driven by a 24in. x 2ft. 6in. engine, an 8in. guide mill driven by a 21in. x 1ft. 8in. engine, an 18in. train for rolling fish bars driven by a pair of horizontal 30in. x 4ft. 6in. engines and a mill train worked by an old beam engine coupled to a horizontal engine.

At this time a 36in. blooming mill was being constructed at Victoria powered by a pair of 36in. x 4ft. 6in. Galloway horizontal engines.[46]

The bigger iron companies with their larger cash reserves were able to survive through some of the lean periods but smaller works were often forced into liquidation. This allowed large concerns such as the Ebbw Vale Iron Company to purchase smaller ironworks during periods of recession. This policy was sometimes carried to extremes but the purchase of the British Ironworks, Abersychan by the Ebbw Vale Iron Company in 1852 must be viewed as somewhat of a bargain for some correspondents believed that the works was sold at ⅕ of its former value.[47]

The Abersychan Ironworks was built by the British Iron Company which had been formed in 1824 and included on its management committee David Mushet and a member of the Recardo family.[48] The British Iron Company was formed with the huge capital of £1.6 million and built a number of works in Wales and the West Midlands. The three managing directors were John Taylor, Robert Small and James Henry Shears. These directors had much experience in the mining and smelting of non-ferrous metals but little knowledge of iron making. The affairs of the company clearly demonstrate mismanagement and a lack of financial prudence. Construction at Abersychan started in 1826 but the backwall of the furnaces was badly built and collapsed. It was held by many that the complete furnace area was unstable and the construction of the works would need an excessive financial outlay. The production of iron at Abersychan started in 1827 with six furnaces which were 48ft. high with a 6,000 cu.ft. capacity. These furnaces were blown by a pair of coupled 52½in. x 8ft. beam blowing engines built by the Neath Abbey Iron Company.[49] The engines blew through a dry regulator and were supplied with steam generated by no less than twenty two boilers. The ironworks also consisted of two refineries, a smiths' shop, a brick yard, a fitting shop, a forge and mills, thirty six puddling furnaces, twenty three heating furnaces, a rolling train for 18in. merchant bars and a rolling train for 12in. merchant bars.[50]

The British Ironworks, Abersychan produced 10,640 tons of iron in 1830.[51] Production consisted solely of merchant bar iron but this proved an unsuccessful strategy with the works later changing to the production of rails. In fact Abersychan did not make any profits until 1838. In 1839 the six furnaces were in blast being blown by the Neath Abbey engines which provided 28,800 cu. ft. of air per minute at a pressure of 2½-3 psi. The blowing engines also provided the blast for five refineries.[52] After some financial difficulties in the 1840s the company was reorganised under the title of the New British Iron Company.[53] The reorganisation led to some development of the works with hot blast being applied to the furnaces in 1848. However, the new company fared little better than the old with only two furnaces in blast during 1850 and the company became bankrupt in 1851. In the following year the Abersychan Ironworks was purchased by the Ebbw Vale Iron Company and by 1856 all six furnaces were in blast.[54] This state of employment continued until 1860 when two of the furnaces were put out of blast.[55] The drop in demand for iron during the early 1860s resulted in the Ebbw Vale Company putting the Abersychan furnaces out of blast during 1862-63.[56] In 1864 four furnaces were in blast and in the following year the Neath Abbey Iron Company repaired a 40in. engine at the works.[57] Production of rails at Abersychan continued during the remaining years of the decade and in 1869 the works was examined and described in some detail.[58] The Abersychan Ironworks had five of their six furnaces in blast at that time with materials coming up from the Monmouthshire Railway by means of an incline powered by a stationary engine constructed in 1858. On the works' site itself five locomotives were employed to move materials around the property. The furnaces were 48ft. high with 17 to 18ft. across the boshes and were each capable of producing 200 tons of hot blast iron per week. Waste gases from the furnaces were used for heating the blast and firing the boilers. There were fifty two puddling furnaces serving three forges and twenty four balling furnaces supplying five mills. A large beam engine powered two forge trains, a rail mill and two other mills for producing iron for rails. Another beam engine powered a forge train and a mill for roughing down iron for the top and bottom of rail piles. A mill for blooming the rail piles was driven by a horizontal engine. These forges and mills were able to produce between 800 and 1,100 tons of rails each week. Also installed at the works was a small inverted engine used for driving two double presses and another of the same type powered two punches for punching and notching rails. Steam for the engines was generated in eighteen boilers.

The Abersychan Ironworks continued to produce rails during the early 1870s. It appears that the Ebbw Vale Iron Company was willing to continue to invest money at Abersychan for one of the beam blowing engines was rebuilt in 1870 and the second blowing engine received similar treatment in 1875.[59] Despite this the drop in demand for wrought iron rails forced the closure of the Abersychan Ironworks in September 1876.[60] However, the works was reopened in April 1877 and two furnaces were put in blast.[61] The works was now producing spiegeleisen for the Ebbw Vale Ironworks. Spiegeleisen was an alloy of iron, manganese and carbon used in steel making. In 1880 there were four furnaces in blast at Abersychan but in the following year the works was finally closed down.[62]

The Pentwyn Ironworks was also absorbed by the Ebbw Vale Iron Company in the 1850s. The three furnaces at Pentwyn had been built by the Hunt brothers in 1825. The cost of building the works, offices, roads and forty houses had amounted to £35,000. During 1830 the Pentwyn Ironworks produced 5,391 tons of iron but the organisation of this works changed in 1838 when it merged to be jointly run with the Golynos Ironworks.[63] This joint stock company was based at Bath and drew their main funding from investors in Somerset and Devon. However, by 1850 this joint working had been abandoned with the three furnaces at Pentwyn lying idle.[64] The works was acquired by the Ebbw Vale Iron Company in 1857 but the furnaces remained out of blast until 1865.[65] During that year there were four furnaces capable of operation with two being put into blast. The two furnaces remained in blast until 1868 and in the following year the dismantling of the Pentwyn Ironworks commenced.[66]

The Pontypool Ironworks was the fifth ironworks to become associated with the Ebbw Vale concern. A charcoal ironworks, owned by the Hanbury family, had been in operation at Pontypool during the eighteenth century. In 1794 this works consisted of an old charcoal furnace, three fineries, two chaferies, a rolling mill, a slitting mill and a tin mill.[67] Another ironworks had also been set up in the Pontypool area in the late eighteenth century. This works had been built at Blaendare by David Tanner.[68] The Blaendare Ironworks boasted one coke fired furnace which was able to produce 1,500 tons of iron in 1796.[69] However, Tanner's widespread business interests later failed and he became bankrupt in 1799. The Blaendare property was sold to John Barnaby who concentrated on coal mining and later leased the furnace to the Hanbury family.[70]

Meanwhile the Pontypool Ironworks was being operated by Capel Hanbury Leigh who had altered the furnace to be coke fired.[71] Hanbury Leigh took Watkin George as a partner in the works in around 1807. George had recently been a partner in the Cyfarthfa Ironworks and brought much practical knowledge and skill to the Pontypool enterprise. George helped Capel Hanbury Leigh to remodel the Pontypool Ironworks (sometimes known as the Race works). However, the works continued to specialise in the production of tinplate and wire. George introduced some new machinery to the works including a giant waterwheel which was probably used to blow the furnaces in a similar way to the great wheel built by George at Cyfarthfa. In 1823 there were three furnaces at the Pontypool Ironworks which produced 3,173 tons of iron while 2,421 tons were produced in 1830.[72] The waterwheel method of blowing the furnace was superseded in 1828 when a 52½in. beam blowing engine was purchased from the Neath Abbey Iron Company.[73]

The Pontypool Ironworks continued to successfully produce iron for manufacturing wire, tinplate and sheet iron with a fourth furnace being constructed during 1839.[74] The works remained in the hands of the Hanbury Leigh family until sold in 1851 to Dimmach and Thompson of South Staffordshire who, while operating the works, termed themselves The Pontypool Iron Company.[75] The four furnaces were kept in blast by the new company until the works was sold to the Ebbw Vale Iron Company in 1864.[76] The Pontypool Ironworks with its own mills and forges were able to process most of the iron produced at their furnaces into wire, sheet and tinplate. The guaranteed market for Pontypool cold blast iron explains the longevity of the works whose furnaces continued to operate after the closure of the Sirhowy, Pentwyn and Abersychan Ironworks.

References.

1. John Lloyd, *The Early History of the Old South Wales Iron Works 1760-1840*, 1906, pp.150-157.
2. Harry Scrivenor, *History of the Iron Trade*, 1854, p.96.
3. John Lloyd, op. cit., pp.150-157.
4. Birmingham Reference Library, Boulton & Watt Collection, List of Furnaces in Great Britain, 1806.
5. Harry Scrivenor, op. cit., p.134.
6. Harry Scrivenor, op. cit., p.134.
7. Glamorgan Record Office, Neath Abbey Ironworks' Collection, D/D N.A.I., L.26-l.28. Drawings for Locomotives for Harfords Davies and Co., Ebbw Vale.
8. David Mushet, *Papers on Iron and Steel*, 1840, pp.414-415.
9. John Lloyd, op. cit., pp.150-157.

10. Gwent Record Office, Cwmbran, Ebbw Vale Ms., D454 516, p.25, Sale Catalogue of Ebbw Vale and Sirhowy Ironworks, 18th April 1844.
11. John Lloyd, op. cit, pp.150-157.
12. *Mining Journal*, July 30th 1859, p.539.
13. John Percy, *Metallurgy, Iron and Steel*, 1864, pp.760-761.
14. E.H. Brooke, *Chronology of the Tinplate Works of Great Britain*, Cardiff, 1944, pp.50-55.
15. Robert Hunt, *Mineral Statistics, 1864*.
16. E.H. Brooke, op. cit., pp.50-55.
    The Engineer, January 18th 1867, p.71.
17. *The Engineer*, November 3rd 1865, p.292.
    The Engineer, March 15th 1867, p.245.
18. Robert Hunt, *Mineral Statistics, 1869 & 1870*.
19. F. Kohn, *Iron and Steel Manufacture*, 1869, pp.47-48.
20. Robert Hunt, *Mineral Statistics, 1870 & 1872*.
21. *The Engineer*, November 3rd 1876, p.319.
22. Robert Hunt, *Mineral Statistics, 1878*.
23. *The Engineer*, July 1st 1881, p.13.
24. *Proceedings of the Institution of Mechanical Engineers*, 1884, pp.386-392.
25. *Journal of the Iron and Steel Institute*, 1885, p.218.
26. John Lloyd, op. cit., pp.145-150.
27. BRL, B&W, List of the Different Iron Works in England, Wales, Scotland, Ireland to the year 1792. Copied from the papers of the late Mr. Wilkinson.
28. John Lloyd, op. cit., pp.145-150.
29. Harry Scrivenor, op. cit., p.96.
30. BRL, B&W, Portfolio No.685, Blowing Engine Drawings for Fothergill & Co., Sirhowy Ironworks.
31. Harry Scrivenor, op. cit., p.98.
32. *Svedenstierna's Tour of Great Britain, 1802-03*, Newton Abbot, 1973, pp.59-60.
33. BRL, B&W, List of Furnaces in Great Britain, 1806.
34. Harry Scrivenor, op. cit., p.134.
35. GRO, NAI, D/D. N.A.I., M/181/1-1/181/2. drawings for a Blowing Engine for Sirhowy Iron Company, 1839. These drawings are for a 38in. engine but from the later sale catalogue it would appear that a 60in. beam blowing engine was in fact constructed at Sirhowy.
36. GWRO, Cwmbran, Ebbw Vale Ms., D454 516, p.25, Sale Catalogue of Ebbw Vale and Sirhowy Ironworks, 18th April 1844.
37. Robert Hunt, *Mineral Statistics, 1854-1870*.
38. *The Engineer*, January 3rd 1879, p.17.
39. Alan Birch, *The Economic History of the British Iron and Steel Industry, 1784-1879*, 1967, p.203.
40. David Mushet, op. cit., pp.414-415.
41. Laurence Ince, *The Neath Abbey Iron Company*, Eindhoven, 1984, p.106.
42. GWRO, Cwmbran, Sale Catalogue of Victoria Ironworks, 1849, Ebbw Vale Ms., D454 516.
43. Robert Hunt, *Mineral Statistics, 1869*.
44. Robert Hunt, *Mineral Statistics, 1880*.
45. *The Engineer*, July 20th 1883, p.57.
46. *Proceedings of the Institution of Mechanical Engineers*, 1884, pp.386-392.
47. Arthur Clark, *The Story of Monmouthshire*, Vol.2, Monmouth, 1979, p.82.
48. Alan Birch, op. cit., p.204.
49. GRO, NAI, D/D N.A.I., M/8/10-M/8/11, M/28/3, Drawings for $52\frac{1}{2}$in. Beam Blowing Engines for British Iron Co., Abersychan, 1826-27.
50. Kim Colebrook, A History of the British Ironworks, Abersychan, *Gwent Local History*, Vol.54, Spring 1983, pp.6-29.
51. Harry Scrivenor, op. cit., p.134
52. David Mushet, op. cit., pp.342-344.
53. Kim Colebrook, op. cit., pp.6-29.
54. Robert Hunt, *Mineral Statistics, 1854-56*.
55. Robert Hunt, *Mineral Statistics, 1860*.

56. Robert Hunt, *Mineral Statistics, 1862-1863*.
57. GRO, NAI, D/D. N.A.I., M/8/9. Nozzles for 40in. engine, Abersychan, 1865.
58. *Mining Journal*, October 23rd 1869, p.802.
59. *The Engineer*, December 9th 1870, p.404.
    Kim Colebrook, op. cit., pp.6-29.
60. *The Engineer*, September 8th 1876, p.177.
61. *The Engineer*, March 8th 1877, p.174.
62. Kim Colebrook, op. cit., pp.6-29.
63. Harry Scrivenor, op. cit., p.134.
64. *Official Descriptive and Illustrated Catalogue of the Great Exhibition, 1851*, Vol.1, pp.150-159.
65. Robert Hunt, *Mineral Statistics, 1857-1865*.
66. *Mining Journal*, October 23rd 1869, p.802.
67. BRL, B&W, List of Ironworks, 1794.
68. Arthur Clark, op. cit., pp.81-82.
69. Harry Scrivenor, op. cit., p.96.
70. Arthur Clark, op. cit., pp.81-82.
71. John P. Addis, *The Crawshay Dynasty - A Study in Industrial Organisation and Development, 1765-1867*, Cardiff, 1957, pp.12-13.
72. Harry Scrivenor, op. cit., p.134.
73. GRO, NAI, D/D. N.A.I., M/117/1, Drawing of Engine House for $52\frac{1}{2}$in. Engine for Leigh and George, 1828.
74. David Mushet, op. cit., pp.414-415.
75. Arthur Clark, op. cit., p.84.
    Samuel Griffiths, *Guide to the Iron Trade of Great Britain*, 1873, p.136.
76. Robert Hunt, *Mineral Statistics, 1864*.

Plate Twenty Five The massive beam of the Darby blowing engine at the Ebbw Vale Ironworks. (Courtesy Ironbridge Gorge Museum Trust)

Plate Twenty Six   The middle chamber of the Darby engine house. (Courtesy Ironbridge Gorge Museum Trust)

Plate Twenty Seven   *A plate encased furnace at the Sirhowy Ironworks. (Courtesy of Welsh Industrial & Maritime Museum, Cardiff)*

Plate Twenty Eight A house for a beam pumping engine at the British Ironworks, Abersychan. The engine was situated in the centre of the ironworks and helped drain the surrounding mineral property.

Chapter Ten.

The Ironworks of the Eastern Outcrop.

The most notable of the ironworks dealt with in this chapter must be the Blaenavon Ironworks whose foundation dates from 1789. Although this concern operated well into the twentieth century its history contains much evidence of under investment and mismanagement.

The land for the works was leased from the Earl of Abergavenny in 1789 by Thomas Hill of Dennis, Staffordshire, Thomas Hopkins and Benjamin Pratt.[1] This was a very well balanced and experienced grouping for Hopkins had experience of operating ironworks, Pratt was an ironmaster from Stourport and Hill was a Stourport banker.[2] The partnership erected three furnaces possibly blown by a mixture of water and steam power.[3] Output can be gauged from the recorded figure of 4,318 tons for 1796.[4] In an attempt to boost production a Boulton & Watt beam blowing engine was purchased for Blaenavon in 1800. This was a 40in. x 8ft. engine with an 80in. blowing cylinder and a 26ft. iron beam.[5] The purchase of this engine might well be related to the fact that a fourth furnace was present at Blaenavon by 1805 when three of the four furnaces produced 7,846 tons of iron for that year.[6] The Blaenavon Ironworks was, at that time, being operated by Thomas Hill and Samuel Hopkins, the son of one of the original partners.

On the death of Samuel Hopkins in 1815 Hill took as a partner a gentleman named Wheeley.[7] This move must have led to an influx of money for in the next year a forge was built at Garnddyrys. Until this time Blaenavon had only produced pig iron and the works had been at a serious disadvantage as other South Wales ironworks exploited the demand for wrought iron. The Garnddyrys site was on a hill side 1½ miles to the north of the Blaenavon Ironworks. One of the main reasons for siting the forge in this position was to allow access through inclines to the local canal system at Llanfoist. This must be viewed as a retrogressive step for the South Wales ironworks were benefiting at this period from being able to bring together all the manufacturing processes onto one site. Further developments were also taking place at the main site with the purchase in 1819 of a 52½in. beam blowing engine manufactured by the Neath Abbey Iron Company.[8]

By 1823 there were five furnaces in blast at Blaenavon producing 16,882 tons for that year. One of these furnaces was out of blast during 1826 when the furnaces produced 14,560 tons of iron and in 1830 the production was 13,843 tons.[9] Members of the Hill family continued as managing partners until the Blaenavon Ironworks was sold in 1836. The ironworks was taken over by the Blaenavon Coal and Iron Company, a joint stock company with a capital of £500,000.[10] A member of the Hill family remained on the board with William Unwin Sims as chairman and James

Ashwell as managing director.[11] One of the other directors was Robert Kennard who was later to have an important role in the running of the Blaenavon Iron Company.

It was obvious to the new directors that the Garnddyrys site was inconvenient and could not cope with the demands made by the main works. The company thus made a decision to build a new works on the other side of the valley at the Coity. The plan was to construct three furnaces at the new site and then develop new forges and mills once iron was being produced. Two furnaces were under construction in 1839 and in 1840 a 52½in. beam blowing engine was purchased from the Neath Abbey Ironworks.[12] During 1840 the five furnaces at Blaenavon were blown by cold blast and produced 400 tons of iron each week. Of the iron produced half was puddled with some cable iron being produced from it with the rest being sold for tinplate and foundry work.[13]

It was clear by the end of 1840 that the company did not have the resources to complete the new works or put any of the furnaces into blast. Production continued at the old works but one notable decision was made during the 1840s and that was to start producing wrought iron rails. In 1850 three of the five furnaces at the old works were in blast with the new works still not completed and the furnaces standing idle. The output of the Blaenavon Ironworks for the year ending May 1850 was 22,616 tons of pig iron, 3,081 tons of refined iron and 9,412 tons of bars and rails.[14] A healthier position was maintained by the company throughout the 1850s with enough profit made to complete the new works. This development led to a lack of dividends for the investors which resulted in an inquiry in 1855 which revealed bad business practice by the directors.

The first part of the new works to be finished was the forge which was opened in 1859.[15] In the following year the mill was completed which contained a pair of horizontal 36in. x 6ft. engines built by James Watt & Co. which could work a rail mill or heavy bar and plate mill.[16] At about the same time the company built their own 18in. horizontal engine to work a rail mill and also cast a twenty five ton flywheel for a blowing engine.[17] In the autumn of 1860 a 30in. x 4ft. 6in. high pressure horizontal engine started work powering a pair of roughing down rolls and a three high train of blooming rolls.[18] Developments were coming quickly with a railway tyre mill commencing work in 1861 driven by a 34in. engine built by James Watt & Co.[19]

The old furnaces continued to operate at Blaenavon with one example being described in some detail in 1863.[20] It was 46ft. 8in. high, 9ft. across the top, 14ft. across the boshes and possessed a 4ft. 10in. hearth. Each furnace had a 5,540 cu.ft. capacity and consumed weekly 50,000,000 cu.ft. of air in producing 104 tons of iron. This low production figure needed improving and during the period 1867-68 the three furnaces at the new works were blown in. The Blaenavon Iron Company's undertakings were described in some detail in 1869.[21] During that year there were six furnaces at the old works each being 48ft. high. Of these there were five in blast blown with cold air. The furnaces were all open topped but there was some collection of waste gas. The blast was provided by a 52½in. x 8ft. beam blowing engine with a 104in. blowing cylinder and two horizontal engines with a single flywheel moving the pistons of two 90in. x 7ft. blowing cylinders. The new works possessed three furnaces each 50ft. high with 15ft. boshes. The furnaces were closed with cup and bells and were blown using a hot blast with each furnace capable of producing from 180 tons of grey iron to 300 tons of forge iron each week. The blast was provided by a beam blowing engine with a 120in. x 10ft. blowing cylinder producing 18,840 cu.ft. of air per minute. The works plant included seventy two coke ovens, seventy two puddling furnaces, three steam hammers, twenty five balling furnaces, four forge trains and five rolling mills. One large beam engine drove a rail mill, a mill for merchant iron and a roughing down mill. One horizontal engine drove a blooming mill with a guide mill being powered by a small engine. There was also present a number of small engines for powering presses, punches, saws and shears. One important part of the works was the patent tyre mill which could produce steel tyres from 2ft. 9in. diameter (trucks) to 7ft. diameter (locomotives). The Blaenavon Ironworks at this time produced 850 tons of iron per week with ⅚ of this being rails or railway iron.

In 1872 the Blaenavon property was purchased by a new company trading under the name of the Blaenavon Iron and Steel Company Limited.[22] This company took over the two works which then possessed ten furnaces, one hundred and seventeen puddling furnaces and eight rolling mills. However, this company was forced into liquidation in 1878 when the West of England Bank collapsed.[23] There were 8,074 shares issued by the company of which Messrs. Kennard, Waring and Laing held 4,380 and were guarantors for £20,000 more. At the time of the liquidation the company employed 5,000 people and had just spent £90,000 in adding a steel works which contained two 8 ton converters.[24] Within a short time a new company, in which Kennard and Laing were still involved, took over the whole enterprise. By 1881 five furnaces had been returned to blast and in 1883 a pair of reversing horizontal high speed 36in. x 4ft. mill engines by Davy Brothers were installed in the steel works.[25]

Activity at the old works continued until 1900 while the new works was kept in operation until 1938. However, the Blaenavon Ironworks is often remembered for the part it played in the development of the British steel industry. It was at Blaenavon in 1878 that Sydney Gilchrist Thomas in conjunction with his cousin Percy Gilchrist, who was the works' chemist, successfully made steel using a basic lining in a converter. Until this time ores which had a phosphoric content made iron which could not be processed into steel using Bessemer converters. The discovery of using a basic lining to absorb the phosphorus meant that the great bulk of British, French, German and Belgium ores could be used to make iron for use in steelmaking.

Another ironworks situated on the eastern outcrop of the coalfield was also to work into the twentieth century. This was the Cwmbran Ironworks whose development was a more minor affair when compared with the Blaenavon Ironworks. The Cwmbran Ironworks was built in the late 1840s by F.J. Blewitt of Llantarnam Abbey. During the 1850s the furnace is listed at different times as being under the ownership of the Cwmbran Iron Company, J. Lawrence and Roper & Son.[26] In 1862 a second furnace was built by John Lawrence acting for Roper & Son.[27] This second furnace was put into blast for the first time in 1863 and in the same year a nearby forge was taken over by Weston & Grice of West Bromwich and Bristol.[28] They altered the forge to produce nuts, bolts and fishplates and later the partnership reorganised to become the Patent Nut and Bolt Company. This company from 1866 onwards attempted to gain control of the Cwmbran Ironworks and so secure their own supply of iron. This was resisted until 1872 when the Patent Nut and Bolt Company absorbed the Cwmbran Ironworks with its two furnaces, twenty puddling furnaces and three mills.[29] The Cwmbran Ironworks was able to survive well into the twentieth century because of the assured market for its iron provided by the Patent Nut and Bolt Company.

A less successful concern was the Varteg Ironworks which commenced production with a single furnace in 1803. The owners of the works in 1805 were Knight & Co. who produced 900 tons of iron at Varteg in that year.[30] The main partner was John Knight who was a member of an important family of ironmasters based in the Stour Valley of the English Midlands.[31] However, Knight soon retired from the company to pursue his Stour valley interests. In 1823 the works possessed two furnaces which produced 6,513 tons of iron. A third furnace was built in 1824 and a fourth furnace added in 1826. During that year the furnaces were under the control of Kenricks & Co. who produced 7,800 tons of iron at Varteg.[32] A fifth furnace was added in 1830 and during that year 13,536 tons of iron were produced.[33] The furnaces remained under the ownership of Kenricks and Co. until 1837 when the Varteg Iron Company took over the site. The Varteg Ironworks was occupied by Williams & Co. in 1854 and this company also held the Golynos Ironworks giving it a total of seven furnaces of which four were in blast.[34] In 1855 Varteg was reported as being unoccupied and was being plundered for stone.[35] However, Golynos and Varteg were leased to Crawshay Bailey and William Morgan in 1858 when four of the six furnaces were returned to blast.[36] This state of activity did not last for long with both ironworks described as being in a bad state in 1860 although a furnace briefly operated at Varteg in 1861.[37] In the following year the Varteg Ironworks was taken over by Partridge & Jones who put a furnace into blast in 1863.[38] The works was relinquished by Partridge & Jones in 1864 when G.E Bevan & Co. of Golynos took over and put one furnace into blast until the end of the year when iron making operations at the site were abandoned.[39]

The Golynos Ironworks had started production in 1837 with two furnaces blown by a 52½in. x 8ft. Neath Abbey beam blowing engine.[40] The owners were termed the Golynos Iron Company but after one year of operation the Golynos and Pentwyn Ironworks merged to be jointly managed. By 1854 the Golynos Ironworks had become linked with the Varteg Ironworks and in 1858 the two works were under the ownership of Crawshay Bailey and William Morgan.[41] During 1860 certain machinery was removed from Golynos and taken to Varteg after an attempt to sell Golynos failed.[42] The Golynos Ironworks with three furnaces, a blowing engine, nine kilns and thirty two coking ovens had been offered for sale in conjunction with forges and mills at Pontnewynydd.[43] The Pontnewynydd Ironworks was advertised as being capable of producing 400 tons of finished iron each week. In 1863 G.E. Bevan & Co. took over the lease of the Golynos Ironworks at a rental of £650 per year.[44] One furnace was put into blast with a second one commissioned in 1864.[45] G.E. Bevan &

Co. had taken Golynos and later Varteg to prove the worth of their Northampton iron ores; with this achieved they ceased their iron making operations at Golynos in January 1866.[46] An attempt was made to sell the Golynos property in 1867 but no interest was shown at the auction.[47]

References.

1. John Lloyd, *The Early History of the Old South Wales Iron Works, 1760-1840*, 1906, pp.160-165.
2. A.H. John, *The Industrial Development of South Wales, 1750-1850*, Cardiff, 1950, p.25.
3. BRL, B&W, List of Ironworks, 1794.
4. Harry Scrivenor, *History of the Iron Trade*, 1854, p.96.
5. BRL, B&W, Portfolio No.673, Drawings for Blowing Engine for Thomas Hill, Blaenavon, 1800.
6. BRL, B&W, List of Ironworks, 1806.
7. Tom Grey Davies, *Blaenavon and Sydney Gilchrist Thomas*, 1978, p.13.
8. GRO, NAI, D/D. N.A.I., M/24/2-M/24/3, Drawings of 52½in. Engine for Blaenavon, 1819. Laurence Ince, *The Neath Abbey Iron Company*, Eindhoven, 1984, p.104.
9. Harry Scrivenor, op. cit., p.134.
10. Alan Birch, *The Economic History of the British Iron and Steel Industry, 1784-1879*, 1967, p.204.
11. *Blaenavon Ironworks*, Ironworks of Torfaen No.1, Torfaen Museum Trust, p.7.
12. David Mushet, *Papers on Iron and Steel*, 1840, pp.414-415. GRO, NAI, D/D. N.A.I., M/24/4-M/24/6. Drawings of 52½in. engine for Blaenavon, 1839-40.
13. Tom Grey Davies, op. cit., p.22.
14. *Mining Journal*, May 4th 1850, p.208.
15. *Mining Journal*, September 24th 1859, p.672.
16. *Mining Journal*, January 21st 1860, p.44.
17. *Mining Journal*, March 3rd 1860, p.148.
18. *Mining Journal*, October 6th 1860, p.680.
19. *Mining Journal*, July 20th 1861, p.472.
20. John Percy, *Metallurgy, Iron and Steel*, 1864, p.557 & p.560
21. *Mining Journal*, October 30th 1869, pp.821-822.
22. Robert Hunt, *Mineral Statistics, 1872*.
23. *The Engineer*, December 20th 1878, p.456.
24. Robert Hunt, *Mineral Statistics, 1878*.
25. *The Engineer*, November 30th 1883, p.417 & p.424.
26. Robert Hunt, *Mineral Statistics, 1854-1860*.
27. *Mining Journal*, July 19th 1862, p.489.
28. *Mining Journal*, June 20th 1863, p.432, July 4th 1863, p.472.
29. Robert Hunt, *Mineral Statistics, 1872*.
30. BRL, B&W, List of Ironworks, 1806.
31. Laurence Ince, *The Knight Family and the British Iron Industry*, Solihull, 1991.
32. *The Engineer*, February 3rd 1860, p.82.
33. Harry Scrivenor, op. cit, p.134.
34. Robert Hunt, *Mineral Statistics, 1854*.
35. *Mining Journal*, 1855, p.418.
36. Robert Hunt, *Mineral Statistics*, 1858.
37. *Mining Journal*, February 11th 1860, p.91
    Mining Journal, March 23rd 1861, p.187.
38. *Mining Journal*, January 31st 1863, p.80.
39. *Mining Journal*, September 17th 1864, p.21.
40. GRO, NAI, D/D. N.A.I., M/95/1-M/95/4. Drawings for 52½in. engine for Golynos, 1836-37.
41. Robert Hunt, *Mineral Statistics, 1858*.
42. *Mining Journal*, June 9th 1860, p.392.

43. *Mining Journal*, February 25th 1860, p.130.
    GWRO, Cwmbran, Ebbw Vale Ms., D394 p.12, Cl, Sale Catalogue of Golynos Ironworks, December 20th 1867.
44. GWRO, Cwmbran, Sale Catalogue of Golynos Ironworks, December 20th 1867.
    Mining Journal, January 17th 1863, p.43.
45. *Mining Journal*, April 23rd 1864, p.300.
46. *The Engineer*, January 5th 1866, p.19.
47. *The Engineer*, November 29th 1867, p.470, & December 27th 1867, p.540.

Plate Twenty Nine   The ruined Blaenavon Ironworks.

Chapter Eleven.

The Ironworks of the Northern Outcrop.

One of the oldest iron making establishments on the northern outcrop of the coalfield was the Beaufort Ironworks whose foundation dates from 1779. In that year land was leased for the works from the Duke of Beaufort after whom the ironworks was named. The original partners were Jonathan Kendall of Drayton, Shropshire, Henry Kendall of Alverston, Lancaster, Edward Kendall of Worlingham, Cheshire and Jonathan Kendall of Seaforge, Gloucestershire.[1] The Kendalls were one of the most important group of charcoal ironmasters in Britain holding extensive interests in the Midlands and the Lake District. At Beaufort one coke fired furnace was constructed which was blown by a Smeaton waterwheel erected in 1780. Two years later this was augmented by the building of a Smeaton atmospheric steam engine to return water to the furnace pool.[2] Two melting fineries were added to the works in 1787 and during 1796 the Beaufort furnace produced 1,660 tons of iron.[3]

Joseph Latham joined the Beaufort partnership in the 1790s and took a 2/32 share in the company. The remaining shares were divided between Edward Kendall (17/32) and Jonathan Kendall (13/32). A second furnace was built in around 1801-02 and in 1805 the Beaufort Ironworks produced 4,696 tons of iron.[4] Edward Kendall died in 1807 leaving a son, Edward, and two stepchildren. His stepson, William Hibbs Bevan, was placed at Beaufort under the instruction of Joseph Latham who was the managing partner. On reaching the age of twenty four W.H. Bevan was then admitted into a share of the Beaufort concern.[5] The partnership was again altered in 1816 with the retirement of Joseph Latham from business.

The works grew steadily with three furnaces in blast in 1823 when 5,243 tons of iron were produced.[6] A fourth furnace was built in 1824 and in 1830 Kendall, Bevan & Co. produced 7,276 tons of iron.[7] This company held the furnaces until 1833 when the Beaufort Ironworks was sold for £45,000 to Joseph and Crawshay Bailey. The partners at the time of the sale were Edward Kendall of Clifton, Gloucestershire, William Henry West of Beaufort Ironworks, William West Jones of Crickhowell and William Hibbs Bevan of Crickhowell.[8]

The Beaufort Ironworks was purchased purely to supply pig iron to the puddling furnaces and rolling mills of the Nantyglo Ironworks. The faltering early history of the Nantyglo Ironworks starts in 1791 with the partners of the Blaenavon Iron Company deciding that their mineral ground was far too large for them to exploit alone. In the following year a partnership was set up between Hill & Co. of Blaenavon and Harford, Partridge & Co. to erect an ironworks on the Nantyglo portion of the mineral ground with Richard Summers Harford as manager.[9] The Nantyglo Ironworks was completed in 1794 and the furnaces were put into blast in 1795. However, as soon as the ironworks began to operate a dispute broke out between the two factions which resulted in the Nantyglo Ironworks remaining idle until 1802. In that year the Nantyglo Iron Company was set up consisting of the partners of the Blaenavon Ironworks plus Joseph Harrison. The new company immediately contracted to supply Samuel Homfray at Penydarren with fifteen tons of iron weekly for six months and then three hundred and ninety tons of iron quarterly for twenty one years. This contract, however, later became part of a legal dispute and in 1805 the two furnaces at Nantyglo were again idle.[10] In 1811 Thomas Hill and Samuel Hopkins sold the works to Joseph Bailey and Matthew Wayne. This new partnership immediately invested money in modernising the Nantyglo machinery. There is a possibility that a Neath Abbey engine was installed at Nantyglo in 1811 and certainly a Boulton & Watt engine was purchased in 1812.[11] This was a 46in. x 8ft. beam blowing engine with a 100in. blowing cylinder.[12]

Matthew Wayne was replaced in the partnership by Crawshay Bailey in 1820 and under the Baileys' management the Nantyglo Ironworks thrived with the five furnaces producing 17,750 tons of iron in 1823.[13] Further furnaces were added in 1826 and 1827 with 23,883 tons of iron produced in 1830.[14] The Nantyglo Ironworks was now entering into a most prosperous period with the Beaufort Ironworks being purchased in 1833 to increase the supply of pig iron to the Nantyglo forges and mills. The Baileys were cousins to the Crawshays and had learnt much from their time of employment at the Cyfarthfa Ironworks.[15] They were shrewd businessmen and exploited fully the demand for wrought iron rails during the 1830s and 1840s with the firm of Bailey Brothers becoming one of the largest suppliers of rails to the home market.

To aid a period of expansion at the two works a 60in. beam blowing engine was purchased from the Neath Abbey Iron Company in 1836 and in 1843 a 45in. rotative beam engine was supplied from the same source.[16] During 1839 Bailey Brothers operated eight furnaces at Nantyglo and six at Beaufort while during the 1850s and 1860s there were seven furnaces capable of production at each site.[17] The manufacture of rails continued at Nantyglo but during the late 1860s it became clear that the Bailey family wished to retire from the iron trade. A sale was agreed and in 1871 the Beaufort and Nantyglo Ironworks were transferred to the ownership of the Blaina Iron & Coal Co.[18] This transaction took place at an ideal time for the Bailey family for the early 1870s saw a boom in iron production in South Wales. This increased demand for iron allowed the Bailey family to sell Beaufort and Nantyglo for a reported sum of no less than £4,000,000. For this money the Blaina Iron & Coal Co. received fourteen furnaces, sixty seven puddling furnaces and four rolling mills.[19]

Unhappily for the Nantyglo and Blaina Iron Works Company (Limited) the boom conditions in the iron trade soon evaporated with the closure of the Beaufort Ironworks taking place at the end of 1873.[20] For the year ending November 1873 the company lost £50-60,000 with £30,000 being lost during the months of the great strike.[21] February 1874 saw the closure of the Nantyglo Ironworks and with continued losses it was decided to sell off the assets of the company in 1878.[22] The associated collieries were taken over by J. Lancaster & Co. of Wigan while in 1879 the ironworks were leased by Spence & Co. of Liverpool who put a furnace into blast at Blaina and started to convert the Nantyglo buildings into a tinplate works.[23]

The Blaina Ironworks dates from 1823 when land for the works was leased by George Jones, the South Staffordshire ironmaster.[24] The works was completed in 1824 when two furnaces were put into blast.[25] These furnaces produced 4,905 tons of iron during 1830.[26] By 1831 the Blaina Ironworks was under the control of Russell & Co. with John Russell and Thomas Brown being the main partners.[27]

A merger took place in 1839 between the Blaina Ironworks and the newly constructed Cwm Celyn Ironworks with its four furnaces.[28] A new company named the Cwm Celyn and Blaina Iron Company was formed to operate both works. There appears to have been an early involvement in this company by the Stothert family who were engineers in Bath (Stothert & Pitt).[29] The Stotherts certainly purchased two 46in. x 9ft. steam cylinders and two 94in. blowing cylinders from Harvey & Co. of Hayle in 1839 for blowing engines to be erected at Cwm Celyn.[30] Robert Pitt seems to have been employed at Cwm Celyn in 1841-42 in the erection of these engines. Thomas Macauley Cruttwell, a Bath solicitor, also took an important role within the company in its early years.

In 1844 the Cwm Celyn and Blaina Iron Company was bought by a new grouping of nine partners who included John and Henry Stothert.[31] Frederick Levick was employed to manage the ironworks. The Cwm Celyn and Blaina Ironworks were owned by Cruttwell, Allies & Co. in 1851 and at the Great Exhibition they displayed pieces of iron, forge and refined metal, puddled, merchant and beat bar iron plus a finished rail.[32] Frederick Levick had bought into the company by 1855 when Cruttwell, Levick & Co. purchased an 0-4-0 standard gauge 12in. x 16in. tank locomotive from Tulk & Ley of the Lowca Foundry.[33] At this time the company was also operating the three furnaces of the Coalbrookvale Ironworks. This works had been founded in around 1820 with one furnace being completed in 1821. The Coalbrookvale Ironworks produced 2,704 tons of iron in 1823 and in the following year a second furnace was put into blast.[34] The works was owned from the 1820s to the 1840s by Brewer & Co. and in 1849 there were three furnaces present on the site.[35]

Frederick Levick became the sole owner of the three ironworks in 1858 when each site possessed two furnaces capable of operation. Levick was born in London in 1803 and started his career in the iron trade in 1825 at the Chillington Ironworks near Wolverhampton. He later managed the Spring Vale Ironworks until 1844 when called to manage the Cwm Celyn and Blaina Ironworks. Levick was one of the first managers to carry out successfully the utilisation of waste gases from blast furnaces which he started in 1849. At about the same time he increased his iron make to two hundred and seventy tons per week from each furnace.[36] In fact the two furnaces at Cwm Celyn produced 22,114 tons of iron for the year ending March 1857.[37] Levick was the first ironmaster to roll Barlow rails, of which he made large quantities with some examples weighing 100 lbs per yard and measuring 27ft. in length.

Robert Simpson, Levick's son-in-law, was admitted as a partner in the three ironworks in 1861.[38] However, conditions in the iron trade worsened during the early

1860s and in 1865 Levick and Simpson suspended payments. The furnaces continued in operation during 1866 but the three ironworks were put up for sale in 1867. The large size of Levick's business empire can be gauged from the following descriptions of the works taken from the sale catalogue.[39] There were two furnaces at Cwm Celyn, one being 60ft. high with a 20ft. diameter across the boshes. This furnace was capable of turning out 250 to 300 tons of iron each week and attached to it were eight hot blast stoves and a refinery. The second furnace was built in 1866 and was 42ft. high with a 18ft. diameter across the boshes. This furnace could produce 200 tons of iron weekly and was also fitted with hot blast stoves. The furnaces were blown by two beam blowing engines which could provide the blast for four furnaces. The engines were 46¼in. x 8ft. 10in. beam blowing engines with 94in. blowing cylinders. Their nine boilers were heated by waste gases from the blast furnaces. The Cwm Celyn Ironworks also boasted kilns, a charging stage with a hydraulic lift and coke ovens. The Blaina Ironworks had a single furnace in blast blown by a 45in. x 7ft. 6in. beam engine with a 94in. blowing cylinder. The ironworks also possessed hot blast stoves, calcining kilns and sixty open coke ovens. The Coalbrookvale Ironworks had a hot blast furnace blown by a 36in. x 6ft. 6in. beam blowing engine with a 69in. blowing cylinder. At nearby Trostrae was a cold blast furnace blown by a 38in. x 8ft. beam blowing engine with a 76in. blowing cylinder. The boilers for this engines were fired by waste heat. The forges and mills at Coalbrookvale were served by fifty two puddling furnaces, two trains of puddling rolls, two squeezers and two shears capable of turning out 900 tons of puddled iron each week. No.1 mill possessed a pair of slabbing rolls with reversing gear, a pair of roughing rolls with reversing gear, a pair of finishing rolls and two pairs of shears all worked by a 40in. x 6ft. beam engine and an auxiliary 26in. x 6ft. horizontal engine. The mill was served by nine balling furnaces and three heating furnaces. No.2 mill contained a pair of slabbing rolls with reversing gear, a pair of roughing rolls, a pair of finishing rolls, eight balling furnaces and three second heating furnaces. No.3 mill had a pair of roughing rolls, a pair of finishing rolls, two pairs of shears, four balling furnaces, a guide mill and two heating furnaces for the guide mill. The rolls in No.2 and No.3 mill were driven by a 36in. x 6ft. high pressure beam engine. Also present were two circular saws for cutting iron with their own steam engines, a range of five straightening and four punching benches for No.1 mill with a separate steam engine and a second range of fourteen benches for straightening, punching, shearing and pressing driven by a separate steam engine. This department also contained a large blacksmith's shop. Attached to the Coalbrookvale Ironworks was a large engineering works whose machinery was powered by a horizontal engine, a repair shop with a horizontal high pressure engine and a factory for making coal cutting machines. The three works in the six years ending 30th September 1865 had produced on average 39,000 tons of iron per year.

No bid for the works was received at the sale and during 1868 the works were idle. During 1869 the Blaina Iron and Coal Company was formed to resuscitate the Blaina Ironworks and two furnaces and four puddling furnaces were put into production.[40] In 1871 the company purchased the Nantyglo and Beaufort Ironworks and was renamed the Nantyglo and Blaina Iron Works Company (Limited) with John

Richardson as managing director.[41] However, the worsening conditions saw all the assets of the company sold off in 1878.[42] The Blaina Ironworks was purchased by Spence and Company of Liverpool who put a furnace into blast in 1880.[43]

Another of the early ironworks was situated in the north eastern corner of the coalfield. This was the Clydach Ironworks built in around 1794 by Edward Frere and Thomas Cooke.[44] The narrow valley site was chosen because of the abundant supply of water and water power although, with the later development of the works, this situation proved to be a costly disadvantage.

Cooke and Frere had both been managers at Crawshay's Cyfarthfa Ironworks. A single coke furnace was put into blast at Clydach during 1794-95 and in the following year it produced 1,625 tons of iron.[45] There was some expansion in the concern during the late eighteenth century when the partners took over the neighbouring Llanelly Ironworks. This provided the Clydach furnaces with a forge to transform the pig iron into wrought iron. A second furnace was built in the early 1800s and in 1805 the two furnaces made 2,802 tons of iron.[46] Further figures are available for this period for in the week ending 24th February 1805, No.2 furnace produced 50 tons 16 cwt. of iron and in the week ending 3rd March 1805, the same furnace produced nearly 52 tons of iron.[47] The Llanelly Forge was also modernised at this time and a Trevithick engine was purchased from the Penydarren Ironworks to provide a blast for the puddling furnaces.[48] A rolling mill was also constructed in 1805 but the money for this development had to be borrowed from Richard Crawshay of Cyfarthfa. Under capitalization was to be a continual problem for the Clydach Iron Company.[49]

An unsuccessful attempt was made to sell the works in 1813 when the property was described as containing two well constructed furnaces each capable of making seventy tons of iron per week and blown by two capital machines worked by water. The company at this time also owned a rolling mill and forge with a mineral ground of 600 acres. The forge at this time was held from Capel Hanbury Leigh and contained a Trevithick engine for occasional blowing. The forge possessed two hammer wheels, a blowing machine, two fineries, three hollow fires, an air chafery, three puddling and balling furnaces, a charcoal house, a smiths' shop, a warehouse, an agent's house and twenty houses for workmen.[50]

The two furnaces produced 5,200 tons of iron in 1823 and during the week ending 17th September 1825, No.1 furnace produced 40 tons of iron and No.2 produced 45 tons.[51] A third furnace was built in 1826 and in 1830 the output of the furnaces was 10,190 tons.[52] By this time the works was being managed by John Scale. In 1832 Edward Frere sold his share in the Clydach Iron Company to John Powell Jnr. of Brecon. His father, John Powell, had invested money in the company at an earlier date and this example was followed by his son who became a part owner. Powell & Co. then attempted to sell the works in 1833. The works was described as possessing three blast furnaces, 44ft. high and 14 ft. across the boshes, capable of making 240 tons of iron each week. A Boulton & Watt type engine and a 42ft. high waterwheel supplied the blast. The site also included twenty six coking ovens, three running out fineries, a foundry air furnace and two cupolas. Included in the sale was the forge for the manufacture of charcoal blooms and puddled bars and a rolling mill, worked by a 42ft high waterwheel, capable of making 120 tons of finished bars each week.[53]

No sale was concluded but in 1834 John Powell and John Jones managed to mortgage the works to Wilkins, the Brecon bankers.[54] The works continued in operation with Launcelot Powell as the resident managing partner. There were four furnaces at the Clydach Ironworks in 1839 and the works was further modernised in 1840 by the addition of a second steam blowing engine. This was a 52½in. beam blowing engine purchased from the Neath Abbey Iron Company.[55] During the 1850s three out of the four furnaces remained in blast but the general depression in the iron trade forced a complete closure in 1861.[56] The result of this was that the Clydach Ironworks was again put up for auction. At this time the works was described as consisting of four blast furnaces capable of turning out 400 tons of pig iron each week, spacious bridge houses, cast houses, mine kilns, coke yards, seventy three coke ovens, a foundry cupola, an air furnace, two stoves, a crane, a carpenters' shop and a smiths' and fitting shop with slide lathe, drilling and boring machines. The blast was supplied by two beam blowing engines, one was a 52½in. x 8ft. engine with a 104 in. blowing cylinder while the second was a 40in. x 8ft. engine with an 80in. blowing cylinder. Additional blast was obtained from a blowing machine worked by a 42ft. high waterwheel. The works also contained a forge worked by a 42ft. waterwheel with puddling furnaces attached. Also included in the sale were valuable mines and collieries worked by levels, two counting houses, an agent's house, spacious shops and warehouses, a shopkeeper's house, stables, forty eight houses for workmen and a 12in. steam engine to wind materials and iron along an inclined plane between the furnaces and rolling mill. The steam engines at the collieries and mines consisted of two 20in. high pressure winding engines, a 12½in. winding engine and a 15in. high pressure pumping engine. These premises were held from Joseph and Crawshay Bailey, lessees of the Duke of Beaufort for seventy six years from 1801.

The second batch of ground was leased from Capel Hanbury Leigh for eighty one years from 1797. This property included the Llanelly Forge which was capable of making 26 tons of charcoal blooms each week. A Trevithick engine was used for blowing which then exhausted into a beam engine which drove a hammer. Two blowing machines and two hammers were worked by water. The forge contained two double charcoal refineries and a balling furnace. A charcoal house, a smiths' shop, brick stoves, kilns, a warehouse and twenty three houses for workmen completed the inventory.

The third parcel of land in the sale was freehold. This contained the rolling mill which was served by a 24in. x 6ft. high pressure steam engine. The mill was capable of producing 300 tons of finished bars or rails each week. A puddling forge was situated next to the mill and was served by a 42ft. high waterwheel and an auxiliary 20in. engine. Also included on this land were balling furnaces, puddling furnaces and a weighing machine.[57]

There was an auction reserve of £22,000 on the whole property but no bids were forthcoming. The Clydach Ironworks was one of the first casualties in the decline of the South Wales iron industry. Its narrow site was a hindrance to expansion and its layout with a rolling mill situated on a hill side and a forge some distance away meant that extra costs were accrued in respect of transportation of materials and products.

In 1863 Jayne and Meadhouse leased part of the Llanelly works to manufacture tinplate and a company called the New Clydach Sheet & Bar Iron Company (Limited) was formed in 1865 to take over the Clydach Ironworks.[58] No furnaces were put into blast and the operations of the company were suspended in 1866 with assets of £21,000 and liabilities of £24,000.[59] Some of the main investors in this enterprise were Thomas Brassey, George Findley and John Jayne who was the former truckmaster of the Nantyglo Ironworks.[60] The Clydach Ironworks was again up for sale in 1867 and was purchased from Chancery for £6,000 by Isaac A. Lewis of Clydach House.[61] Lewis seems to have disposed of the works to John Jayne but no operations were commenced on the site. The Llanelly Forge was sold out of Chancery in 1870 and in 1872 it was owned by the Llanelly Charcoal Iron company but its ten puddling furnaces and single rolling mill were lying idle.[62]

The Clydach Ironworks was later owned by the Brynmawr Coal and Iron Company (Limited) who in 1881 dismantled the buildings and sold off the iron rails from the site.[63]

The Tredegar Ironworks is an example of one of the large northern enterprises which was able to continue in operation after the collapse of the Welsh wrought iron trade. A forge had operated at Tredegar during the eighteenth century and this was occupied by Harford and Partridge in 1794 when it consisted of two fineries and a chafery.[64] However, the large scale development of the Tredegar Ironworks dates from 1800 when land was leased to Samuel Homfray, Richard Fothergill of Sirhowy Furnace, Matthew Monkhouse of Sirhowy Furnace, William Thompson of London and William Forman of London.[65] One coke fired furnace was constructed and in 1801 a steam blowing engine was built at the works. This was a Boulton & Watt 40in. x 8ft. beam blowing engine which at Tredegar was connected to a 52ft. diameter waterwheel which worked hammers and turned rolls.[66]

A visitor to Tredegar in 1803 saw one furnace in blast and a few score puddling furnaces being built. The large number of puddling furnaces were needed for it was planned to use Tredegar to convert into wrought iron the pig iron produced by the Sirhowy Ironworks, in which Fothergill and Monkhouse had a share. It was estimated that the setting up of the Tredegar Ironworks had cost the partners £100,000.[67]

In 1802 a second engine was made for Tredegar by Boulton & Watt. This was a rotative 56 h.p. engine designed to power some rolling mills. However, this engine was probably sold off before it was set to work at Tredegar.[68] Samuel Homfray, by this time, had become a partner with Richard Trevithick and both men were promoting Trevithick's high pressure patent engine for use in industry. Instead of the Boulton & Watt engine, a 28in. x 6ft. Trevithick engine with a vertical cylinder was installed in 1804 to work puddle rolls.[69] This engine had been built at the Penydarren Ironworks and it is possible that a second Trevithick engine built by the Neath Abbey Iron Company was also installed at this time.[70]

The Tredegar Ironworks grew steadily with two furnaces in blast during 1805 which produced 4,500 tons of iron.[71] In 1823 there were five furnaces in blast which produced 16,385 tons of iron and in 1830, 18,514 tons were produced.[72] Homfray's early interest in steam locomotives encouraged the partners to buy a locomotive to transport iron along the Sirhowy Tramroad. This locomotive was named *Britannia* and was purchased in 1829 from Robert Stephenson and Company. *Britannia* was an 0-6-0 locomotive which cost the Tredegar Iron Company £550.[73] This early use of a locomotive encouraged the Tredegar engineers to build no less than eleven locomotives themselves during the period 1832-53.[74] The design of these locomotives owed much to the arrangement of the original Stephenson locomotive with its highly inclined cylinders.

The Tredegar Iron Company expanded its undertakings in the late 1830s and early 1840s. A 42in. beam blowing engine with a 122in. blowing cylinder was purchased from the Neath Abbey Iron Company in 1839 and two furnaces were under construction in 1840.[75] At this time the furnaces were producing 400 to 450 tons of iron each week.[76] This iron was made into bars, rods and rails. Expansion continued with nine furnaces in blast at the end of the 1840s and in 1849 a large rolling mill was opened.[77] Developments continued with a large blowing engine being constructed at the Tredegar Ironworks in 1860.[78] This was a 57in. x 13ft. beam blowing engine with a 144in. x 12ft. blowing cylinder. This engine was partly built by the Tredegar engineers and partly by Charles Jordan of the Pillgwenlly Foundry, Newport. Certainly the 50ft. beam which weighed 70 tons was cast at Newport.

For most of its working life the Tredegar Ironworks was owned by the Homfray, Fothergill and Forman families. In 1867 the Forman family held 10½ shares in the concern, the Homfray family 8 shares and Rowland Fothergill owned 5½ shares.[79] During the following year the Homfray shares were purchased by Forman and Fothergill.[80] The Tredegar Ironworks was described in some detail in 1869.[81] There were nine blast furnaces on the site with each furnace being 45ft. high with 16-17ft. boshes. Seven of these furnaces were closed and were making hot blast iron using ores from Wales, Northampton, Forest of Dean, Mwyndy and Spain. These furnaces were served by three hundred coke ovens. The furnace blast could be provided by five blowing engines although only three were in operation. No.1 blowing engine was a 40in. x 7ft. condensing beam blowing engine with no flywheel which worked at eighteen strokes per minute. This was probably the original Boulton & Watt engine. No.2 engine was a 50in. x 8ft. beam blowing engine which was not at work. No.3 engine was a smaller example which was standing idle while No.4 engine was the Neath Abbey 42in. x 10ft. beam blowing engine with a 122in. blowing cylinder. That blowing engine was making sixteen strokes each minute and delivering 25,132 cu. ft. of air per minute. No.5 engine was the 1860 57in. x 13ft. beam blowing engine with a 144in. blowing cylinder. This engine had the connecting rod between the steam cylinder and the centre of the beam with the flywheel weighing no less than fifty tons. The output of this beam blowing engine was 35,286 cu. ft. of air per minute. The four forge trains were served by eighty puddling furnaces. Two of these forge rolls were driven by an old 36in. x 8ft. condensing beam engine. The other two trains were driven by a 33in. x 4ft. horizontal engine. In the older part of the mills were two rail mills, two blooming mills and a mill for merchant iron all driven by a 45in. x 8ft. beam engine working at 50 psi. Also in these buildings were two small engines working two saws and a pair of shears, thirty five balling furnaces and a recently added merchant mill and a guide mill driven by a 28in x 3 ft. horizontal engine. The machinery and plant was completed by a further seven balling furnaces, two small engines for shearing and bending cramp iron and an engine working twelve presses and two large shears. One of the small engines was an inverted vertical 10in. x 10in. engine supplied by the Neath Abbey Iron Company in 1867.[82] The works was producing 1,000 to 1,100 tons of railway iron each week during 1869.

The Tredegar Ironworks continued to sell large amounts of rails, particularly in the export market. Rails were exported to Galveston and Rio de Janeiro in 1872 when the works was operating eighty puddling furnaces and five rolling mills.[83] In 1873 the works was bought by the Tredegar Iron Company Limited.[84] The new owners wisely made the decision to manufacture steel and in 1882 two 8 ton Bessemer converters were put into operation although the official opening ceremony did not take place until 1883.[85] The machinery for the steel department was built by Davy Brothers and at the time of opening the works employed 2,000 which included 500 to 600 women and girls. The manufacture of steel rails guaranteed the survival of the Tredegar Iron and Steel Works into the 1890s.

For another of the Welsh ironworks the change over to the manufacture of steel did not prove to be a success. This was the Rhymney Ironworks which built a steel making department in 1877 but was forced to cease iron and steel making in around 1891. The Rhymney Ironworks has a most interesting but complicated early history. The first ironworks to be built in the Rhymney Valley was the Union Ironworks which dates from 1800. The works received its name because the furnace was constructed at a point where the counties of Brecon, Monmouth and Glamorgan met.[86] The partners in this enterprise were David Evans, Thomas Williams, John Ambrose and Richard Cunningham, this company being a Bristol based concern.[87] One furnace was constructed and a 24in. x 5ft. Boulton and Watt beam blowing engine with a 55in. blowing cylinder was purchased to provide the blast. This engine was rated at 20 h.p. and was provided with a wooden beam. In fact, this was a second-hand engine having originally been installed at the Barnetts Leasow Ironworks, Shropshire in 1797 as a 23¾in. x 5ft. beam blowing engine with a 48in. blowing cylinder.[88] The reconditioning of the engine was undertaken by Boulton & Watt at their Soho Foundry.

Soon the Crawshay family of Cyfarthfa was buying into the concern and in 1803 the works was owned by Richard Crawshay, Watkin George, Benjamin Hall, Richard Cunningham and Thomas Williams.[89] At that time new furnaces were being constructed further down the valley. It was intended that the output of these furnaces would supply the hungry forges and mills of Cyfarthfa. In 1804 the Rhymney Ironworks, as it came to be known, was being operated by Crawshay, George and Hall with Hall becoming the sole owner in 1810.

On Hall's death in 1817 a sale of the Rhymney Ironworks was negotiated with Crawshay Bailey. However, the transfer of the works did not take place.[90] Presumably the works continued under the ownership of the Hall family for in 1823 the three furnaces of the Rhymney Ironworks produced 5,500 tons of iron.[91] Forman & Co.

purchased the ironworks in 1825 for £147,000. This money was raised through a loan from Coutts, the Marquis of Bute's bankers.[92] The previous year had seen Forman & Co. build the Bute Ironworks with three furnaces on the opposite bank of the River Rhymney. The Marquis of Bute, who was the landowner, had actively encouraged this development on a site opposite the Rhymney Ironworks.[93] The partners in this enterprise were William Forman, Thomas Seton Forman and Thomas Johnson.[94]

From 1825 Forman & Co. operated both concerns as one works with the six furnaces producing 7,608 tons of iron in 1830.[95] A second lease for the land that the ironworks stood on was granted to the Rhymney Iron Company in 1837. The partners at that time were Henry Rowles, William Thompson and John Pirie.[96] After this further lease was obtained a large scale expansion programme was embarked upon by the company. In 1837 a 25in. x 8ft. beam engine was purchased from Harvey & Co. of Hayle for £628 and in the following year two 34in. beam engines were supplied from the same source.[97] Also in 1838 the Neath Abbey Iron Company supplied Rhymney with an 18in. beam engine and two 15in. x 2ft. 6in. high pressure beam engines. This was followed in the next year by the purchase of two 52½in. beam blowing engines and a 38in. 'A' frame beam engine manufactured by the Neath Abbey Iron Company.[98] This expansion also involved an increase in iron making capacity for two further furnaces were being built in 1839 and it is obvious from the beam engines being bought that the Rhymney Iron Company was developing a number of rail mills.[99] The transport of raw materials and products were also improved at this time with the purchase of two locomotives built by the Neath Abbey Iron Company.[100]

Furnace output at Rhymney was 93.4 tons each week in 1846 and this had been improved to 106.4 tons each week in 1847.[101] At the end of the 1840s the Rhymney Ironworks possessed ten furnaces although this was reduced to nine in the mid 1850s.[102] For most of the 1860s seven furnaces were kept in blast with further machinery being added to the works in 1865-67.[103] In 1865 a 70in. beam engine was supplied to the Rhymney Iron Company by the St. Blazey Foundry, Cornwall and in 1867 a 2-4-0 side tank locomotive with 8in. x 16in. cylinders was purchased from the Neath Abbey Iron Company.[104]

Rails were the main product of the Rhymney Ironworks with much of the output being exported. To service this demand for wrought iron rails the Rhymney Iron Company in 1872 was operating ninety two puddling furnaces and seven mills.[105] The title of the company was changed in 1874 to the Rhymney Iron Company Limited and in 1876 the decision was made to produce steel rails.[106] During that year a loss of £4,000 was made with many directors puzzled, when with the company owning eight hundred houses, shops and a brewery and 4/5 of what was paid out returning, why losses were being sustained.[107] Two Bessemer converters were installed in 1877 with the machinery being built by Tannett & Walker of Leeds, the boilers constructed by Adamson and Company of Hyde and the engines built by Galloways of Manchester. It was estimated that the works would be able to turn out five hundred tons of steel rails each week.[108] The Rhymney Ironworks was listed in 1878 as working three 7 ton Bessemer converters and two further converters were built in the following year to work with the Gilchrist Thomas process.[109] To deal with the increased steel making capacity new reversing mill engines were installed at the works in 1880. These were unusual engines for they were manufactured by Cockerill of Belgium.[110]

During 1884 the Rhymney Iron Company ceased making wrought iron.[111] It was also in that year that the works was visited by members of the Institution of Mechanical Engineers.[112] They saw three furnaces at work on the Monmouthshire side of the river. These masonry furnaces had been 42ft. in height but had been raised by 13ft. for the production of Bessemer pig. Materials were brought up to the furnace tops by means of two steam lifts. The furnaces were blown by two engines, one being a 52½in. x 10ft. beam blowing engine with a 104in. blowing cylinder, while the second engine was a 50in. x 12ft. beam blowing engine with a 90in. blowing cylinder although a further 72in. x 6ft. blowing cylinder had been added to this engine. The blowing engines for the converters were built by Galloways and consisted of two 45in. x 5ft. engines with 54in. blowing cylinders and two 30in. x 4ft. engines with 40in. blowing cylinders. Galloways had also constructed two pairs of 16in. x 1ft. 3in. hydraulic engines for the steel making department. In the rolling mills there was a cogging mill with a pair of 30in. rolls driven by a 50in. x 4ft. inverted engine with a 28ft. diameter flywheel weighing 70 tons. There was also present in this building a 26in. roughing down mill driven by two 60in. x 4ft. non condensing engines. The nucleus of these engines was a 50in. x 4ft. inverted engine which was enlarged with a replacement 60in. cylinder and the addition of a 60in. horizontal cylinder. The cylinders and parts for the conversion had been supplied by Tannett & Walker of Leeds. The company also possessed a 24in. finishing mill driven by a pair of 40in. x 4ft. horizontal engines made by Cockerill of Belgium. On the Glamorgan side of the river were six furnaces whose height ranged from 45 to 60ft. Only two furnaces were in blast and these could be blown by three engines. These beam blowing engines consisted of a 56in. x 8ft. engine with a 120in. blowing cylinder, a 60in. x 8ft engine with a 120in. blowing cylinder and a 38in. x 8ft. engine with a 100in. blowing cylinder. There was an old rail mill on this side of the river which contained a 30in. blooming mill driven by a pair of 25in. reversing engines made on the premises. Other mills in the building were driven by a 48in. x 8ft beam engine geared to a shaft. Unhappily for the company the move to steel production does not seem to have been a profitable venture. In around 1891 the Rhymney Ironworks gave up making steel rails with the furnaces and plant being dismantled.[113] The company, however, did continue in operation but only as a coal mining enterprise.

References.

1. John Lloyd, *The Early History of the Old South Wales Ironworks, 1760-1840*, 1906, pp.178-192.
2. *A Catalogue of the Civil and Engineering Designs, 1741-1792, of John Smeaton*, 1950.
3. Harry Scrivenor, *History of the Iron Trade*, 1854, p.96.
4. BRL, B&W, List of Ironworks, 1806.
5. John Lloyd, op. cit., p.178-192.
6. &
7. Harry Scrivenor, op. cit., p.134.

8. &
9. John Lloyd, op. cit., pp.178-192.
10. BRL, B&W, List of Ironworks, 1806.
11. &
12. GRO, NAI, D/D. N.A.I., M/144/2, Plans of Engine House and Boiler for Nantyglo Ironworks, 24th May 1811.
BRL, B&W, Portfolio No. 682, Drawings for Blowing Engine for Bailey and Wayne, Nantyglo Ironworks, 1811-12.
13. &
14. Harry Scrivenor, op. cit., p.134.
15. Margaret Stewart Taylor, *The Crawshays of Cyfarthfa Castle*, 1967, pp.25-26.
16. GRO, NAI, D/D. N.A.I., M/144/1- M/144/4, Drawings for Engines for Nantyglo Ironworks, 1836-43.
Laurence Ince, *The Neath Abbey Iron Company*, Eindhoven, 1984, pp.106-107.
17. David Mushet, *Papers on Iron and Steel, 1840*, pp.414-415.
Robert Hunt, *Mineral Statistics, 1854-69*.
18. *The Engineer*, July 28th 1871, p.66.
19. Robert Hunt, *Mineral Statistics, 1872*.
20. *The Engineer*, November 7th 1873.
21. *The Engineer*, November 21st 1873, p.348.
22. *The Engineer*, January 4th 1878.
23. *The Engineer*, February 27th 1880, p.168
24. Arthur Clark, *The Story of Monmouthshire*, Vol.2, Monmouth, 1979, p.79.
25. &
26. Harry Scrivenor, op. cit., p.134.
27. Arthur Clark, op. cit., p.79.
28. Tom Grey Davies, *Blaenavon and Sydney Gilchrist Thomas*, 1978, p.14.
29. Hugh Torrens, *The Evolution of a Family Firm: Stothert and Pitt of Bath*, Bath, 1978, p.31.
30. D.B. Barton, *The Cornish Beam Engine*, Truro, 1969, p.280.
31. Hugh Torrens, op. cit., p.31.
32. *Official Descriptive and Illustrated Catalogue of the Great Exhibition*, Vol.1, 1851, p.147.
33. James W. Lowe, *British Steam Locomotive Builders*, Cambridge, 1975, p.651.
34. Harry Scrivenor, op. cit., p.134.
35. Alan Birch, *The Economic History of the British Iron and Steel Industry*, 1967 Appendix II.
36. *Proceedings of the Institution of Mechanical Engineers*, 1868, p.17.
37. John Percy, *Metallurgy, Iron and Steel*, 1864, p.558.
38. Robert Hunt, *Mineral Statistics, 1861*.
39. GWRO, Cwmbran, Sale Catalogue of Cwm Celyn, Blaina and Coalbrookvale Ironworks, June 5th 1867. D. 1089.2.
40. *The Engineer*, August 20th 1869, p.110.
41. *The Engineer*, July 28th 1871, p.66.
42. *The Engineer*, January 4th 1878.
43. *The Engineer*, February 27th 1880, p.168.
44. John Lloyd, op. cit., pp.192-197.
45. Harry Scrivenor, op. cit., p.96.
46. BRL, B&W, List of Ironworks, 1806.
47. John Lloyd, op. cit., pp.192-197.
48. Laurence Ince, Richard Trevithick's Patent Steam Engine, *Stationary Power*, Vol 1, p.69.
49. John Van Laun, *The Clydach Gorge*, 1980, p.9.
50. John Lloyd, op. cit., pp.192-197.
51. &
52. Harry Scrivenor, op. cit., p.134.
53. John Lloyd, op. cit., pp.192-197.
54. John Van Laun, op. cit., p.9.

55. GRO, NAI, D/D. N.A.I., M/47/1-M/47/6, Drawings for 52½in. Engine for Clydach Iron Company, 1839-40.
    Laurence Ince, *The Neath Abbey Iron Company*, Eindhoven, 1984, p.106.
56. Robert Hunt, *Mineral Statistics, 1854-61*.
    Mining Journal, October 5th 1861, p.652.
57. *Mining Journal*, September 13th 1862, p.630.
58. *Mining Journal*, May 9th 1863, p.324.
    Robert Hunt, *Mineral Statistics, 1865*.
59. *The Engineer*, November 16th 1866, p.389.
60. John Van Laun, op. cit., p.9.
61. *The Engineer*, October 25th 1867, p.369.
62. *Mining Journal*, February 5th 1870, p.109.
    Robert Hunt, *Mineral Statistics, 1872*.
63. *The Engineer*, September 16th 1881, p.213.
64. BRL, B&W, List of Ironworks, 1794.
65. John Lloyd, op, cit., pp.134-144.
66. BRL, B&W, Portfolio No.698, Drawings for a Blowing Engine for Homfray and Fothergill, Tredegar Ironworks, 1801.
67. *Svedenstierna's Tour of Great Britain, 1802-03*, Newton Abbot, 1973, pp.59-71.
68. BRL, B&W, Portfolio No.327, Drawings for an Engine for Tredegar Ironworks, 1802.
69. Laurence Ince, Richard Trevithick's Patent Steam Engine, *Stationary Power*, Vol.1, p.69.
70. Arthur Clark, op. cit., p.73
71. BRL, B&W, List of Ironworks, 1806.
72. Harry Scrivenor, op. cit., p.134.
73. Michael R. Bailey, Robert Stephenson & Co. 1823-1829, *Transactions of the Newcomen Society*, Vol.50, 1978-79, p.129.
74. James W. Lowe, op. cit., pp.645-646.
75. GRO, NAI, D/D. N.A.I., M/193/2- M/193/4, Drawings for a 42in. Engine for the Tredegar Ironworks, 1839.
    David Mushet, op. cit., pp.414-415.
76. W.W. Tasker, *Railways in the Sirhowy Valley*, Blandford, 1978, pp.3-4.
77. *Mining Journal*, April 6th 1850, p.164.
78. *Mining Journal*, September 29th 1860, p.664.
79. *The Engineer*, January 18th 1867, p.71.
80. *The Engineer*, January 1st 1869, p.24.
81. *Mining Journal*, November 20th 1869, p.882.
82. GRO, NAI, D/D. N.A.I., M/193/1, Drawing of a 10in. Engine for Tredegar Iron Company, 1867.
83. Robert Hunt, *Mineral Statistics, 1872*.
    The Engineer, May 10th 1872, p.340.
84. *The Engineer*, April 4th 1873, p.212.
85. Robert Hunt, *Mineral Statistics, 1882*.
    The Engineer, May 11th 1883, p.370.
86. BRL, B&W, James Watt Jnr.'s Journal of a Visit to Ironworks in South Wales, c.1800.
87. John Lloyd, op. cit., pp.129-130.
88. BRL, B&W, Portfolio No.691, Drawings for Blowing Engine for Union Company, Rhymney, 1800.
89. John Lloyd, op. cit, pp.129-130.
90. Charles Wilkins, *The History of the Iron, Steel, Tinplate and Other Trades of Wales*, Merthyr Tydfil, 1903, p.186.
91. Harry Scrivenor, op. cit., p.134.
92. John Davies, *Cardiff and the Marquesses of Bute*, Cardiff, 1981, p.223.
93. John Davies, op. cit., p.223.
94. John Lloyd, op. cit., pp.129-130.
95. Harry Scrivenor, op. cit., p.134.
96. John Lloyd, op. cit., pp.129-130.
97. D.B. Barton, op. cit., p.280.

98. GRO, NAI, D/D. N.A.I., M/172/1-M/172/35, Drawings for Rhymney Iron Company, 1837-39.
99. David Mushet, op. cit., pp.414-415.
100. GRO, NAI, D/D. N.A.I., L/40/1- L/40/4, Drawings for Locomotives for the Rhymney Iron Company, 1837-1840.
101. A.H. John, *The Industrial Development of South Wales, 1750-1850*, Cardiff, 1950, p.155.
102. Robert Hunt, *Mineral Statistics, 1854-56*.
103. Robert Hunt, *Mineral Statistics, 1860-69*.
104. D.B. Barton, op. cit., p.161.
    GRO, NAI, D/D. N.A.I., L/39/1, Drawing for a Locomotive for the Rhymney Iron Company, 1867.
105. Robert Hunt, *Mineral Statistics, 1872*.
106. *The Engineer*, September 15th 1876.
107. *The Engineer*, June 29th 1877, p.458 & November 23rd 1877, p.382.
108. *The Engineer*, December 7th 1877, p.417.
109. Robert Hunt, *Mineral Statistics, 1878-79*.
110. *The Engineer*, July 2nd 1880, p.20.
111. *The Engineer*, April 22nd 1884, p.136.
112. *Proceedings of the Institution of Mechanical Engineers*, 1884, pp.381-386.
113. John Lloyd, op. cit., pp.129-130

Plate Thirty A cast iron tramroad bridge built in 1824 to serve the Clydach Ironworks.

Plate Thirty One   The Tredegar Ironworks photographed in the 1890s. Clearly visible are five furnaces including two metal cased ones. (Courtesy Welsh Industrial & Maritime Museum, Cardiff)

Chapter Twelve.

The Ironworks of the Southern Outcrop.

Although the South Wales iron industry was concentrated along the northern borders of Glamorgan and Monmouthshire, there were also a number of ironworks founded on the southern outcrop of the coalfield. It is true to say that these works were much smaller than their northern counterparts but the development of the iron industry on the southern outcrop exhibits an equally long history when compared with the developments in the north.

The oldest of the iron making enterprises sited on the southern outcrop was the Pentyrch Ironworks. There had been an iron furnace working at Pentyrch during the sixteenth century but the redevelopment of the works can be dated to a lease of land in 1740. The Pentyrch Ironworks, consisting of a charcoal fired furnace and a forge, was built by Nicholas Price, a tanner and publican of Caerphilly, his son also called Nicholas and Thomas Lewis of Llanishen.[1] During the 1780s and 1790s the Pentyrch Ironworks was owned by William Lewis who introduced puddling to the works in around 1792 and also built up a considerable trade by selling iron to the nearby Melingriffith Tinplate Works. In 1805 the Pentyrch Ironworks was sold to Harford, Partridge and Company, the Quaker owners of the Melingriffith Tinplate Works. However, a dissolution of this partnership commenced in 1808 with the ownership of Melingriffith and Pentyrch being transferred to Richard Blakemore, Thomas Prichard of Ross and Richard Jones Tomlinson of Bristol. The Harford connection with the two works seems to have been finally severed in 1810.[2]

Richard Blakemore, who was born in Darlaston, Staffordshire in 1775, became the managing partner. He was the son of Thomas Blakemore, a merchant who had married Ann the daughter of John Partridge. Blakemore set about modernising the Pentyrch Ironworks by reconstructing the furnace and modernising the forge. This reconstruction of the furnace may well indicate the change-over from being charcoal fired to coke fired. In 1823 the Pentyrch Ironworks produced 1,235 tons of iron with production rising to 2,412 tons in 1830.[3] This iron would have been used for the manufacture of tinplate at the partners' Melingriffith works.

During the 1830s the Pentyrch Ironworks experienced some expansion for a second furnace was constructed at that time. Blakemore retired from business in around 1834 with T.W. Booker taking over as managing partner. T.W. Booker was Blakemore's nephew and on Blakemore's death in 1855 Booker inherited the ownership of Melingriffith and Pentyrch. Booker held the Pentyrch Ironworks for a short period and his death saw the concern inherited by his sons Thomas William Booker and John Partridge Booker. By 1866 John Partridge Booker had ceased to take an active role in the affairs of the two works with the management resting solely on the shoulders of Thomas Booker. Under Booker's control the Pentyrch Ironworks built up an excellent reputation for its tinplate iron and in 1866 T.W. Booker & Co. won a prize medal at the Dublin International Exhibition for its display of sheet, wire, cable, tin and terne.[4] At that time some foreign markets were cultivated by the company for a number of shipments of sheet iron were sent to Holland.[5]

In 1873 the ownership of the works was converted into a limited liability company known as Thomas W. Booker and Company Limited. The assets of the Pentyrch part of the concern consisted of two furnaces, seven melting furnaces, nine fineries in the charcoal department, eleven puddling furnaces, seven balling furnaces and fitting, smiths', millwrights' and pattern making shops. The new company was able to invest additional money at Pentyrch for in 1874 No.2 furnace was renovated and a third furnace constructed. However, in 1879 the company failed.[6] This was the direct result of the failure of the West of England and District Bank as Thomas W. Booker and Company was one of its heaviest debtors. Efforts were made by the liquidator to sell the assets of the company but this did not meet with success until 1882 when Spence & Co., a firm of Liverpool metal merchants purchased Melingriffith and Pentyrch.[7] Both works were put back into operation for a short time but the last furnace at Pentyrch was blown out in 1885 with Melingriffith commencing the manufacture of tinplate from steel bars purchased from the Dowlais Ironworks.

Part of the Pentyrch Ironworks was leased in 1890 to Waterhouse Brothers a Midland firm specialising in producing iron hollow ware. The company manufactured sheet iron at Pentyrch spasmodically until 1915. The buildings were then abandoned, although, during the period 1930-31 the Pentyrch Steel and Tinplate Company operated at the site.

There was also an early attempt to exploit the mineral wealth in the eastern part of the region when land at Cefn Cribwr was leased in 1772 by John Bedford of Worcestershire.[8] John Bedford was an experimenter in iron making techniques but it appears that he was no businessman. He intended to build several structures on the land at Cefn Cribwr but a full scale furnace was not completed until 1790.[9] This furnace, which was waterwheel blown, seems to have been little in blast and in 1794 the Cefn Cribwr Ironworks was listed as being occupied by Green and Price.[10]

After John Bedford's death in around 1791 the ownership of the furnace passed to his brother Thomas Bedford, a cutler of Birmingham.[11] There is no record of the furnace being in blast during the early nineteenth century. Bryant & Co. took over the Cefn Cribwr Ironworks in 1824 and rebuilt the furnace.[12] William Bryant was a native of Merthyr Tydfil and a brewer.[13] However, after the reconstruction of the furnace there seems to have been little activity at the works although the company continued for some time with William Bryant's son taking on a major role. A report was drawn up in 1836 which detailed the extent of the Cefn Cribwr iron making operations. The property at this time was made up of a blast furnace, a 50 h.p. beam blowing engine, a blast regulator, bridge house, cast house, store, two smitheries, carpenters' shop, ten coke ovens, coke yard, four mine kilns, a finery, cupola, two hot blast apparatus, double saw pit, sixteen cottages, public house, shop, office and store house. There is no record of any attempt to work the concern after this report was drawn up.[14]

Further attempts to successfully make iron in the area date from the late 1830s. Two furnaces were constructed at Cefn Cwsc in 1839 by Malins and Rawlinson who also termed themselves the Porthcawl Iron and Coal Company.[15] Malins and Rawlinson had extensive interests in the iron trade including the ownership of works in London and West Bromwich. The first furnace at Cefn Cwsc was blown in during 1840 with the blast being supplied by a beam blowing engine constructed by the Copperhouse Foundry, Hayle, Cornwall.[16] The activities of the Porthcawl Iron and Coal Company must have met with success for a third furnace was operating at the Cefn Ironworks in the later 1840s and a second ironworks had been built by the partners in 1847 at Garth, Maesteg.

The initial success of the Cefn and Garth Ironworks was not a prolonged phenomenon with the company failing and its assets being put up for sale in 1852.[17] The Cefn property consisted of ground which could yield from 2,000 to 3,000 tons of coal weekly, three blast furnaces, an 80 h.p. beam blowing engine, hot air stoves, a small forge, fifty coke ovens, mine ovens, extensive workshops, numerous branch railways and abundant machinery which included ten steam engines and numerous trams. No purchaser came forward and the works was again offered for sale by the Royal British Bank in 1857.[18] The lack of interest in the concern was thought to be the result of bad communications between the works and any major dock system.[19] A belated attempt to resuscitate the works was made in 1872 probably initiated by C.R.M. Talbot, the landowner.[20] A 42in. beam blowing engine was built or repaired at the works by the Neath Abbey Iron Company and two hundred men were employed to start production of iron.[21] These actions do not seem to have met with success and no furnaces are listed as being put back into blast at the Cefn Ironworks. A little interest in the site was shown in 1880 with the floating of the Pyle Works Company with a capital of £10,000 made up of £10 shares.[22] This enterprise wanted to purchase the Cefn Ironworks to smelt ores and manufacture spiegeleisen. The attempted launch of this company, however, met with little interest from British investors. However, a foreign based partnership did take over the works and spiegeleisen was made there until the early years of the twentieth century.

One of the more successful works in this region was the Tondu Ironworks whose construction dates from 1836. Although this enterprise was a fairly long lived affair its early history was fraught with commercial uncertainty. The origin of the Tondu Ironworks lies with the ambitions of Sir Robert Price of Foxley Court, Yazor, Herefordshire. Price was born in 1786 and was destined to become Member of Parliament for Hereford. He possessed the desire to become an ironmaster although he had no experience within the industry. Price began to lease land at Tondu for an ironworks and raw materials during the 1830s. His one industrial contact with the area was that he had invested heavily in the Duffryn, Llynvi and Porthcawl Railway.[23]

Price formed a partnership with Sir Francis Knowles of Vaynor Park, Montgomeryshire and Frederick Beckford Long of Hampton, Surrey with the three partners' interests being organised into the Glamorgan Iron and Coal Company. Construction of the Tondu Ironworks started in 1836 although a shortage of capital meant a slow development of the site with the works being finished in the early 1840s. One furnace was built and in 1846 the Duffryn, Llynvi and Porthcawl Railway carried 2,637 tons of iron for the company. By 1849 there were two furnaces in blast but during the early 1850s it was obvious to all that the company was labouring under a shortage of capital. The Glamorgan Iron and Coal Company was forced to sell the Tondu Ironworks in 1854 to John Brogden and Sons of Manchester who were builders of railways and merchants in Furness haematite.[24] The works was greatly developed by the Brogdens and was extended to consist of two blast furnaces, twenty three puddling furnaces, four rolling mills, eleven balling furnaces, a forge and one hundred coke ovens. The two furnaces remained in blast until one was made idle in 1871.[25] In 1872 a new company was formed which was named the Llynvi, Tondu and Ogmore Coal and Iron Company. Alexander Brogden was the chairman with Henry Brogden later becoming managing director.[26] The new company had a capital of £550,000 which it used to take over the properties of John Brogden & Sons and the Llynvi Vale Coal & Iron Co. These assets included 14,000 acres of mineral ground, two blast furnaces, forges and mills at Tondu, four blast furnaces, forges and mills at Llynvi and three blast furnaces at Maesteg.

The Tondu furnaces were put out of blast in 1877 with the company collapsing in the following year.[27] A new company was formed by the receiver and both furnaces at the Tondu Ironworks were returned to production. However, the new company also failed in 1885 which resulted in the final closure of the Tondu Ironworks.

The southern outcrop was to have the honour of providing the location of one of the last ironworks to be developed on the South Wales Coalfield. This was the Brynna Ironworks, near Pencoed, which was under construction in 1860.[28] A single furnace was built but the ancillary buildings had not been completed when in 1862 the Brynna Gwynnon (Gwynion) Collieries and iron ore mines were offered for sale.[29] The property consisted of 397 acres of mineral land and the furnace. Also included in the sale were the other parts of the ironworks which were close to completion, namely an engine house, engine and boiler. In 1863 there were reports that the furnace was about to be blown in with any cold blast iron produced being sold to the Pontnewynydd Ironworks in Monmouthshire.[30] It is hard to believe that this was a serious proposition and there is strong evidence to suggest that the works was, in fact, never commissioned. The projected conversion of iron at the Pontnewynydd forge indicates that the ironworks of the southern outcrop were handicapped through the use of inferior coals compared with their northern counterparts.

References.

1. J.B. Davies, The Parish of Pentyrch, *Glamorgan Historian*, Vol.1, Cowbridge, 1963, p.84.
2. Edgar L. Chappel, *Historic Melingriffith: An Account of Pentyrch Ironworks and Melingriffith Tinplate Works*, Cardiff, 1940, p.54.
3. Harry Scrivenor, *History of the Iron Trade*, 1854, p.134.
4. *The Engineer*, February 2nd 1866, p.97 (terne was an inferior tinplate alloyed with lead).
5. *The Engineer*, May 10th 1872, p.340.

6. *The Engineer*, September 12th 1879, p.212.
7. *The Engineer*, January 6th 1882, p.15.
8. William Rees, *Industry Before the Industrial Revolution*, Vol.1, Cardiff, 1968.
9. &
10. BRL, B&W, List of Ironworks, 1794.
11. D.M. Rees, *Mines, Mills, and Furnaces*, 1969, p.79.
12. Harry Scrivenor, op. cit., p.134.
13. A. H. John, op. cit., p.38.
14. D.M. Rees, op. cit., p.80.
15. David Mushet, op. cit., pp.414-415.
16. W.H. Pascoe, *The History of the Cornish Copper Company*, Redruth, p.97.
17. *Mining Journal*, October 16th 1852, p.504.
18. *Mining Journal*, 1857, p.410.
19. *Mining Journal*, June 27th 1857, p.464.
20. *The Engineer*, July 5th 1872, p.16.
21. GRO, NAI, D/D. N.A.I. M/42. Drawing for a 42in. Engine for Cefn Ironworks, 21st February 1872.
22. *The Engineer*, November 12th 1880, p.373.
23. A.J. Flint, 'Neither a Borrower ....', Sir Robert Price, Bart. M.P., *Glamorgan Historian*, Vol.11, Cowbridge, 1976, pp.82-97.
24. Leonard S. Higgins, John Brogden and Sons: Industrial Pioneers in Mid-Glamorgan, *Glamorgan Historian*, Vol.10, Cowbridge, 1974, p.148.
25. Robert Hunt, *Mineral Statistics, 1872*.
26. &
27. Leonard S. Higgins, op. cit., p.154.
28. *Mining Journal*, May 26th 1860, p.356.
29. *Mining Journal*, March 22nd 1862, p.198.
30. *Mining Journal*, November 7th 1863, p.800.

Chapter Thirteen.

The Iron Industry of the Central Anticlinal District.

This region was one of the last to be developed on the main South Wales Coalfield with its first ironworks being founded in 1819. In that year a blast furnace was built at Cwmavon by the Quaker, Samuel Fothergill Lettsom.[1] The furnace was built at an existing forge but Lettsom soon got into financial difficulties and was forced to sell the Cwmavon Ironworks.[2] The works was purchased in 1820 by Leonard Smith and John Vigurs who further developed the site by building bar and sheet mills. In 1823 the Cwmavon Ironworks produced 1,560 tons of iron with output rising to 1,950 tons in 1830.[3]

Smith severed his connection with the works in 1835 and his place was taken by two Cornishmen called Batten and James. The reorganisation also saw the arrival of William Brunton as works' manager. One of Brunton's first tasks was to erect a copper works which came into production in 1838.[4] The ironworks also received some additional investment for a second furnace was in blast by 1839.[5] New machinery was also purchased at this time, including a 60in. rotative beam engine built by Harvey & Co., of Hayle, Cornwall which arrived in 1838 and cost £1,145.[6]

In 1840 the Cwmavon Iron and Copper Works were purchased by the Governor and Company of Copper Miners who appointed William Gilbertson as their manager.[7] The Cwmavon Ironworks was considerably enlarged and capital was expended on the purchase of the Pontrhydyfen Ironworks and the assets of the failed Oakwood Iron and Coal Company.

The Pontrhydyfen Ironworks with its two furnaces had been built in 1826 by John Reynolds whose use of water power seems to indicate a lack of investment and a lack of knowledge of modern methods.[8] It is not surprising that little production is recorded for these furnaces. The new company invested heavily in machinery for in 1845 the Neath Abbey Iron Company supplied the Cwmavon Ironworks with a 60in. rotative beam engine to drive rolling mills, two coupled 15in. beam engines and a locomotive with 10½in. cylinders.[9]

Perhaps the company was too enthusiastic in its investment for it experienced financial difficulties in 1847. An attempt was made to sell the property in 1849 when it was advertised as consisting of seven blast furnaces, five at Cwmavon and two at Oakwood, which were capable of making 850 to 900 tons of iron each week. The Cwmavon Ironworks also consisted of three puddling mills and five rail and bar mills capable of producing 3,000 tons of bars or rails each month.[10] No sale was achieved but the property was mortgaged to the Bank of England who had been running the works since 1847 and this situation continued. The works had been managed by John Biddulph the agent of the Swansea branch of the bank.[11] However, this soon changed as his management techniques seem to have aggravated several groups of workers at Cwmavon and he was replaced in 1849 by a committee of shareholders.[12] These financial and managerial problems did not stop the company from displaying its products at the 1851 exhibition. Cwmavon's display included bar iron, sheet iron, tinplate, rails and minerals with the company securing a prize medal for their railway iron.[13]

In 1852 the Governor and Company of Copper Miners were reorganised with new capital of £200,000 to be raised through the sale of 8,000 shares each valued at £25.[14] The Governor was named as Sir John Dean Paul with John Henry Pelly as his deputy. This resuscitation proved to be successful with the result that the Cwmavon undertakings were reorganised. The company now appeared to be on a firm footing for in 1857 the Oakwood furnaces were put back into blast after a considerable period of inactivity.[15] The production of rails seems to have been an important facet of Cwmavon's output with the company being awarded a Grand Medaille d'Honneur in 1855 for its display of railway iron at the Paris Exhibition.[16]

William Price Struve was appointed as manager at Cwmavon in 1859 and under his leadership the works continued to operate successfully during the 1860s. The Cwmavon Ironworks continued its tradition of entering exhibitions by sending a display to the 1862 exhibition. This consisted of an iron flange rail which was 90ft. long and weighed 58lbs. to the yard, a model flange rail which was 63ft. long and weighed 3¾lbs. to the yard and a copper and yellow metal rail.[17]

During the period 1867-71 there were only three furnaces in blast at Cwmavon and for the year ending January 1871 the company lost £12,584.[18] In the better conditions of 1872 the company was operating fifty puddling furnaces and four mills, but within a few years the worsening conditions in the iron trade forced the Cwmavon Ironworks to reduce its output.[19] The works had only three furnaces in blast during 1874 and the subsidiary Oakwood Ironworks was at that time being dismantled.[20] There were only two furnaces in blast during 1876 and in the following year the works was sold to a new syndicate which continued to operate with the old company's name.[21] In 1881 the Cwmavon enterprises were reorganised under the title of the Cwmavon Estate and Works Company (Ltd.) with a single furnace being kept in blast during the year.[22] Iron production seems to have ended in 1882 when the Furness Iron Co. filed a petition to wind up the Cwmavon Estate and Works Company.[23]

By coincidence another of the district's ironworks also had early contacts with the non-ferrous metal industries. This was the Cambrian Ironworks, Maesteg. The land on which the works was built was leased in 1830 or 1831 from the Coegnant Estate by J.H. Allen of Neath who wished to build a zinc smelting works on the site.[24] Allen later sold the lease to the Cambrian Iron & Spelter Company which had been formed by a group of London businessmen in 1837.

The company built two furnaces on the property with the blast being supplied by a 52½in. beam blowing engine purchased from the Neath Abbey Iron Company in 1838.[25] In the mid 1840s the works was owned by a joint stock company called the Llynvi Iron Company with the works being renamed the Llynvi Ironworks. This company was operating four furnaces at the Llynvi Ironworks by the end of the 1840s.[26] The works was put up for sale in 1852 and was taken over by the Llynvi Vale Iron Company.[27] This new company invested some capital in the enterprise for in 1855 the site boasted four blast furnaces, thirty puddling furnaces, two squeezers, two muck rolls and four rolling mills with the necessary power being supplied by ten steam engines.[28] An additional 40in. beam blowing engine was also purchased in 1855 from the Neath Abbey Ironworks.[29] The Llynvi Vale Iron Company considerably expanded their undertakings when in 1862 they purchased the Maesteg Ironworks.[30]

The Maesteg Ironworks had been built in 1828 and in 1830 its single furnace produced 2,430 tons of iron.[31] A second furnace was constructed in 1831 and during the late 1830s the works was listed as being owned by Smith & Co.[32] Ownership of the works had possibly changed by 1844 when it was in the hands of a joint stock company with a capital of £100,000.[33] This venture did not meet with success for the company became bankrupt and was forced to sell the works in 1848. At this time the works consisted of three blast furnaces, two blast engines capable of blowing four furnaces, cast houses, refineries, a foundry for making railway chairs, two cupolas, two winding engines, seventy two coke ovens, dwelling houses and cottages for workmen. The works' property also included 946 acres of mineral ground and it was estimated that the furnaces could produce 15,000 tons of pig iron each year. A valuation of £51,045 was placed on the ironworks and its plant.[34]

No sale appears to have taken place because of a disagreement between the owners. There was no activity at the Maesteg Ironworks until 1853 when the assets of the previous company were purchased by R.P. Lemon & Co.[35] This company seems to have possessed widespread business interests for they are listed as ironmasters, coalminers, grocers and drapers! By 1860 R.P. Lemon & Co. was in some financial difficulties and was trying to form a joint stock company to operate the furnaces. At this time the Maesteg Ironworks was exploiting 1,345 acres of mineral ground and had produced on average 20,000 tons of iron each year for the past seven years.[36] The attempt to float a joint stock company failed and the furnaces remained out of blast until 1862 when the Maesteg Ironworks was bought by the Llynvi Vale Iron Co.

The Maesteg furnaces were immediately reduced to three in number although at no time did the Llynvi Vale Iron Co. keep more than a total of four furnaces in blast at the two site.[37] In 1872 the two Maesteg ironworks were absorbed by a new company initiated by the Brogden family. This was the Llynvi, Tondu and Ogmore Coal and Iron Company.[38] This resulted in some expenditure being directed to the Llynvi Ironworks where in 1872 a new rail mill driven by a horizontal engine was built.[39] During the great strike of 1873 the Brogdens' company settled their dispute at an early stage with a type of productivity agreement. The Brogdens' ironworks were some of the few iron making enterprises to operate at that time which had the effect of attracting experienced men to the workforce from the larger iron companies.[40] The Llynvi, Tondu and Ogmore Coal & Iron Co. did not suffer as badly as others during the great strike but the recession in the South Wales iron trade still forced a closure in 1878.

A new company was formed by the receiver in 1878 and a single furnace was put in blast at Maesteg. By 1881 there were no puddling furnaces or rolling mills operating at the Llynvi Ironworks which in 1872 had thirty three puddling furnaces and four rolling mills at work. The company was unable to produce rails at an economic price and a final closure of the three connected works (Tondu, Maesteg and Llynvi) took place in 1885.[41]

For a short period a third ironworks was operating in Maesteg. This was the Garth Ironworks founded by Malins and Rawlinson in 1847. This works was operated jointly with the Cefn Ironworks which had been built by the same partners in 1839. Two furnaces were originally constructed with a third being added within two years. This venture did not meet with success and little production of iron is recorded from the Garth Ironworks. The ironworks was advertised for sale in 1852 and was described as consisting of three blast furnaces, hot air stoves, coke ovens, trams and other plant. The blast was supplied by a powerful double acting engine which had cost upwards of £6,000. The land was held on a long lease with moderate royalties to be paid.[42] No prospective purchasers came forward and the works was dismantled with the beam blowing engine probably being purchased by the Briton Ferry Ironworks.

References.

1. &
2. E.H. Brooke, *Chronology of the Tinplate Works of Great Britain*, Cardiff, 1944, pp.40-42.
3. Harry Scrivenor, op. cit., p.134.
4. Charles Wilkins, op. cit., p.335.
5. David Mushet, op. cit., pp.414-415.
6. D.B. Barton, op. cit., p.280.
7. Charles Wilkins, op. cit., p.335.
8. Harry Scrivenor, op. cit., p.134.
9. GRO, NAI, D/D. N.A.I., L/10/1-L/10/2, M/55.
   Laurence Ince, *The Neath Abbey Iron Company*, Eindhoven, 1984, p.107 & p.117.
10. *Mining Journal*, June 30th 1849, p.305.
11. &
12. *Mining Journal*, June 22nd 1850, p.294.
13. *Official Descriptive and Illustrated Catalogue of the Great Exhibition*, Vol.1, p.150.
14. *Mining Journal*, 1852, p.70.
15. Robert Hunt, *Mineral Statistics, 1857*.
16. *The International Exhibition of 1862. The Illustrated Catalogue of the Industrial Department*, Vol.1, exhibit 1255.
17. *Mining Journal*, March 22nd 1862, p.195.
18. *The Engineer*, April 21st 1871, p.278.
19. Robert Hunt, *Mineral Statistics, 1872-78*.
20. Robert Hunt, *Mineral Statistics, 1874*.
21. *The Engineer*, November 2nd 1877, p.325.
22. *The Engineer*, January 7th 1881.
    Robert Hunt, *Mineral Statistics, 1881*.
23. *The Engineer*, June 30th 1882, p.479.

24. Charles Wilkins, op. cit., p.353.
25. GRO, NAI, D/D. N.A.I., M/37/4, Drawing for a 52½in. Engine for the Cambrian Iron & Spelter Company, 1838.
26. Charles Wilkins, op. cit., pp.353-355.
27. *Mining Journal*, March 20th 1852, p.132.
28. Charles Wilkins, op. cit., p.355
29. GRO, NAI, D/D. N.A.I. M/148/1.
    Laurence Ince, *The Neath Abbey Iron Company*, Eindhoven, 1984, p.108.
30. *Mining Journal*, September 27th 1862, p.664.
31. Harry Scrivenor, op. cit., p.134.
32. David Mushet, op. cit., pp.414-415.
33. Alan Birch, *The Economic History of the British Iron and Steel Industry, 1784-1879*, 1967, p.204.
34. GRO, Sale Catalogue of the Maesteg Ironworks, October 27th 1848, D/D. XIV 2.
35. GRO, Deeds of Partnership for R.P. Lemon & Co., 1853-59, D/D. Ybt 5/13-25.
36. *Mining Journal*, August 25th 1860, p.576 & p.582.
37. Robert Hunt, *Mineral Statistics, 1862-72*.
38. Leonard S. Higgins, op. cit., p.154.
39. *The Engineer*, April 19th 1872.
40. *The Engineer*, February 21st 1873, p.122 & March 28th 1873, p.196.
41. Leonard S. Higgins, op. cit., p.154.
42. *Mining Journal*, October 16th 1852, p.504.

Plate Thirty Two   The remains of a furnace at the Llynvi Ironworks, Maesteg.

Plate Thirty Three *The blowing engine house of the Llynvi Ironworks, Maesteg. This held two beam blowing engines and has now been converted into a reception hall of a sports centre.*

Plate Thirty Four   John Brogden, founder of the company.

Plate Thirty Five   James Brogden.

Chapter Fourteen.

The Iron Industry of West Wales.

The development of the iron industry in West Wales is closely linked with the discovery of the ability to make iron using anthracite coal. This innovation was pioneered by George Crane of the Ynyscedwyn Ironworks in 1836. Anthracite is a hard stone coal of metallic lustre with a low proportion of volatile matter. It burns at high temperatures without a yellow flame or smoke and is unsuitable for the manufacture of coke. The occurrence of anthracite coals increase as you travel westwards through the South Wales Coalfield. The approximate boundary of bituminous coals and anthracite is usually given as the valley of the River Neath. Although the West Wales area is dominated by anthracite there are semi-anthracite and bituminous coals present in the higher seams.

An early attempt to smelt iron using anthracite was made by the British Iron Company during the years 1824-26.[1] A single furnace was built at Abercrave in the Swansea Valley to use anthracite as the fuel but the enterprise proved unsuccessful. However, a furnace was later used to smelt iron with anthracite at Abercrave. This may well have been the original furnace built by the British Iron Company. The furnace was in blast during the period 1845-61 when the ironworks was owned by T. Walters who was a colliery owner in the Swansea Valley.[2] During the period 1862-65 the Abercrave Ironworks did not produce any iron and after this date there is no mention of the works in any published statistics.

It was to be at the Ynyscedwyn Ironworks in the Swansea Valley that the problems associated with using anthracite for producing iron were solved. The Ynyscedwyn Ironworks possesses a long history and it is the only South Wales ironworks' site to have produced iron using charcoal, bituminous coals and anthracite as fuels. A charcoal fired furnace was in blast at Ynyscedwyn during the eighteenth century when for part of the time it was a component in the iron making empire of the Crowley family. During the 1770s the furnace was leased to Thomas Price of Neath and in 1782 it was in the hands of John Miers.[3]

David Tanner, who had widespread interests in the Welsh iron industry, owned the furnace for a short period before passing it to Richard Parsons, who was his son-in-law. The furnace continued to be charcoal fired and during 1796 produced 800 tons of iron.[4] However, the date of change-over to coke firing is not documented and so the 1796 figure could possibly represent the output of coke iron. The furnace at Ynyscedwyn was still in blast during 1805 but the Parsons' family were forced to close the works in 1817. The ironworks remained unoccupied until the early 1820s when it was purchased by George Crane of Bromsgrove. Certainly by this time it was coke fired. In 1823 the single furnace at Ynyscedwyn produced 1,498 tons of iron with a second furnace being built in 1830.[5] Crane and his works' manager, David Thomas, set about experimenting with the use of local anthracite as a fuel in the furnace. The results of these experiments was the successful production of iron using anthracite with a hot blast and the granting of a patent in 1836.[6] Crane seems to have continued using a proportion of bituminous coals in his furnaces and this may explain the longevity of the enterprise when compared with the many unsuccessful anthracite ironworks in South Wales. A third furnace had been constructed by 1839 and in 1840 the blast was being provided by a 45in. x 8ft. beam blowing engine with a 90in. blowing cylinder.[7] Two further beam blowing engines were constructed at the works with 60in. x 6ft. blowing cylinders supplied by Harvey & Co. of Hayle, Cornwall.[8]

During the early 1850s the works was owned by the Ynyscedwyn Iron Company.[9] In 1856 the number of furnaces on the site were reduced from seven to six although by 1862 only a single furnace was in blast.[10] A complete closure of the works took place in August 1863 but conditions in the iron trade improved which led to a reopening in the early part of 1864.[11] During 1866 the number of furnaces at Ynyscedwyn was reduced to two with another closure taking place in 1869.[12] The Ynyscedwyn ironworks was then purchased by a new company who started iron production in 1870. The principal promoter of this enterprise was T. Challender Hinde with Mr. Creswick, formerly of the Plymouth Ironworks, being appointed as works' engineer.[13] The new company put the two furnaces back into blast and plans were drawn up to build a steel department at the works. The operating company took the title of the Ynyscedwyn Iron, Steel and Coal Company but in November 1876 the venture was wound up with the buildings of the steel department unfinished.[14] The machinery at the works was sold off in February 1878 with the site being abandoned until 1889 when a tinplate works was built on the property.[15]

The great disadvantage with anthracite was that this fuel caked on burning and could not be used in the puddling process. For some of the anthracite ironworks which had no access to bituminous coals this meant the production of only pig or foundry iron. Some of the larger concerns in and around the Swansea Valley which had some access to bituminous coals could use the puddling process. These works often specialised in producing tinplate iron and some operated their own tinplating operation on the same site. The Ystalyfera Ironworks is an example of this type of enterprise for it operated a tinplate works attached to the main iron producing plant. The Ystalyfera Ironworks dates from 1838 when a single anthracite fired furnace was built by Benjamin Treacher and Evan James of Swansea.[16] In the following year the works was sold to Brancker & Co. which consisted of Sir Thomas Brancker, J.J. Hogan of Liverpool and Edward Budd of Swansea.[17] This change of ownership seems to have led to additional investment at Ystalyfera, for a second furnace was under construction in 1839.[18] It is probable that a 24in. Neath Abbey blowing engine was purchased at that time.[19] Furnaces were periodically added to the works and in 1845 a 52½in. beam blowing engine was purchased from the Neath Abbey Iron Company.[20]

James Palmer Budd, the son of Edward Budd, later became general manager and then owner of the Ystalyfera Ironworks. Under his guidance the works was to expand to contain six blast furnaces by 1846 and then to be diversified by the addition of a tinplate works. This grew to consist of twelve mills in 1848 and was said to be the largest tinplate works in the world.[21] Budd also experimented with new iron making techniques. In the middle of the 1840s Budd perfected a system of using heat from waste gases generated in the furnaces to heat the air blast from the blowing engines. Each furnace at Ystalyfera was producing from 50 to 60 tons of iron each week during 1848 and the six furnaces were linked by arches upon which five hot blast stoves were constructed.[22]

The expansion of the works continued with Ystalyfera possessing ten furnaces during the 1850s although in 1854 only seven were in blast.[23] During the 1860s the Ystalyfera Ironworks was able to keep six furnaces in production and in 1872 the property boasted forty two puddling furnaces and sixteen mills.[24] The presence of the puddling furnaces obviously indicates the use of bituminous coals at the works. There was a gradual decline in the fortunes of the Ystalyfera Iron Company from the mid 1870s with only four furnaces in blast in 1877 and the men only working two weeks out of three.[25] The death knell of the works was sounded when Budd retired from the management of the works in 1880 and then withdrew his financial interest in the company in 1883.[26] The Ystalyfera Ironworks closed in 1885 and a later attempt to reopen the venture failed.

Before we leave the Swansea Valley there are several small iron making enterprises to be examined. During the 1820s a small cupola furnace operated at Morriston, owned by a gentleman named Bevan.[27] The furnace was 46ft. high and the blast was provided by a beam blowing engine with a 50in. x 6ft. 3in. blowing cylinder. Unfortunately little is known about this concern. There also appears to have been a small furnace at Millbrook owned by Sir G.B. Morris and it could be that this is the earlier Morriston furnace with a different name. A furnace was also under construction at Pontardawe in 1863.[28] The Pontardawe furnace was owned by J. Lewis & Sons but no statistics of production are available. References to this furnace in the technical press seem to indicate that it was kept out of blast during the 1860s and 1870s.

The Brynamman Ironworks in Carmarthenshire was another example of an ironworks which developed its own tinplate making department. The works was built by Llewellyn Llewellyn who owned several tinplate works in South Wales.[29] This enterprise was named the Amman Iron Company and two anthracite furnaces were built in 1847 with the blast being supplied by a 36in. beam blowing engine purchased from the Neath Abbey Iron Company.[30] In 1859 the ironworks was taken over by G.B. Strick who was Llewellyn's brother-in-law, W.H. Francis, Henry Strick and W. Llewellyn. The mid 1860s saw some expansion at the Brynamman Ironworks with a forge being added in 1865 and a third furnace constructed in 1867. During the period 1869-70 all three furnaces were in blast but in 1871 the furnaces were altered for firing with bituminous coal.[31] In the following year a three mill tinplate works was built at the Brynamman Ironworks. During 1881 the Amman Iron Company was operating ten puddling furnaces but only one mill. Using their own iron for tinning meant that the works survived through the 1880s but finally succumbed to closure in 1891. The tinplate works continued in operation until its final closure in 1897.[32]

An earlier attempt had been made to establish an iron industry in Carmarthenshire based on the bituminous coals of the Llanelli area. Alexander Raby operated a furnace at Llanelli in the late eighteenth century with a second furnace being constructed in around 1801.[33] Raby was an experienced forgemaster who was moving his operations from the Weald to South Wales. In 1805 the Llanelli Ironworks produced 2,267 tons of iron.[34] However, Raby's business career was not to flourish for his industrial enterprises led him into bankruptcy in the second decade of the nineteenth century. Another attempt at making iron with bituminous coal was made at Pembrey. An ironworks with two furnaces was completed in 1824 with the blast for the furnaces being supplied by a 30in. beam blowing engine built by the Neath Abbey Ironworks.[35] Little is known of this venture and it would appear that the works did not prosper and soon closed down.

Further efforts were made to successfully produce iron with anthracite as the fuel at the Gwendraeth and Trimsaran Ironworks. The Gwendraeth Ironworks seems to date from around 1839 when a 24in. high pressure beam blowing engine was purchased from the Neath Abbey Ironworks.[36] The works consisted of three furnaces and was operated by the Watney family. In 1851 at the Great Exhibition, Alfred Watney displayed a specimen of anthracite coal from Gwendraeth, two models of blast furnaces and pig iron which could be used in a foundry or for tinplate or boiler plate.[37] From 1854 onwards only two furnaces are listed as being present at the Gwendraeth Ironworks and until 1860 the owner is listed as T. Watney & Co.[38] During the period 1857-59 no furnaces were in blast at the site but in 1860 a single furnace was in production under the ownership of Daniel Watney.[39]

Two years later three furnaces are again listed as present at the Gwendraeth Ironworks but none were in blast. The furnaces remained out of blast until the listing completely disappears from the statistics in 1871. However, the dimensions of one of the furnaces at Gwendraeth were recorded in the early 1860s.[40] It was 30ft. high, 8ft. across the top, 12ft. across the boshes, 4ft. across the hearth and had a capacity of 1720 cu. ft.

It would appear that the Trimsaran Ironworks dates from 1846 when a 32½in. beam blowing engine was supplied to the works by the Neath Abbey Iron Company.[41] This venture, which consisted of three furnaces, seems to have met with little success for the works had ceased to produce iron by 1850. The Trimsaran property was offered for sale in 1852 when it consisted of two furnaces, collieries and Trimsaran Mansion.[42] The owner of the ironworks in 1854 was listed as Nortole & Co. but no furnaces were in blast.[43] In the following year the property was owned by E.H. Thomas but again no iron was being produced.[44] The Trimsaran property was again offered for sale in 1859 and was advertised as an ironworks with two furnaces, a 120 h.p. blast engine, cast houses, refineries and 750 acres of mineral ground.[45] The Trimsaran Ironworks and associated collieries were purchased by Frederick Harrison but again no furnaces were put into blast and their listing in statistics disappear after 1860.

The expansion of the Welsh iron industry even spread as far as the Pembrokeshire part of the coalfield. The construction of an anthracite ironworks at Kilgetty near Saundersfoot began in 1848, the year after the formation of the operating company which was called the Pembrokeshire Iron and Coal Company.[46] The partners in this company included William Chadwick, W.T. Longbourne and C.R. Vickerman. J.B. Hosgood who had been trained at the Neath Abbey Ironworks was appointed manager. The ironworks consisted of two furnaces with the first furnace being put into blast in 1849. However, the operations of the company was soon disrupted by a row between shareholders which resulted in an action at the Court of Chancery. The outcome of the action was that Chadwick was dismissed as a trustee and the board reconstituted to consist of W.T. Longbourne, C.R. Vickerman, C. Ranken, J. Disney and E. Church.

To add to the problems of the company a gas explosion severely damaged a furnace in 1850 and trade was so bad in 1852 that only a single furnace was in blast. After this time the furnaces were inactive for a considerable time although in 1857 a single furnace was in blast for three months. From 1863 C.R. Vickerman was the sole owner with one furnace in blast during 1864. During that year 2,933 tons of iron were exported from Saundersfoot. In 1866 both furnaces were in blast at various times and one furnace was kept in blast during the period 1867-68. Some iron produced at Kilgetty was sold to other South Wales ironworks for making steel which suggests that haematite was being imported for iron making. There was also a market for Kilgetty iron in the foundry trade and for use in the manufacture of saddlers' ironmongery. After 1868 the furnaces were never seriously put back into blast. A report on the ironworks was drawn up in 1872 which listed the plant and buildings present at Kilgetty.[47] The ironworks consisted of two furnaces, No.1 was 35ft. high and 12ft. in the boshes with No.2 being 53ft. high and 12ft. in the boshes. No.1 was open topped while No.2 was closed with a cup and cone. The blast was supplied by two beam blowing engines, one was a 34in. x 7ft. engine with a 64in. blowing cylinder while the second was a 30in. x 7ft. engine with a 58in. blowing cylinder. Both engines had 16ft. diameter flywheels. The 30in. blowing engine was a conversion from a colliery pumping engine. Also in the same engine house was a 24in. x 5ft. condensing beam engine which could be used for taking materials from the bottom level to mine kilns or for working a forge. The plant and buildings also included a 60ft. blast regulator of 7ft. diameter, hot air stoves, a cast house which was 67ft. by 73ft. with a corrugated iron roof, two cupolas, a reverberatory furnace, a refinery capable of turning out 80 tons of refined metal each week, mine kilns and limekilns. The workshops included smitheries, a fitting shop and lathe room containing an 11in. centre lathe and one other large lathe, a 4ft. circular saw mill, a carpenters' shop with a lathe and a further smithery with four fires blown by a Lloyd's patent fan. The machinery in the workshops was driven by an 11in. high pressure engine.

After several years of inactivity at the Kilgetty Ironworks, the Bonvilles Court Coal and Iron Company Ltd. was set up in 1873 to take over the ironworks and associated collieries. In 1878 the property of this company was in the hands of the receiver who sold it to C.R. Vickerman for £10,000. The ironworks was never worked again and the buildings were dismantled by 1889. Although one furnace was briefly lit in 1873 it is probable that no iron production took place at Kilgetty after 1868.

The story of iron making in West Wales clearly illustrates the unsuccessful nature of the anthracite iron industry in Wales. The output of Welsh anthracite furnaces never achieved the high levels recorded for their American counterparts. In America anthracite furnaces were large and were blown at a very high pressure. Welsh anthracite furnaces were small with a maximum output of no greater than 60 tons of iron each week. These furnaces had to be blown at a higher pressure, sometimes as high as 7 psi, which produced an overall increase in the expense of producing each ton of iron. Also contributing to the general frailty of the Welsh anthracite industry was the inability of many of these ironworks to manufacture wrought iron. It is no wonder that the histories of the Welsh anthracite ironworks are punctuated by numerous changes of ownership, bankruptcies and proceedings in the Chancery Court.

References.

1. Alan Birch, *The Economic History of the British Iron and Steel Industry, 1784-1879*, 1967, p.169.
2. Robert Hunt, *Mineral Statistics, 1854-61*.
3. William Rees, *Industry Before the Industrial Revolution*, Vol.1, Cardiff, 1968, pp.306-308.
4. Harry Scrivenor, *History of the Iron Trade, 1854*, p.96.
5. Harry Scrivenor, op. cit., p.134.
6. D. Morgan Rees, *Mines, Mills and Furnaces*, 1969, p.82.
7. Stationary Steam Engines in Swansea, c. 1840, *Bulletin of the South West Wales Industrial Archaeology Society*, No.34, September, 1983, p.4.
8. D.B. Barton, *The Cornish Beam Engine*, Truro, 1969, p.280.
9. Robert Hunt, *Mineral Statistics, 1854*.
10. Robert Hunt, *Mineral Statistics, 1856-62*.
11. *Mining Journal*, April 25th 1863, p.287 and April 30th 1864, p.315.
12. Robert Hunt, *Mineral Statistics, 1866-69*.
13. *The Engineer*, May 27th 1870, p.340.
14. *The Engineer*, November 24th 1876, p.373.
15. *The Engineer*, January 25th 1878, p.72.
16. D. Morgan Rees, op. cit., p.82.
17. &
18. David Mushet, *Papers on Iron and Steel*, 1840, pp.414-415.
19. GRO, NAI, D/D. N.A.I., M/210/4, Drawings of a 24 inch Engine and Blowing Apparatus for the Ystalyfera Ironworks, 1839-40.
20. GRO, NAI, D/D. N.A.I., M/210/2-M/210/3, Drawings for a $52\frac{1}{2}$ inch Engine for the Ystalyfera Ironworks, 1844-45.
21. E.H. Brooke, *Chronology of the Tinplate Works of Great Britain*, Cardiff, 1944, p.131.
22. James Palmer Budd, On the Advantageous Use of the Gaseous Escape from the Blast Furnaces at Ystalyfera Ironworks, *Report of the British Association for the Advancement of Science*, 1848, pp.75-84.
23. Robert Hunt, *Mineral Statistics, 1854*.
24. Robert Hunt, *Mineral Statistics, 1860-72*.
25. *The Engineer*, June 8th 1877, p.404.
26. D. Morgan Rees, op. cit., p.83.
27. *The Engineer*, February 3rd 1860, p.82.
28. W. Fordyce, *A History of Coal, Coke, Coalfields and Iron Manufacture in Northern England*, 1860, p.156.

29. E.H. Brooke, op. cit., pp.135-136.
30. Laurence Ince, *The Neath Abbey Iron Company*, Eindhoven, 1984, p.108.
31. Robert Hunt, *Mineral Statistics, 1871*.
32. E.H. Brooke, op. cit., pp.135-136.
33. Harry Scrivenor, op. cit., p.98.
34. BRL, B&W, List of Ironworks, 1806.
35. GRO, NAI, D/D. N.A.I., M/97/4, Drawing for a 30in. blowing engine for Guant and Company, Pembrey, 1823. Various other sources give the title of the company as Gaunt and Company or Grant and Company.
36. GRO, NAI, D/D. N.A.I. M/100, Drawing for a 24in. Blowing Engine for the Gwendraeth Ironworks, 1839.
37. *Official Descriptive and Illustrative Catalogue of the Great Exhibition*, Vol.1, 1851, p.147.
38. Robert Hunt, *Mineral Statistics, 1854-59*.
39. Robert Hunt, *Mineral Statistics, 1860*.
40. John Percy, *Metallurgy, Iron and Steel*, 1864, p.559.
41. GRO, NAI, D/D. N.A.I., W/3/1, Inventory of the Neath Abbey Ironworks, 31st April 1846.
42. *Mining Journal*, November 27th 1852, p.569.
43. Robert Hunt, *Mineral Statistics, 1854*.
44. Robert Hunt, *Mineral Statistics, 1855*.
45. *Mining Journal*, August 13th 1859, p.574.
46. M.C.R. Price, *Industrial Saundersfoot*, Llandysul, 1982, pp.140-154.
47. M.C.R. Price, op. cit., pp.221-226.

Plate Thirty Six   The charging platform of the Ynyscedwyn Ironworks pictured in the early 1970s. The part of the site was cleared soon after the photograph was taken.

Plate Thirty Seven   The remains of the unfinished steel department at the Ynyscedwyn Ironworks.

Appendix One.

Pig Iron Production in South Wales 1788-1885.

Year	Tons	Percentage of British Total
1788	12,500	18.3%
1796	34,101	27.3%
1805	73,933	29.5%
1806	78,045	30.2%
1820	154,000	38.5%
1823	182,325	40.0%
1826	223,520	38.4%
1827	272,000	39.4%
1828	279,812	39.8%
1830	277,643	41.0%
1839	453,880	36.3%
1840	505,000	36.2%
1842	317,430	28.9%
1843	457,350	37.6%
1847	706,680	35.3%
1848	631,280	30.1%
1850	700,000	31.0%
1852	666,000	24.6%
1854	750,000	24.4%
1855	840,070	26.1%
1856	877,150	24.5%
1857	970,727	26.5%
1858	886,478	25.7%
1859	985,290	26.6%
1860	969,025	25.3%
1861	886,300	23.9%
1862	893,309	22.6%
1863	847,753	18.8%
1864	937,821	19.7%
1865	845,035	17.6%

Year	Tons	Percentage of British Total
1866	927,454	20.5%
1867	886,284	18.6%
1868	894,255	18.0%
1869	800,972	14.7%
1870	979,193	16.4%
1871	1,045,916	15.8%
1872	981,826	14.6%
1873	817,789	12.5%
1874	714,724	11.9%
1875	541,809	8.5%
1876	756,121	11.5%
1877	710,958	10.8%
1878	741,136	11.6%
1879	669,858	11.2%
1880	889,738	11.5%
1881	910,965	11.2%
1884	851,391	10.9%
1885	792,784	10.7%

Sources for the Statistics.

Harry Scrivenor, *History of the Iron Trade*, 1854, pp.87- 88, pp.95-96, p. 99, pp.134-135, p.295 & p.302.

BRL, B&W, List of Furnaces in Great Britain, 1806 (statistics of production in 1805 given).

A. Birch, *The Economic History of the British Iron and Steel Industry, 1784-1879*, 1967, p.124 & p.130.

The Engineer, February 3rd 1860, p.82.

R. Meade, *The Coal and Iron Industries of the United Kingdom*, 1882, p.610.

David Mushet, *Papers on Iron and Steel*, 1840, pp.414-415.

Official and Descriptive and Illustrated catalogue of the Great Exhibition, 1851, pp.150-159.

Robert Hunt, *Mineral Statistics of the United Kingdom of Great Britain and Ireland, 1855-1882.*

The Journal of the Iron and Steel Institute, 1885, p.567.

The Journal of the Iron and Steel Institute, 1886, p.1027.

Philip Riden, The Output of the British Iron Industry before 1870, *Economic History Review*, 1977, 30, 2nd Series (3), pp.442-459.

Appendix Two.

British Railway Companies Supplied with Rails by the South Wales Iron Industry.

Bishop Auckland and Weardale Railway - Rails supplied by Dowlais Ironworks. Act for railway granted in 1837.

Stockton and Darlington Railway - Railway opened in 1825 with one third of the rails supplied by the Neath Abbey Ironworks. These were cast iron rails.

Bodmin and Wadebridge Railway - Opened in 1834 with rails supplied by the Ebbw Vale Ironworks.

Glasgow, Paisley, Kilmarnock and Ayr Railway - Rails supplied by Nantyglo and Beaufort in 1838 at £11. 7s. 6d. and in 1839 at £10. 18s. 0d. per ton.

Great North of England Railway - Some of the rails supplied by the British Iron Company, Abersychan. Act for railway granted in 1836.

Hull and Selby Railway - Rails supplied by Dowlais, Cyfarthfa and Rhymney Ironworks. Act for railway granted in 1836.

Lancaster and Preston Railway - Rails bought from the Ebbw Vale Ironworks and Beaufort and Nantyglo Ironworks. 4,000 tons of rails were purchased at an average cost of £11 per ton. Railway opened in 1840.

Manchester, Bolton and Bury Canal and Railway Company - Dowlais Ironworks supplied rails in 1835.

London and Birmingham Railway - Rails supplied by several Welsh ironworks. Nantyglo and Beaufort Ironworks contracted for rails in 1835 at £12. 10s. 0d. per ton and also contracted in 1836 for 1,000 tons of rails at £14. 2s. 6d. per ton. They also supplied 1,000 tons of rails in 1837 at £9. 5s. 0d. per ton. The British Iron Company contracted for 75 tons in 1836 at £13 per ton. 1,000 tons were ordered from the Varteg Ironworks in 1835 at £11 per ton. The Dowlais Ironworks supplied 4,150 tons of rails, the orders being received between April 1836 and May 1837. The Plymouth Ironworks contracted for 1,000 tons in 1836 at £13. 5s. 6d. a ton. The Varteg Ironworks received a further order of 1,000 tons in 1836. There is also a possibility that the Rhymney Ironworks supplied rails to this company after these dates.

Great Western Railway - Rails ordered from the Dowlais Ironworks, 1837-47. Ebbw Vale also supplied rails in 1837 and 1838. The British Iron Company, Abersychan supplied rails in 1837-38. A comparatively late order of rails was placed with the Plymouth Ironworks in 1872.

Manchester and Birmingham Railway - Opened in 1840 with rails partly supplied by the Dowlais Ironworks.

North Midland Railway - Rails partly supplied by the Dowlais Ironworks. Acts for the formation of the railway date from 1836.

Sheffield and Rotherham Railway - Rails supplied by Nantyglo and Beaufort Ironworks. Railway opened in 1838.

Brighton, Croydon and Dover Joint Railway - Rails ordered from the Dowlais Ironworks in 1842.

Slamannan Railway - 1,000 tons of rails supplied by the Dowlais Ironworks at £11. 10s. 0d. per ton. Railway opened in 1840.

Ulster Railway - Rails supplied by the Dowlais Ironworks at £12 per ton. Railway opened in 1839.

York and North Midland Railway - Rails supplied by the Cyfarthfa Ironworks. Railway opened 1839-40.

Dover and Eastern Counties Railway - Rails ordered from the Dowlais Ironworks in 1842.

Dublin and Drogheda Railway - 100 tons of rails ordered from the Dowlais Ironworks in 1842.

Eastern Counties Railway - Act granted for railway in 1836. Rails supplied by Cyfarthfa Ironworks.

St. Helens and Runcorn Gap Railway - Rails ordered from Dowlais Ironworks in 1842.

Midland Railway - Rails supplied by the Cyfarthfa Ironworks in the mid 1840s.

Stanhope and Tyne Railway. Rails supplied by the Ebbw Vale Ironworks before 1838.

Great Southern and Western Ireland Railway - Rails ordered from the Dowlais Ironworks in 1845.

Lancashire and Yorkshire Railway - Rails ordered from the Dowlais Ironworks in 1857.

Liverpool and Manchester Railway - Rails partly supplied by the Penydarren Ironworks. Railway opened in 1830.

Durham Railway - Opened in 1830 with rails supplied by the Nantyglo and Beaufort Ironworks.

South Eastern Railway - In the early 1840s rails were obtained from the Rhymney Ironworks, Dowlais Ironworks and the British Iron Company, Abersychan.

Great Northern Railway - At the end of the 1840s rails were obtained from the Nantyglo and Beaufort Ironworks and the Ebbw Vale Ironworks.

Stamford and Essendine Railway - Payments for rails were being made in 1856 to the Rhymney Ironworks.

Preston and Wyre Railway - Rails supplied by the Cyfarthfa Ironworks.

This is not a complete list of rails supplied by the South Wales iron industry to domestic railway companies. However, the scope of the entries does demonstrate the important part played by the industry in the supply of railway iron in the home market. The main sources for the list are:

Frances Whishaw, *The Railways of Great Britain and Ireland*, 1842.

A.H. John, *The Industrial Development of South Wales, 1750-1850*, Cardiff, 1950.

M. Elsas, *Iron in the Making, Dowlais Iron Company Letters, 1782-1860*, 1960, p.xviii.

G.R. Hawke, *Railways and Economic Growth in England and Wales, 1840-1870*, Oxford, 1970, pp.213-245.

Appendix Three.

Some Furnace Dimensions in the South Wales Iron Industry.

1767 - Cyfarthfa furnace described as 50ft. high and 36ft. square.[1]

1793 - The Neath Abbey furnaces had the dimensions of about 60ft. high and 38ft. square although a drawing of 1829 shows them as 53ft. high and 65ft. high.[2]

1831 - A furnace at the Dowlais Ironworks was 48ft. 9in. high and 2ft. 10in. across the hearth. It was able to contain 8,220cu. ft. of material.[3]

1833 - The furnaces at the Clydach Ironworks were described as being 44ft. high and 14ft. across the boshes.[4]

1837 - The Victoria Ironworks was built with four furnaces each 45ft. high, 16ft. across the boshes and 8ft. across the top.[5]

1839 - The Dyffryn furnaces were 40ft. high, 18ft. across the boshes and 9 or 10ft. across at the filling place.[6]

1859 - The six furnaces of the Penydarren Ironworks were 45ft. high and 16ft. across the boshes.[7]

1863 - No.12 furnace at the Dowlais Ironworks was built in this year at a height of 42ft. It was 10ft. 6in. across the top, 18ft. across the boshes, 8ft. across the hearth with a 6,160cu. ft. capacity.[8]

1864 - An anthracite furnace at the Gwendraeth Ironworks was described as being 30ft. high, 8ft. across the top, 12ft. across the boshes and with a 4ft. hearth. The capacity of the furnace was 1,720cu. ft.[9]

1864 - No.3 furnace of the Ebbw Vale Ironworks was 44ft. 6in. high, 9ft. across the top, 17ft. 6in. across the boshes, 7ft. 6in. hearth with a capacity of 5,890cu. ft.[10]

1864 - No.17 furnace of the Ebbw Vale Iron Company was 44ft. 6in. high, 10ft. across the top, 20ft. across the boshes, 8ft. hearth with a capacity of 8,000cu. ft.[11]

1867 - The furnace at the Cwm Celyn Ironworks was 60ft. high and 20ft. across the boshes.[12]

1869 - The furnaces at Dyffryn and Plymouth were from 40 to 50ft. high and the largest measurement across the boshes was 16ft.[13]

1869 - The three furnaces at the Llwydcoed Ironworks were 42ft. high and 18ft. across the boshes.[14]

1869 - One furnace at Abernant was 40ft. high and 19ft. across the boshes. A newly built furnace was 52ft. high and 18ft. across the boshes.[15]

1869 - The six furnaces at Abersychan were 48ft. high and 17 to 18ft. across the boshes. The furnaces each produced 200 tons of iron each week.[16]

1869 - The furnaces at Tredegar were 45ft. high and 16 to 17ft. across the boshes.[17]

1874 - The Cyfarthfa furnaces were described as being 52ft. high and 14½ to 16ft. across the boshes.[18]

1874 - A new furnace at the Ivor Ironworks was 55ft. high and 18ft. across the boshes. This furnace was capable of producing 300 tons of iron weekly.[19]

1880 - The Stuart Iron, Steel and Tin Plate Company remodelled their furnaces at Hirwaun so that they were 54ft. high and 16ft. across the boshes. The furnaces were blown through six tuyères.[20]

1880 - A new furnace built at Treforest following the Middlesbrough pattern was 70ft. high, 17ft. across the boshes with a 7ft. hearth. It produced 80 tons of iron daily.[21]

1883 - A new furnace was built at the Victoria Ironworks. It was 60ft. high and blown through seven tuyères. It could produce 700 tons of iron per week in combination with another furnace.[22]

References.

1. D.M. Rees, *Mines, Mills and Furnaces*, 1969, p.72.
2. Laurence Ince, *The Neath Abbey Iron Company*, Eindhoven 1984, p.91.
3. John Percy, *Metallurgy: Iron and Steel*, 1864, p.651.
4. John Lloyd, *The Early History of the Old South Wales Iron Works*, 1906 p.122.
5. GWRO, Cwmbran, Sale Particulars of the Victoria Ironworks, 1849, D.454. 516 (Ebbw Vale Collection).
6. Harry Scrivenor, *History of the Iron Trade*, 1854, p.251.
7. GRO, Dowlais Iron Company Papers, D/D/G, Section E, Box 8, Valuation of Penydarren Ironworks, March 1859.
8. Percy, op. cit., p.561.
9. Percy, op. cit., p.559.
10. Percy, op. cit., p.559.
11. Percy, op. cit., p.561.
12. GWRO., Cwmbran, Sale Document of Cwm Celyn, Blaina and Coalbrookvale Ironworks, 5th June 1867, D1089.2
13. *Mining Journal*, October 2nd 1869, pp.742-743.
14. &
15. *Mining Journal*, October 6th 1869, p.762.
16. *Mining Journal*, October 23rd 1869, p.802.
17. *Mining Journal*, November 20th 1869, p.882.
18. *Proceedings of the Institution of Mechanical Engineers*, 1874, p.239.
19. *Proceedings of the Institution of Mechanical Engineers*, 1874, pp.239-241.
20. *The Engineer*, April 23rd 1880, p.310.
21. *The Engineer*, October 15th 1880, p.293.
22. *The Engineer*, July 20th 1883, p.57.

Appendix Four.

The South Wales Iron Industry in 1796.

Works	Furnaces	Production (tons)
Clydach	1	1,625
Blaendare	1	1,500
Blaenavon	3	4,318
Sirhowy	1	1,930
Beaufort	1	1,660
Ebbw Vale	1	397
Hirwaun	1	1,050
Melinycwrt	1	503
Ynyscedwyn	1	800
Caerphilly	1	695
Cyfarthfa	3	7,204
Plymouth	1	2,200
Penydarren	2	4,100
Dowlais	3	2,800
Llanelly	1	1,560
Neath Abbey	2	1,759

Source: Harry Scrivenor, *History of the Iron Trade*, **1854, p.96.**

Appendix Five.

The South Wales Iron Industry in 1823.

Works	Furnaces	Production (tons)
Aberdare	3	}
Abernant	3	5,676
Blaenavon	5	16,882
Beaufort	3	5,243
Coalbrookvale	1	2,704
Cyfarthfa	8	24,200
Clydach	2	5,200
Dowlais	8	22,287
Hirwaun	2	4,160
Nantyglo	5	17,750
Pentyrch	1	1,235
Plymouth	3	6,387
Penydarren	5	15,547
Rhymney	3	5,500
Pontypool	3	3,173
Sirhowy & Ebbw Vale	6	20,425
Tredegar	5	16,385
Varteg	2	6,513
Cwmavon	1	1,560
Ynyscedwyn	1	1,498
Neath Abbey	2	--

Source: Harry Scrivenor, *History of the Iron Trade***, 1854, p.134.**

Appendix Six.

The South Wales Iron Industry in 1839.

Works	Furnaces in blast	not in blast	building
Landore	1	-	-
Ynyscedwyn	3	-	-
Ystalyfera	1	-	1
Neath Abbey	1	1	-
Venallt	-	-	2
Maesteg	2	-	-
Cambrian	-	-	4
Tondu	-	-	?
Cefn Cwsc	-	-	2
Cwmavon	2	-	-
Oakwood	-	2	-
Gadlys	1	-	-
Hirwaun	4	-	-
Aberdare & Abernant	6	-	-
Pentyrch	1	1	-
Cyfarthfa	7	-	-
Ynysfach	2	-	2
Plymouth	4	-	-
Dyffryn	3	-	1
Penydarren	6	-	-
Dowlais	14	-	4
Rhymney & Bute	6	-	2
Tredegar	5	-	-
Sirhowy	4	-	-
Ebbw Vale	3	-	1
Beaufort	6	-	-
Victoria	2	-	2
Nantyglo	8	-	-
Coalbrookvale	2	-	1
Blaina	2	-	-
Cwmcelyn	-	-	4

Works	Furnaces in blast	not in blast	building
Llanelly	4	-	-
Blaenavon	5	-	2
Varteg	5	-	-
Golynos	2	-	-
Abersychan	4	2	-
Pentwyn	2	1	-
Pontypool	3	-	1

Source: David Mushet, *Papers on Iron and Steel*, 1840, pp.414-415.

Appendix Seven.

The South Wales Iron Industry in 1861.

Works	Total Furnaces	Furnaces in Blast
Abercrave	1	1
Ynyscedwyn	6	2
Brynamman	2	1
Gwendraeth	2	1
Kilgetty	2	0
Aberaman	3	3
Aberdare & Abernant	6	5
Briton Ferry	2	2
Cwmavon	5	2
Cyfarthfa	7	7
Dowlais	17	15
Dyffryn	5	5
Gadlys	4	4
Llynvi Vale	4	3
Oakwood	2	1
Pentyrch	2	1
Penydarren	7	0
Plymouth	5	5
Pontypridd	3	0
Tondu	2	2
Ynysfach	4	4
Beaufort	7	6
Clydach	4	3
Hirwaun	4	0
Onllwyn	2	1
Abersychan	6	4
Blaenavon	6	5
Blaina, Cwmcelyn & Coalbrookvale	6	6*

Works	Total Furnaces	Furnaces in Blast
Cwmbran	1	1
Ebbw Vale	4	3
Nantyglo	12	12
Pentwyn	3	0
Pontypool	4	4
Rhymney & Bute	9	6
Sirhowy	5	3
Tredegar	9	7
Varteg & Golynos	5	0
Victoria	4	3

* For part of year only.

Source: Robert Hunt, *Mineral Statistics, 1861.*

Appendix Eight.

The South Wales Iron Industry in 1881.

Works	Total Furnaces	Furnaces in Blast
Ystalyfera	11	2½+
Brynamman	3	2*
Aberdare & Abernant	5	0
Briton Ferry	2	1*
Cwmavon & Oakwood	2	1
Cyfarthfa & Ynysfach	10	6
Dowlais	16	13
Llynvi	7	1
Gadlys	4	0
Pentyrch	3	1
Plymouth & Penydarren	17	0
Treforest	3	2
Tondu	2	2
Hirwaun	4	0
Abersychan	6	3½+
Pontypool	4	2
Sirhowy	4	3
Ebbw Vale	4	4
Victoria	1	1
Blaenavon	8	5
Cwmbran	2	2
Nantyglo	2	0
Coalbrookvale	1	0
Blaina	3	2
Rhymney	9	7½+
Tredegar	8	5

* = part of year only, + = in blast for six months.

Source: Robert Hunt, *Mineral Statistics, 1881.*

Appendix Nine.

Rolling Mills and Puddling Furnaces in the South Wales Iron Industry, 1871.

Works	Mills	Puddling Furnaces
Brynamman	3	9
Margam	6	-
Clydach	1	12
Gadlys	2	15
Llynvi	4	33
Abernant & Llwydcoed	5	55
Aberaman	0	17
Pentyrch & Melingriffith	12	17
Penydarren	0	13
Treforest	5	6
Briton Ferry	4	44
Cyfarthfa	6	72
Dowlais	14	150
Plymouth & Dyffryn	7	46
Cwmavon	4	50
Ystalyfera	16	42
Tondu	4	23
Ebbw Vale Co.'s Works	12	161
Blaina	4	37
Nantyglo	4	67
Blaenavon	8	117
Pontnewynydd	3	30
Rhymney	7	92
Tredegar	5	80
Oakfields	2	23
Cwmbran	3	20
Llanelly	1	10

Source: Robert Hunt, *Mineral Statistics, 1871.*

Appendix Ten.

Rolling Mills and Puddling Furnaces in the South Wales Iron Industry, 1881.

Works	Mills	Puddling Furnaces
Brynamman	1	10
Llynvi	4	34
Pentyrch	4	7
Briton Ferry	4	42
Cyfarthfa	5	81
Dowlais	15	71
Ystalyfera	16	42
Pontardawe	6	9
Tondu	3	23
College	3	12
Ebbw Vale	18	64
Pontypool	4	20
Blaenavon	3	0
Rhymney	6	64
Tredegar	5	72
Oakfields	2	15
Cwmbran	4	23

Source: Robert Hunt, *Mineral Statistics, 1881*

Bibliography.

Manuscript Sources

Birmingham Reference Library: Boulton & Watt Collection, lists of ironworks, letters, diaries, agreements and engine drawings.
Cardiff Central Library: Sale catalogue of the Aberdare Iron Company, June 11th 1846.
Glamorgan Record Office: Cardiff and Swansea; Neath Abbey Ironworks Collection.
Sale catalogue of the Maesteg Ironworks, October 27th 1848.
Deeds of partnership for R.P. Lemon & Co., 1853-59.
Dowlais Iron Company Collection.
Sale catalogue of Plymouth Collieries and Ironworks, August 16th 1882.
Penllyn Castle Papers.
Gwent Record Office, Cwmbran: Ebbw Vale Collection.
Sale catalogue of the Golynos Ironworks, December 20th 1867.
Sale catalogue of Cwm Celyn, Blaina and Coalbrookvale Ironworks, June 5th 1867.
Kidderminster Public Library: Homfray notebook.
National Library of Wales, Aberystwyth: Homfray Accounts and Papers.
Maybery Papers.

Contemporary Printed Material.

Annales Des Mines.
The Cambrian.
The Engineer.
Chris Evans and G.G.L. Hayes (Eds.), *The Letterbook of Richard Crawshay, 1788-1797*, Cardiff, 1990.
W. Fordyce, *A History of Coal, Coke, Coalfields and Iron Manufacture in Northern England*, 1860.
Samuel Griffiths, *Guide to the Iron Trade of Great Britain*, 1873.
Robert Hunt, *Mineral Statistics of the United Kingdom of Great Britain and Ireland.*
The International Exhibition of 1862. The Illustrated Catalogue of the Industrial Department.
Iron and Coal Trades Review.
Journal of the Iron and Steel Institute.
Frederick Kohn, *Iron and Steel Manufacture*, 1869.
R. Meade, *Coal and Iron Industries of the United Kingdom*, 1882.
Mining Journal.
David Mushet, *Papers on Iron and Steel*, 1840.

Official Descriptive and Illustrated Catalogue of the Great Exhibition, 1851.
John Percy, *Metallurgy: Iron and Steel*, 1864.
Proceedings of the Institution of Mechanical Engineers.
Reports of the British Association for the Advancement of Science.
Harry Scrivenor, *History of the Iron Trade*, 1854.
Svedenstierna's Tour of Great Britain, 1802-03, Newton Abbot, 1973.
William Truran, *The Iron Manufacture of Great Britain*, 1855 & 1863 editions.

Later Printed Material.

John P. Addis, *The Crawshay Dynasty*, Cardiff, 1957.
T.S. Ashton, *Iron and Steel in the Industrial Revolution*, 1963.
M. Atkinson & C. Baber, *The Growth and Decline of the South Wales Iron Industry 1760-1880*, Cardiff, 1987.
Michael R. Bailey, Robert Stephenson and Company, 1823-1829, *Transactions of the Newcomen Society*, Vol.50, 1978-79.
D.B. Barton, *The Cornish Beam Engine*, Truro, 1969.
A.R. Bennett, *The Chronicles of Boulton's Siding*, Newton Abbot, 1971.
A. Birch, *The Economic History of the British Iron and Steel Industry, 1784-1879*, 1967.
Blaenavon Ironworks, Ironworks of Torfaen, No.1, Torfaen Museum Trust, (ND).
E.H. Brooke, *Chronology of the Tinplate Works of Great Britain*, Cardiff, 1944.
Duncan Burn, *The Economic History of Steel Making, 1867-1939*, Cambridge, 1961.
A Catalogue of the Civil and Mechanical Engineering Designs (1741-1792) of John Smeaton, 1950.
Edgar L. Chappel, *Historic Melingriffith: An Account of the Pentyrch Iron Works and Melingriffith Tinplate Works*, Cardiff, 1940.
Arthur Clark, *The Story of Monmouthshire*, Vol.2, Monmouth, 1979.
Kim Colebrook, A History of the British Ironworks, Abersychan, *Gwent Local History*, Vol.54, Spring 1983, pp.6-29.
S.M. & M.V. Cooksley, Watermills and Water-powered Works on the River Stour, Worcestershire and Staffordshire, Part 5, The Smestow Brook, *Wind and Water Mills*, No.2, 1981
M.V. Cooksley, Watermills and Water-powered Works on the River Stour, Part 2, Wolverley and Kinver, *Wind and Water Mills*, Vol.5, 1984.
John Davies, *Cardiff and the Marquesses of Bute*, Cardiff, 1981.
Tom Grey Davies, *Blaenavon and Sydney Gilchrist Thomas*, 1978.
Dictionary of Welsh Biography, 1959.
M. Elsas (Ed.), *Iron in the Making; Dowlais Iron Company Letters, 1782-1860*, Cardiff, 1960.
M.W. Flinn, *Men of Iron - The Crowleys in the Early Iron Industry*, Edinburgh, 1962.

A.J. Flint, 'Neither a Borrower ....', Sir Robert Price, Bart., M.P., *Glamorgan Historian*, Vol.11, Cowbridge, 1971.

Dean Forester, Mr. Keeling Buys a Locomotive, *The Industrial Railway Record*, Vol.1.

W.K.V. Gale, *The British Iron and Steel Industry*, Newton Abbot, 1967.

Harry Green, Cwmgwrach Iron and Resolven Coal, *Neath Antiquarian Society Transactions*, 1977.

Harry Green, Penrhiwtyn Ironworks and Eaglesbush Coal, *Neath Antiquarian Society Transactions*, 1978.

Harry Green, Melinycwrt Furnace: Earth, Air, Fire and Water, *Neath Antiquarian Society Transactions*, 1980-81.

H.W. Gwilliam, Mills and Forges on the Wannerton Brook, *Wind and Water Mills*, No.2, 1981.

G.R. Hawke, *Railways and Economic Growth in England and Wales, 1840-1870*, Oxford, 1970.

W.O. Henderson, *Britain and Industrial Europe, 1750-1870*, Leicester, 1965.

Leonard S. Higgins, John Brogden and Sons, Industrial Pioneers in Mid Glamorgan, *Glamorgan Historian*, Vol.10, Cowbridge, 1974.

Stephen Hughes, *The Brecon Forest Tramroads*, Aberystwyth, 1990.

E.W. Hulme, Statistical History of the Iron Trade, 1717-50, *Transactions of the Newcomen Society*, Vol.9, 1928-29.

Laurence Ince, The Beam Blowing Engines of the Neath Abbey Iron Company, *Journal of the Historical Metallurgy Society*, Vol.17, No.1, 1983.

Laurence Ince, *The Neath Abbey Iron Company*, Eindhoven, 1984.

Laurence Ince, Richard Trevithick's Patent Steam Engine, *Stationary Power*, Vol.1, 1984.

Laurence Ince, Water Power and Cylinder Blowing in Early South Wales Coke Ironworks, *Historical Metallurgy*, Vol.23, No.2, 1989.

Laurence Ince, *The Knight Family and the British Iron Industry*, Solihull, 1991.

A.H. John, *The Industrial Development of South Wales, 1750-1850*, Cardiff, 1950.

Edgar Jones, *A History of GKN, Vol.1, Innovation and Enterprise, 1759-1918*, 1987.

John van Laun, *The Clydach Gorge: I.A. Trails in a North Gwent Valley*, 1979.

M.J.T. Lewis, Steam on the Penydarren, *Industrial Railway Record*, No.59, 1975.

John Lloyd, *The Early History of the Old South Wales Iron Works 1760-1840*, 1906.

James W. Lowe, *British Steam Locomotive Builders*, Cambridge, 1975.

R.A. Mott, *Henry Cort: The Great Finer*, 1983.

John A. Owen, Chronological Date Sequence of Events for the Dowlais Ironworks, *Merthyr Historian*, Vol.1, 1976.

H.W. Paar and D.G. Tucker, The Old Wireworks and Ironworks of the Angidy Valley of Tintern, Gwent, *Journal of the Historical Metallurgy Society*, Vol.9, No.1, 1975.

R. Ivor Parry, Aberdare and the Industrial Revolution, *Glamorgan Historian*, Vol.4, Cowbridge, 1967.

W.H. Pascoe, *The History of the Cornish Copper Company*, Redruth.
John Pickin, Excavations at Abbey Tintern Furnace, *Journal of the Historical Metallurgy Society*, Vol.16, No.1, 1982.
M.C.R. Price, *Industrial Saundersfoot*, Llandysul, 1982.
Arthur Raistrick, *Quakers in Science and Industry*, Newton Abbot, 1968.
D.M. Rees, *Mines, Mills and Furnaces*, 1969.
D.M. Rees, *The Industrial Archaeology of Wales*, Newton Abbot, 1975.
William Rees, *Industry Before the Industrial Revolution*, Cardiff, 1968.
P.J. Riden, The Output of the British Iron Industry before 1870, *Economic History Review*, 1977, 30, 2nd Series (3).
C.W. Roberts, *A Legacy from Victorian Enterprise, the Briton Ferry Ironworks and Daughter Companies*, Gloucester, 1983.
H.R. Schubert, *The History of the British Iron and Steel Industry, 450-1775*, 1957.
Stationary Steam Engines in Swansea (c1840), *Bulletin of the South West Wales Industrial Archaeology Society, No.34*, September 1983.
W.W. Tasker, *Railways in the Sirhowy Valley*, Blandford, 1978.
Margaret S. Taylor, *The Crawshays of Cyfarthfa Castle*, 1967.
Margaret S. Taylor, The Penydarren Ironworks 1784-1859, *Glamorgan Historian*, Vol.3, Cowbridge, 1966.
Margaret S. Taylor, The Plymouth Ironworks, *Glamorgan Historian*, Vol.5, Cowbridge, 1968.
Hugh Torrens, *The Evolution of a Family Firm: Stothert and Pitt of Bath*, 1978.
Barrie Trinder, *The Industrial Revolution in Shropshire*, Chichester, 1973.
Victoria County History of Staffordshire.
Charles Wilkins, *The History of the Iron, Steel, Tinplate and Other Trades of Wales*, Merthyr Tydfil, 1903.

Index

A

Aberaman Iron Company	41
Aberaman Ironworks	41
Abercarn	33
Aberdare Iron Company	4, 10, 36 - 39, 41 - 42, 55, 59, 94, 105
Aberdare Ironworks	2, 35
Abergavenny, Earl of	121
Abernant Ironworks	12, 34, 36 - 37, 80 - 81, 93
Abersychan Ironworks	106, 111 - 113
Addenbrooke, Edward	74
Ambrose, John	137
Amman Iron Company	163
Ashwell, James	121
Atkinson, Thomas	108 - 109

B

Bacon, Anthony	2, 33, 53, 60, 76
Bacon, Thomas	33 - 34, 53
Bailey, Crawshay	40, 124, 129 - 130, 134, 137
Bailey, Joseph	62, 130
Banwen Ironworks	94
Barrow, William	21, 108 - 109
Beaufort Ironworks	1, 11, 40, 129 - 130, 132, 173 - 174
Bedford, John	146
Bedford, Thomas	146
Bevan, G.E. & Co	124
Bevan, William Hibbs	129
Biddulph, John	151
Birch, James	36, 80
Blackpool	28
Blaenavon Coal and Iron Company	121
Blaenavon Iron and Steel Company Limited	6, 123
Blaenavon Ironworks	121 - 123, 125, 130
Blaendare Ironworks	113
Blaina Iron and Coal Co	132
Blaina Iron Company	6, 131
Blaina Ironworks	6, 131 - 133
Blakemore, Richard	145
Blakeway, Edward	47, 53
Bonvilles Court Coal and Iron Company Limited	165
Booker, John Partridge	145
Booker, T.W.	145 - 146
Booker, Thomas W. and Company Limited	146
Boulton & Watt	7, 11, 13, 22, 34, 36, 57 - 58, 65 - 66, 79 - 82, 91 - 92, 109, 113, 121, 130, 133, 135 - 137
Boulton, Isaac Watt	35
Bowzer, Francis William	34, 60
Brecon	2, 29, 33, 96, 133 - 134, 137
British Iron Company	111, 161, 173 - 174
Briton Ferry Ironworks	22 - 23, 94 - 96, 154
Broadwaters Middle Forge	73 - 74
Broadwaters Upper Forge	74

Brogden, Alexander 148
Brogden, Henry 148
Brogden, John & Sons 148
Brownrigg, William 60, 76
Brynamman Ironworks 163
Brynna Ironworks 148
Budd, Edward 162
Budd, James Palmer 13, 162, 166
Bute Ironworks 138
Bute, Marquis of 35, 41, 138

C

Caerphilly . . . . .27 - 28, 145, 177
Calcutts Ironworks . . . . 75 - 76
Carmarthen Ironworks 28
Caswell, Jeremiah 74
Cefn Cribwr Ironworks 146
Coalbrookdale Ironworks 1, 92
Cockshutt, James 60
Coity 122
Cooke, Thomas 133
Copperhouse Foundry 49, 147
Cort, Henry . . . . 19 - 20, 23, 67, 78, 82
Cossham, Handel 35
Cowles, Joseph 47
Cracroft, Charles 105
Crane, George 161
Crawshay, Francis 35, 41
Crawshay, Richard . . . . .19, 23, 49, 60 - 61, 67, 78, 133, 137
Crawshay, Robert 4, 64
Crawshay, William . . . . 23, 34, 39, 62 - 63
Crocker, Philip 105
Cruttwell, Thomas Macauley 131
Cunningham, Richard 137
Cwm Celyn and Blaina Iron Company 131
Cwm Celyn Ironworks . . . . 13, 131 - 132, 175
Cwmavon Estate and Works Company (Limited) 152
Cwmavon Ironworks . . . . 3, 151 - 152
Cwmbran Ironworks . . . . .123 - 124
Cwmdwyfran . . . . 28 - 29

D

Daniel, Thomas 29
Darby, Abraham . . . . .106 - 107
Davey, Joseph and George 95
Davies, Edward 93
Dickenson, Henry 106
Dimmach and Thompson 113
Dowlais Ironworks . . . . 1 - 4, 8, 11, 22 - 23, 47 - 52, 57, 64 - 65, 146, 173 - 175
Dyffryn Ironworks 54, 57

E

Ebbw Vale Ironworks . . . . .12 - 13, 80, 105 - 109, 112, 173 - 175
Evans, David 137
Evans, Francis 53
Evans, Herbert 91
Evans, James 95

F

Fareham Ironworks ... 19
Forest Iron and Steel Company (Limited) ... 41
Forman, Henry ... 57, 77
Forman, Richard ... 57, 77 - 78, 82
Forman, Thomas ... 36
Forman, William ... 36, 57 - 58, 77, 81, 135, 138
Fothergill, Hankey and Bateman ... 37, 55
Fothergill, Hankey and Lewis ... 37
Fothergill, Richard ... 6, 36 - 37, 39, 57, 59, 81, 107, 109, 135
Fothergill, Rowland ... 37, 136
Fothergill, Thomas ... 36
Fox, Alfred ... 92
Fox, Edward ... 91
Fox, George Croker ... 91
Fox, Robert Were ... 91
Fox, Thomas ... 91
Francis, W.H. ... 163
Frere, Edward ... 133

G

Gadlys Coal and Iron Company Limited ... 40
Gadlys Ironworks ... 6, 40
Garnddyrys ... 121 - 122
Garth Ironworks ... 4, 95, 147, 154
George, Watkin ... 60, 62, 113, 137
Glamorgan Iron and Coal Company ... 147 - 148
Glover, Samuel ... 33, 36
Golynos Ironworks ... 112, 124, 126
Gothersley Slitting Mill ... 73
Gould, John ... 91
Governor and Company of Copper Miners ... 151 - 152
Gregory, W. ... 94
Guest, John ... 47 - 48, 50, 53
Guest, Josiah John ... 48, 50
Guest, Lady Charlotte ... 50
Guest, Sarah ... 53
Guest, Thomas Revel ... 48
Gwendraeth Ironworks ... 10, 164, 167, 175

H

Hall, Benjamin ... 62, 137
Hall, Joseph ... 21
Hanbury, John ... 28 - 29
Harford, James ... 27, 105, 109
Harford, John ... 27
Harford, Samuel ... 27, 105
Harford, Truman ... 28
Harris, Thomas ... 47
Harrison, Frederick ... 164
Hazeldine's Foundry ... 38
Henty, James ... 94
Hill, Anthony ... 54 - 55
Hill, John ... 54 - 55
Hill, Richard ... 53 - 54
Hill, Thomas ... 121, 125, 130

Hinde, Thomas Challender	35
Hirwaun Ironworks	2 - 3, 29, 33 - 35, 42, 80
Hodgett, John	36, 74
Hogan, J.J.	162
Homfray, Francis	19, 57, 60, 73 - 77
Homfray, Jeremiah	14, 34, 36, 57, 75, 77, 79 - 82, 105
Homfray, Jeston	74 - 75
Homfray, Lorenzo	81
Homfray, Samuel	20, 23, 36, 57 - 58, 78 - 82, 130, 135
Homfray, Samuel George	81
Homfray, Thomas	57, 75, 77
Homfray, Watkin	81
Hopkins, Samuel	121, 130
Hopkins, Thomas	121
Howell, John	93
Hudson, Bolton	108
Hyde Mill	74, 78

I

Ivor Ironworks	10, 49, 52, 176

J

James, Evan	162
Jayne, John	135
Jenkins, Richard	47
Jenkins, Thomas	95
Jevons and Wood	94
Johnson, Thomas	138
Jones, George	131
Jones, Henry	93
Jones, Hugh	27
Jones, John	47, 134
Jordan, Charles	136

K

Kendall, Edward	129
Kendall, Henry	129
Kendall, Jonathan	129
Kennard, Robert	122
Kidwelly	28
Kilgetty Ironworks	165
King, William	33
Knowles, Sir Francis	147

L

Latham, Joseph	129
Lean, Joel	95
Leigh, Capel Hanbury	113, 133 - 134
Lethbridge, Sir Thomas Buckler	110
Lettsom, Samuel Fothergill	28, 151
Levick, Frederick	13, 131
Lewis, Thomas	28, 47, 145
Lewis, William	47 - 48, 145
Lightmoor Ironworks	75
Llanelli Ironworks	164
Llanelly	8, 27, 133 - 135, 177, 180, 184
Llewellyn, Llewellyn	163
Llewellyn, W.	94, 163

Llwydcoed Ironworks 35, 37, 175
Llynvi Ironworks . . . . 152 - 154
Llynvi Vale Iron Company 153
Longbourne, W.T. 165
Lower Broadwaters Forge 74

M
Machen 27
Maesteg Ironworks 153, 155
Malins and Rawlinson 147, 154
Maybery, John 2, 27, 33
Maybery, Mary 33
Maybery, Thomas 29
Melingriffith Tinplate Works 8, 145, 148
Melinycwrt 28, 30, 177
Menelaus, William 23, 41, 51, 65
Miers, John and Company 28, 54
Miers, John Nathaniel 28, 54
Miers, Nathaniel 28, 54
Millbrook 163
Monkhouse, Matthew 81, 109, 135
Monmouth . . . . 27, 29, 47, 58, 80 - 81, 105, 110, 112, 114, 137, 139 - 140, 145, 148
Monmouthshire Iron and Coal Company 110
Morgan, George Rowland 40
Morgan, John 29
Morgan, Robert 28
Morgan, Sir Charles Gould 81
Morgan, Thomas 27
Morgan, William 124
Morris, Morgan and Company 29

N
Nantyglo and Blaina Ironworks Company 6
Nantyglo Ironworks . . . . 21, 40, 129 - 130, 135, 140, 173
Neath Abbey Iron Company . 2, 11 - 14, 22 - 23, 34, 37 - 40, 42 - 43, 49, 56, 58 - 59, 63, 65 - 67, 91 - 94
  . . . 96, 105, 109 - 114, 121, 125, 130, 134 - 138, 140 - 141, 147, 151 - 152, 154 - 155, 162 - 164, 167, 176
Neath Abbey Ironworks . . . . 3, 5, 12, 23, 42, 63, 91 - 96, 113, 122, 153, 164 - 165, 167, 173
New British Iron Company 111

O
Oakwood Iron and Coal Company 151
Oliver, Lionel 34
Oliver, Simon 34
Onllwyn Iron and Coal Company 94
Onllwyn Ironworks 94, 96
Overton, George 3, 34

P
Parsons, Richard 161
Parsons, William 94
Partridge, John . . . . 27 - 28, 105, 145
Patent Nut and Bolt Company 124
Paul, Sir John Dean 152
Pembrey 164, 167
Pembrokeshire Iron and Coal Company 165
Penrhiwtyn Ironworks 96
Pentwyn Ironworks 106, 112, 124
Pentyrch Ironworks . . . . 6, 145 - 146, 148

Pentyrch Steel and Tinplate Company ... 146
Penydarren Ironworks ... 3, 6, 11, 14, 20, 36, 57 - 60, 66, 77, 79 - 80, 82, 133, 135, 174 - 176
Perran Foundry ... 12, 50, 56, 107
Perran Wharf Foundry ... 91 - 92
Perritt, William ... 53
Pitt, Robert ... 131
Plymouth Ironworks ... 1, 4 - 5, 11, 23, 37, 49, 53 - 57, 65 - 66, 162, 173
Pontardawe ... 163, 185
Pontnewynydd Ironworks ... 124, 148
Pontypool Iron Company ... 113
Pontypool Ironworks ... 62, 107, 112 - 113
Porthcawl Iron and Coal Company ... 147
Powell Duffryn Steam Coal Company ... 41
Powell, John Jnr. ... 133
Powell, Launcelot ... 134
Pratt, Benjamin ... 121
Pratt, James ... 27
Pratt, Samuel ... 27
Price, Henry Habberly ... 92
Price, Joseph Tregelles ... 92 - 93
Price, Nicholas ... 145
Price, Peter ... 91 - 92
Price, Sir Robert ... 147, 149
Price, Thomas ... 47, 161
Puddling ... 20, 37, 59, 184 - 185
Pytt, Rowland ... 28

R

Raby, Alexander ... 91, 164
Reynolds, John ... 151
Reynolds, Richard ... 29
Rhymney Iron Company Limited ... 138
Rhymney Ironworks ... 4, 7, 137 - 139, 173 - 174
Roberts, Evan ... 95
Roberts, M.G. ... 96
Robinson, Joseph ... 106
Rogers, Samuel ... 21
Rowles, Henry ... 138
Russell, John ... 131

S

Scale, George ... 36
Scale, Henry ... 95
Scale, John ... 36, 133
Scale, Mary ... 37
Scale, Rebecca ... 36
Sealy, John ... 108
Shears, James Henry ... 111
Sims, D.T. ... 96
Sims, William Unwin ... 121
Sirhowy Ironworks ... 1, 105 - 106, 108 - 109, 114, 135
Small, Robert ... 111
Smeaton, John ... 11, 13, 139
Smith, Leonard ... 151
Soho Foundry ... 55, 137
Spence and Company ... 133

Stevens, William 60
Stockton and Darlington Railway 3, 173
Stourton Mill 74
Strick, Henry 163
Struttle, Amos 54
Stuart Ironworks 35
Swindon Forge 75

T
Tanner, Benjamin 29
Tanner, David 29, 60, 77, 113, 161
Tappenden, Francis 36
Tappenden, James 36
Taylor, H.F. 96
Thomas, David 162
Thomas, E.H. 164
Thomas, Sydney Gilchrist 123, 125, 140
Thompson, Robert 29, 47, 64
Thompson, William 36, 58, 81, 135, 138
Tondu and Ogmore Coal and Iron Company 148, 153
Tondu Ironworks .... 147 - 148
Tothill, Francis 106
Townshend Wood and Company 95
Treacher, Benjamin 162
Tredegar .... 175, 178 - 179, 182 - 185
Tredegar Ironworks .... 12, 22, 58, 80 - 81, 109, 135 - 137, 141
Treforest Ironworks 41
Tregelles, Samuel 91
Treharne, Thomas 60
Trevithick, Richard .... 23, 42, 58, 66, 80, 82, 135, 140 - 141
Truran, Samuel 50
Truran, William 42, 49, 65

U
Union Ironworks 137

V
Varteg 173, 178, 180, 182
Varteg Ironworks 124, 173
Vaughan, N.V.E. 94
Venallt 179
Venallt Ironworks .... 4, 93 - 94
Vickerman, C.R. 165
Victoria Ironworks .... 10, 13, 106, 108, 110, 114, 175 - 176
Vigurs, John 151

W
Wasse, John 33
Watkins, Walter 105
Watney, Alfred 164
Watney, Daniel 164
Wayne, Matthew 40, 43, 130
Wayne, Thomas 40
Webb, Nathaniel 47
West of England and District Bank 6, 146
Whitland 28
Wilkins, John 33
Willet, Edward 95

Williams and Company 43
Williams, Edward 41, 64
Williams, Edward Morgan 40
Williams, Thomas 137
Wilson, Thomas 91
Wood, William . . . . 91 - 92

Y

Ynyscedwyn Iron Company 162
Ynyscedwyn Ironworks 161
Ystalyfera Ironworks . . . . 13, 162 - 163, 166